T0155642

Drones to Go

A Crash Course for Scientists and Makers

Julio Alberto Mendoza-Mendoza
Victor Javier Gonzalez-Villela
Carlos Fernando Aguilar-Ibañez
Leonardo Fonseca-Ruiz

Apress®

Drones to Go: A Crash Course for Scientists and Makers

Julio Alberto Mendoza-Mendoza
Centro de Ingenieria Avanzada,
Facultad de Ingenieria UNAM,
Coyoacan, Ciudad de Mexico, Mexico

Victor Javier Gonzalez-Villela
Centro de Ingenieria Avanzada,
Facultad de Ingenieria UNAM,
Coyoacan, Ciudad de Mexico, Mexico

Carlos Fernando Aguilar-Ibañez
CIC, Instituto Politecnico Nacional,
Gustavo A Madero, Ciudad de Mexico, Mexico

Leonardo Fonseca-Ruiz
UPIITA, Instituto Politécnico Nacional,
Gustavo A Madero, Ciudad de Mexico, Mexico

ISBN-13 (pbk): 978-1-4842-6787-5
https://doi.org/10.1007/978-1-4842-6788-2

ISBN-13 (electronic): 978-1-4842-6788-2

Managing Director, Apress Media LLC: Welmoed Spahr
Acquisitions Editor: Aaron Black
Development Editor: James Markham
Coordinating Editor: Jessica Vakili

Distributed to the book trade worldwide by Springer Science+Business Media New York, 1 NY Plaza, New York, NY 10014. Phone 1-800-SPRINGER, fax (201) 348-4505, e-mail orders-ny@springer-sbm.com, or visit www.springeronline.com. Apress Media, LLC is a California LLC and the sole member (owner) is Springer Science + Business Media Finance Inc (SSBM Finance Inc). SSBM Finance Inc is a **Delaware** corporation.

For information on translations, please e-mail booktranslations@springernature.com; for reprint, paperback, or audio rights, please e-mail bookpermissions@springernature.com.

Apress titles may be purchased in bulk for academic, corporate, or promotional use. eBook versions and licenses are also available for most titles. For more information, reference our Print and eBook Bulk Sales web page at www.apress.com/bulk-sales.

Any source code or other supplementary material referenced by the author in this book is available to readers on GitHub via the book's product page, located at www.apress.com/978-1-4842-6787-5. For more detailed information, please visit www.apress.com/source-code.

Printed on acid-free paper

Table of Contents

TABLE OF CONTENTS

About the Authors

Julio Alberto Mendoza-Mendoza is a Mechatronic Engineer, with a Masters in Advanced Technologies from UPIITA IPN and a PhD in Computer Sciences from CIC IPN. He is currently a visiting researcher at the National Autonomous University of Mexico (UNAM). His areas of interest and research are robotics (manipulators, aerial vehicles and wheeled robots, humanoids, haptics, exoskeletons, and teleoperation), programming, analytical and intelligent control, electronics, and mechanical design. His most recent line of development is aerial robotic manipulators. He holds five patents. He has written a couple of books for Apress, including this one.

Victor Javier Gonzalez-Villela received a B.Eng. degree in Mechanical and Electrical Engineering and a M.Eng. degree in Electrical Engineering in 1987 and 1993, respectively, from UNAM, Mexico City, Mexico, and a Ph.D. degree in Kinematics, Dynamics, and Nonlinear Systems applied to Mobile Robot Modelling and Control from Loughborough University, Loughborough, UK, in 2006. He is currently a Titular Professor in the Department of Mechatronics Engineering, UNAM.

He has belonged to the National System of Researchers (SNI) of Mexico since 2013. His research focuses on mobile, hybrid and adaptive robots, and artificial intuition.

Carlos Fernando Aguilar-Ibañez was born in Tuxpan, Veracruz, Mexico. He graduated in Physics at the Higher School of Physics and Mathematics of the National Polytechnic Institute (IPN), Mexico City 1990. From the Research Center and Advanced Studies of the IPN (Cinvestav IPN) he received a M.S. degree in Electrical Engineering in 1994 and a Ph.D. in Automatic Control in 1999. Since then he has been a researcher at the Center of Computing Research of the IPN (CIC IPN). He has belonged to the National System of Researchers (SNI) of Mexico since 2000. His research focuses on nonlinear systems, system identification, observers, automatic control, and chaos theory.

Leonardo Fonseca-Ruiz received a Bachelor's degree in Mechanical and Electrical Engineering from UNAM in 2002 and a M.S. degree from the Department of Electrical Engineering with the Specialty of Bio-Electronics by the Center for Research and Advanced Studies of the National Polytechnic Institute (CINVESTAV-IPN) in 2006. Currently he works as a full-time Research Professor at UPIITA-IPN. He is the author and co-author of 16 works published in magazines and congresses. His areas of interest are PLC, DSP, microcontrollers, automation, design and development of PCBs, and CNC systems.

About the Technical Reviewer

Jesus Vazquez-Nicolas is a mechatronics engineer. He has a Master's of Science in computer engineering from the National Polytechnic Institute, Mexico. He did an academic exchange at the State University of Campinas in Brazil and a research stay at the Institut Polytechnique des Sciences Avancées and the Université d'Évry, both in France.

He is currently pursuing a Ph.D., developing artificial intelligence and control systems for unmanned aerial vehicles (UAV). He is a professor at the Technological University of Mexico, where he was recognized in the circle of academic excellence in 2017, 2018, and 2019. He has had publications in national and international conferences and has indexed scientific journals on robust control and convolutional neural networks applied to UAV. He is very interested in the development of systems that combine mechatronics and artificial intelligence.

Acknowledgments

Julio Mendoza This book was made with the support of the UNAM DGAPA postdoctoral grants program 2018-2020. I also thank IPN, Conacyt, and IMPI, as well as my teachers, students, family, and friends, in particular Humberto Sossa, Jose Antonio Aquino, Gabriel Sepulveda, Rogelio Lozano, Miguel Suarez-Castanon, Marco Butron, Hazur Socconini, Francisco Arteaga-Velasquez, Jamyr Vasquez-Salinas, Carlos Vargas-Luis, David Arvizu-Rondero, Vicente Flores-Gutierrez, Mario Martinez-Ramirez, Artemisa Pedroza, Rodrigo Encinas-Porcel, Rodrigo Pelayo-Ramos, Mauricio Mendez, Tio Fox (Neftali Elorza), Gilberto Castrejon , Rafael Martinez, Manuel Jesus Rodriguez, Orlando Garcia, Carlos Rios Ramirez, Pablo Mendoza-Iturralde, Ernesto Filio-Lopez, our graphic designer Jesus Castillo, our editor Natalie Pao and her team, the Ardupilot team through Philip Rowse and his CubePilot project, the Mathworks book program, among many other people and institutions. I also deeply appreciate my granny Guille that unfortunately could not break her personal record of 100 years. Finally, I appreciate the invaluable help of doctors, nurses, rescuers, food and services providers, researchers, and all the public security teams who are true heroes and who risk their own integrity by supporting us in these truly difficult times for all humanity. In particular, this book is dedicated to all the people who are no longer with us, but whose impact on our formation and life had some meaning including my other grandma Carmen, and also to all the people that in the anonymity of the streets or poverty did not reach a mention in our lists.

Victor J. Gonzalez-Villela would like to acknowledge the financial support from the Support Program for Research and Technological Innovation Projects (PAPIIT) and Postdoctoral Grant Program DGAPA, UNAM, and the National Council of Science and Technology (CONACYT) for its support given via its

ACKNOWLEDGMENTS

National Research System (SNI exp 262253). Also I want to thank to my lovely family, especially my daughter Brenda and my son Andres for their support for all over these years in the good and bad times. Besides, thanks to all the members of the Mechatronics Research Group (MRG) and all the members of the Mechanical Design and Technological Innovation Center (CDMIT), FI, UNAM, who I have shared many personal and professional experiences throughout all these years, working together for a common goal and finally, all who made possible the materialization of this book.

Carlos Aguilar I wish to express my profound appreciation to my colleagues and friends, professors Santiago Suarez, Octavio Gutierrez, Julio Mendoza, Jose de Jesus Rubio, Jose Angel Acosta, Juan Carlos Martinez, Ruben Garrido, Rafael Martinez, Eloisa García, and Nareli Cruz for their interested and unmeasurable support for so many years. I also want to thank my new friends and collaborators, professors Eduardo Javier, Manuel, and Belem for their contributions to my work. I also wish to express my profound gratitude to my mentors and role models, professors Moises Bonilla, Rogelio Lozano, Hebertt Sira, and Romeo Ortega. They have been, for me, an example of effort and dedication in our beloved profession. Last but not least, I want to thank my beloved wife, Erika, my daughters, Daira and Zaida, and my mother, brothers, cousins, and uncles, who are my primary source of love and the motivation to be a better person every day. Finally, I express gratitude to God for letting me do and live off what I love to do.

Leonardo Fonseca-Ruiz I dedicate the book to Aidee, Matilde Amelie, and Leonardo, who are the lights of my life. I also thank the National Polytechnic Institute; my students, who keep me updated; Dr. Julio Alberto Mendoza and MSc. Mauricio Méndez, who have been by my side since they were my students and have always done their best, inspiring me to do the same. I am really grateful to the Interdisciplinary Professional Unit of Engineering and Advanced Technologies (UPIITA) of the IPN for giving me the opportunity to teach new mechatronic engineers for over 14 years.

Foreword

This book can be considered as one of the most complete courses on drones and specifically on multicopters with special attention and focus on quadcopters. It is aimed at an audience ranging from makers to scientists. It contains the necessary elements of design, modeling, control, simulation, and programming, explained in a concise but extended way, especially in points that many texts ignore. Additionally, it merges maker knowledge and technical details with scientific knowledge and design details in a single book.

This book is the result of several years of research in the field. It has a staggered pedagogical design, so that the newcomer to the world of drones or the already embedded can obtain strong basis for learning more knowledge.

Detailed step-by-step deductions not available in other works are included, such as the extensive proof of the controllers and their simulations.

It is clearly indicated and with enough references how to extend the knowledge here developed to a wide variety of aircraft or aerial systems.

Finally, an appendix offers a very complete bibliography for those who like to extend their knowledge on the subject.

The text assumes that the readers have at least a high school or technical bachelor's degree and understand concepts such as derivatives, integrals, basic ordinary differential equations, and notions of algorithms and programming.

Licenses and Copyrights

- MATLAB® and Simulink® are registered trademarks of The MathWorks, Inc. See mathworks.com/trademarks for a list of additional trademarks.

- ArduPilot libraries and Mission Planner software are GPLv3 license-free software. They can be redistributed and/or modified under GNU GPLv3 terms and restrictions as described by the Free Software Foundation (www.fsf.org/). The code and programs are distributed with the hope of being useful but without any guarantee, even without the implied warranty of merchantability or capacity for a particular purpose. See the General Public License section of the GNU project for more details. ArduPilot libraries can be downloaded from http://ardupilot.org/dev/docs/apmcopter-programming-libraries.html.

- PX4 libraries have a BSD 3-clause license (https://opensource.org/licenses/BSD-3-Clause).

- The Pixhawk autopilot has a CC-BY-SA 3.0 license (https://creativecommons.org/licenses/by-sa/3.0/deed.es), which belongs to Lorenz Meier.

- DroneKit-Python is licensed under the Apache License Version 2.0, January 2004 (www.apache.org/licenses/).

- Scilab is available under the GPL License. Xcos is freely available and distributed with Scilab.

With This Book, You Will Learn

- An introduction to the five desirable skills to become a multicopter developer: design, modeling, control, simulation, and programming

- An extended model on the mathematics of a multicopter, not present in any previous work and with a visual and pedagogical development, answering many of the doubts that remain in the air at the time of such explanations

- A novel way to visualize the controllers of a multicopter, that is fully compatible with the existing state of the art

- A detailed description of the controllers and their simulation, which is not widely disseminated in articles or other books and is usually reserved for classrooms

- You can use this book as the basis for future learning in a small, highly visual, and easy-to-understand presentation.

- The goal of this book is to unify the maker world with the scientific world through this type of aircraft, including design tips omitted in scientific books and scientific tips omitted in design books.

- You can extend the acquired knowledge to the design and analysis of other types of vehicles with a moderate but systematic effort.

How to Read This Book

This book is divided into five sections that in our opinion are necessary for an acceptable level of knowledge for a drone designer:

- In the design section, the technical characteristics to be considered when preparing a prototype of a multicopter are shown. This section is based on a compilation of maker-style texts and webpages. Note that this knowledge can be easily extended to other types of vehicles.

- In the modeling section, the mathematics related to a quadcopter (and generic aircraft) are shown, emphasizing the three basic sets of equations: the dynamic set (with this, the control is designed), the kinematic set (with this, the tasks to be executed are designed), and the set of allocation (with this, each motor is programmed and works as the link between theory and practice). Also here, the knowledge shown is moderately easy to be extended to other types of vehicles.

- In the control section, four basic types of multicopter controllers are developed, classifying them into two main branches: vehicle mode control, also known as on-board or first-person mode, and robot mode control, also known as external or third-person mode. This categorization was preferred because these aircraft can be seen as a vehicle or as a robot depending on the application they have. The knowledge in this section can be extended to other types of vehicles under certain mobility conditions.

- The simulation section provides a simplified way (a template) to simulate the previous systems and their controllers, allowing you to understand that only two sections of code are required: the one that contains modeling and control equations, and the one that contains the ODE solver. Although in this book we use MATLAB and Simulink for simplicity, with the concepts outlined, you will be able to use any other programming language or graphic simulator for the same purposes.

- And finally the implementation section, which shows the coding considerations and signal processing currently available or required to use most of the unmanned aerial systems. Also this section may be useful for other types of vehicles.

As you can see, this book and its chapters can be used as the basis for the elaboration of a complete plan for teaching and studying the described subject. This book is by itself a complete course in a pocket size.

This book is aimed at makers, designers, scientists, and researchers related to the drone world and specifically to multicopters. However, if you are a pilot or a hobbyist and you are interested in knowing every corner of your vehicle, this text will be a useful and understandable reading.

If you have the printed version of this book, consider to download also the pdf of the same in order to see detailed close-ups of the equations.

CHAPTER 1

Drone Design Concepts

In this chapter, you will find the most relevant information about what a drone is, including historical and social context. This chapter will cover international standards, some etymologies, and certain safety considerations that you should keep in mind while working with these aircraft. We'll go through a description of generic components and their selection and connection. As a result, you will learn the technical details, international standards, and necessary requirements for the design of drones and other vehicles. Remember that this book is a crash course, so this chapter just provides a fast way for you to assimilate the contents. If you want to extend this knowledge, go to the guided reference appendix.

Historical Context

If you look at the Figure 1-1, you will notice that drones, and particularly multicopters, have centuries of history. They started as sketches designed by DaVinci (at least that's how occidental history reports it). Recently these sketches were carried out in a giant quadcopter in a kind of retrotechnology developed by the University of Maryland where the processor and base engine are the human body (the brain and the extremities, respectively). Multicopters came back around in 1907 with the Breguet brothers and later in the 1920s with Oehmichen and Bothezat.

© Julio Alberto Mendoza-Mendoza, Victor Javier Gonzalez-Villela,
Carlos Fernando Aguilar-Ibañez, Leonardo Fonseca-Ruiz 2021
J. A. Mendoza-Mendoza et al., *Drones to Go*, https://doi.org/10.1007/978-1-4842-6788-2_1

In these drones, the processor and base engine were, respectively, a pilot and a mechanical computer (a mechanism) in charge of coordinating the movements of each propeller and internal combustion motors. They were forgotten until the 2010s, when the commercial and research booms in these vehicles/robots occurred. Currently, the processor and engine base are, respectively, an autopilot and electric motors. Now you that you know some history, let's move on to some useful nomenclatures.

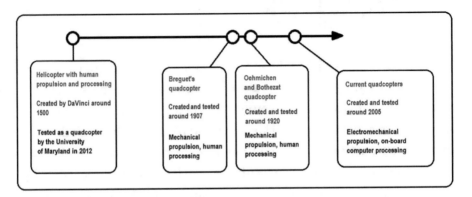

Figure 1-1. *Quadcopter history*

Etymologies and Names in Use

Although the term "drone" is correctly used for any unmanned vehicle, commercial popularization associates it with aerial vehicles, and more specifically, with multicopters. This term comes from insects, very specifically from those whose function in the hive or nest is simply to perpetuate the species.

More professional words to refer to an aerial drone are

- UAV or unmanned aerial vehicle

- UAS or unmanned aerial system

- RPAS or remotely piloted aircraft system

You should also familiarize yourself with the terms "multirotor" and "multicopter," which roughly mean multiple rotating motors. The term "multiple copters" was adapted from the French "hélicoptère," a word invented by Gustave d'Amécourt in 1861 that means spiral wing. The word is based on the Greek "helix," which means helix or spiral, and "pteron," which means wing.

Why is this useful to know? Perhaps it seems trivial, but for those who want to research the classic concepts of drones, the archaic nomenclature is important to know. Of course, if you only need current research and new trends, you only need to know the modern terms. For the vehicles presented in this book, the evolution from classic to current terminologies is

- Multicopter (22,400 results in Google Scholar on May 5, 2020) -> multirotor (10,600 results in Google Scholar on May 5, 2020)

- Quadcopter (37,400 results in Google Scholar on May 5, 2020) -> Quadrotor (35,500 results in Google Scholar on May 5, 2020)

- And, in an unusual way, the word quadricopter (674 results in Google Scholar on May 5, 2020)

Figure 1-2 is based on Google Trends, indicating when the boom of the term "quadcopter" began. In early 2011 approximately, the words "quadrotor" and "quadcopter" were almost equally employed. In fact, it was very frequent to read "quadrotor" in the scientific field, but the use of the "quadcopter" grew as time evolved (including in scientific and technological research). Currently, both terms are more or less equal in use due to a reduction in their use, and the domination and popularization of the term "drone" (Figure 1-3). Curiously, the terms "quadcopter" and "quadrotor" have been relegated to the research field where the growing term now is "UAV."

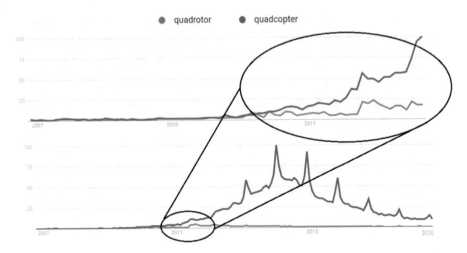

Figure 1-2. *Quadrotor vs. quadcopter search results on Google Trends*

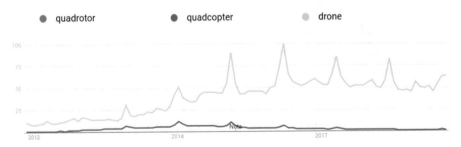

Figure 1-3. *Quadrotor vs. quadcopter vs. drone search results on Google Trends*

In summary, the value of this section is to indicate the trend of certain terms to facilitate any necessary research, and also the way to provide background on how each term should be used in context. Now that you know about etymologies as a tool for searching, let's consider what kind of drone you need.

What Kind of Drone Do You Need?

There are four types of drone users: the specialist researcher, the researcher (who uses a drone as a tool), the designer, and the pilot. Table 1-1 shows some of the characteristics and recommended equipment for each type of user.

Table 1-1. *Types of Drone Users and Characteristics*

User	Most common vehicle	Kind of software (see Chapter 5 regarding ways to program a drone)	What do they need to know?	Examples
Pilot	Closed architectures (prebuilt drones)	Closed architecture GUI	Maker-style technical knowledge, regulations, and unmanned flight courses. The vehicle is a work tool.	Racing pilot or photographer
Researcher who uses a drone as a tool	Mostly closed or limited open architectures	GUI or SDK type 1	Maker-style technical knowledge. The vehicle is still a work tool but with a specialized task unrelated to the drone. The aircraft is a test platform.	Research in artificial vision or artificial intelligence algorithms, including SLAM

(*continued*)

Table 1-1. (*continued*)

User	Most common vehicle	Kind of software (see Chapter 5 regarding ways to program a drone)	What do they need to know?	Examples
Specialist researcher	Kit-like open architectures	SDK type 2 or 3	Scientific knowledge about control and robotic vehicles, and maker-style technical knowledge are desired. Here, the vehicle's flight mode is designed.	Research in automatic control algorithms for aircraft flight
Designer	Open architectures which are selected component by component	SDK type 3 In general, a design component by component is related to open software architectures and conversely, almost all the commercial drones have software with limited capabilities.	Scientific knowledge specialized in aircraft control and design, and advanced technical knowledge are required. Here, the whole vehicle is designed.	Aircraft designer

Now you have an idea about the vehicle that is useful for your purposes, but what about safety and standards? Let's answer this now.

Generic Safety Issues and International Standards

In general, nobody will persecute you for carrying out prototype tests in your home, garden, or in a laboratory with the appropriate equipment and security measures, as long as people, animals, buildings, or property other than your own are not injured. However, in order to reduce risks and accidents, we include a small section with generic recommendations. Note that the impact of these recommendations for each person may vary based on local laws.

Communications

A drone can affect and infringe on local telecommunications in two ways and in both cases you could be penalized.

1. **Telemetry system and remote control system**: Telemetry and remote control transmitters must be compatible with the range of transmission frequencies allowed in your locality. A typical example is that telemetry radios usually come in two presentations: 433 MHz, which is used in Europe and countries with the same standard, and 915 MHz, which is used in the US and countries compatible with the same standard.

2. **Electrical power consumption**: People who design and use quadcopters with high power consumption, especially in high current applications, know that this affects the performance of the vehicle's sensors, and it's necessary to shield the cables, twist them, cover them, or even separate the connections.

This can influence the behavior of a public antenna
or civil communication equipment. So, as a designer
or user, you should be aware that you could be
penalized.

Electrical Safety

Drone operation with wired electrical connections, called tethered,
involves sending medium voltages of around 400V to the vehicle, which in
certain countries (for example, Japan) go beyond what is legally permitted.

Transport and Storage

The tricky topic here is about batteries and fuel tanks, so be sure you know
how to properly store and transport such supplies.

Safety of Use

Any person or property that you damage with your vehicle involves
legal problems. You must be aware that a drone is an object that, even in
small sizes, due to the speeds that it reaches by itself or by its propellers,
represents a risk.

Buying and Selling Problems

You may be interested in a vehicle or perhaps you want to commercialize
a prototype. If so, you need to verify that its components, features, and
materials are permitted in your region. It is possible that something that
represents a small expense to you, once you sell it or buy it in a specific
country or commercial area, will increase considerably in price or taxes or
may even be retained or rejected for the use of illegal components.

Regulations and Standardizations

When you get to Chapter 2, you will notice a non-arbitrary selection of coordinates and angles of rotation, as displayed in Figure 1-4. This selection obeys the ISO 1151-2: 1985 standard and facilitates the link between the described theory and the use of sensors and components already manufactured. However, to simplify equations, we will use the upward Z axis.

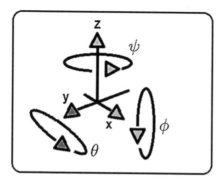

Figure 1-4. *Drone motions as indicated by the ISO 1151-2: 1985 standard*

Notice that in the case of a drone, as you will see later, although the pitch (theta) and roll (phi) angles are measured respectively with the Y and X axes, the motion in X axis depends on controlled tilt rotations in theta, and the motion in the Y axis depends on controlled tilt rotations in phi, as illustrated in Figure 1-5.

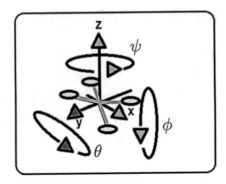

Figure 1-5. *Link between angular and planar motions*

Recommendations

Here are some standard recommendations in order to work with drones:

- Read your local legislation regarding the topics listed here or even additional considerations.

- Verify that your hardware complies with the requirements of said legislations.

- You and your team must use standard protective equipment such as googles or gloves.

- When other people are present during a test, keep in mind that a prototype can cause injuries and it is recommended that you or the person in charge of your laboratory have a license to operate unmanned aerial vehicles.

- Avoid public or private spaces, whether indoors or outdoors, that are not designed for your tests.

- Remember that you are a designer and not necessarily a pilot.

- If you have the necessary permissions, you must prepare the place with walls, protection meshes, or plastic surfaces in case any pieces break or detach from the drone. You should also post warning advisories/ signs to restrict access of non-authorized personnel.

- Perform exhaustive tests without propellers or with the drone anchored before the free flying tests. In order to avoid damaging your motors by testing them without any load, you can replace your propellers with pieces of paper.

- When you have a prototype available, verify that all its components are legal in your specific location and determine if there are functional replacements for the components that are not allowed.

Now it is time to specify the type of drones that we will analyze in the rest of the book.

Types of Drones

According to their displacement, drones can be classified in this way (Figure 1-6):

- **Rotary wings**: They only require propellers to move. In this case, they have vertical takeoff and landing, and are designed for load transport and short- and medium-range applications.

- **Fixed wings**: They require long surfaces in order to move, like most airplanes. In this case, they have applications for horizontal takeoff and landing, and are designed for higher speeds as well as longer flight ranges than rotating wing aircrafts.

- **Flapping wings**: They require oscillating surfaces to fly, like the wings of a bird or an insect. They could be viewed as a fusion of fixed and rotating wings, and similarly have mixed applications.

- **Transformable**: They can go from one configuration to another, as in the case of the tailsitters. These vehicles go from a vertical takeoff and landing using propellers to a fixed-wing flight-mode for long range operations.

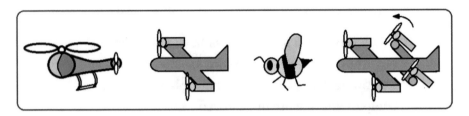

Figure 1-6. *Types of drones*

This book will cover topics about multicopter-type unmanned aerial vehicles, which are based on rotary-wing propulsion. However, most of the concepts can be extended to other types of aircraft under additional restrictions or considerations (including modeling, control, simulation, and programming topics).

Let's move to the drone components.

Components

We will describe the most relevant components of a drone, based on their use: action components, structural components, measurement components, command components, and power ones.

Action Components

There are two types of action components: electromechanical and electrical action. Electromechanical types are motors or servos that simply receive an electrical signal and then transform this signal to a mechanical effect. In the case of the electrical action, they are components that provide an amplification stage or an electrical adaptation.

Electromechanical action elements can have a direct effect on the speed (brushless and brushed motors) or position (servo motors).

Brushed and Brushless Motors

Currently, because of their response time, the most common engines found on multicopters (for makers and scientists) are based on direct current electric motors. These kinds of motors can be brushed or brushless. In both cases, it is required to modify the motor speed by increasing or decreasing it by adjusting values such as the RMS voltage.

In the case of brushed motors, they are the most common electric motor. They are used in very small size drones. The brushes reduce response times due to contact friction. Also, they are not recommended in explosive environments due to the sparks that they produce, and they are not recommended in aquatic environments since they can short-circuit themselves. However, since they work with PWM duty cycle signals (remember that pulse width modulation are various techniques for regulating a signal by varying a percentage of its action, in this case by regulating the on/off percentage of the power signal), this kind of PWM is usual for example in an Arduino board.

Brushless motors are usually found in multicopters because of their faster response times and because of the absence of electrical contacts, which implies a reduction in friction. They are employed in explosive environments due to the absence of sparks and they can be used in aquatic environments because they do not have elements susceptible to short-circuiting (as long as their wires are coated).

On the other hand, they are more expensive compared to the brushed motors and they operate with a special type of PWM called RC, where the on/off percentage is regulated in a different way than brushed motors (here the percentage is a function of the time), requiring additional components.

For the proper use of both types of motors, power stages are required, as you will see in the next section. Note that duty cycle-type PWM and vRC-type PWM are not directly compatible

The main difference is that brushed type motors are usually single-phase while brushless are three-phase or multiphase motors (generally three-phase in aircraft applications).

Figure 1-7 shows an oversized brushed motor compared to a brushless one, but the opposite can also happen; this simply depends on the requirements of the user or the designer. A more remarkable difference that you should notice is the number of cables (electrical phases) and the fact that brushed motors are generally of the inrunner type (rotating inner shaft) while brushless are often outrunner (rotating outer casing).

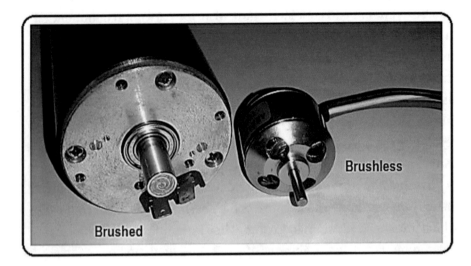

Figure 1-7. *Brushed and brushless motors*

ESCs and Power Stages

ESCs, also called speed variators (Figure 1-8), are the power stages of brushless motors and some brushed motors (for the latter, they are only electronic RC signal to duty cycle adapters).

Basically they are injected with a signal that regulates their on/off states in PWM RC format. By means of that, the single-phase and direct-current power signal is transformed to a kind of three-phase signal that controls the speed of the motor's rotation.

In the case of brushed DC motors, as already explained, an adapter ESC can be used. This takes a PWM RC signal that is converted to a PWM duty cycle signal. Another option that is more commonly used on devices is called an electronic driver, which takes a duty cycle PWM as input and then amplifies the signal to obtain the necessary current or voltage to regulate the motor speed.

Both ESC and electronic drivers are called power stages because they are electronic circuits that amplify electrical signals sent by autopilots or processing units (which are unable to supply enough electrical power) to drive the motors. Observe that if you try to move a motor directly from a processing unit without using the proper power stage, you can burn or break this processing unit.

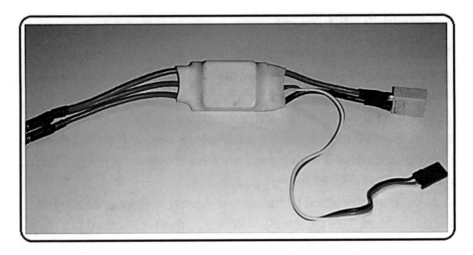

Figure 1-8. *ESC*

Servos

Servo motors (widely known as just "servos") are position motors that receive a PWM RC type signal that is converted into the position of an axis coupled to the motor. See Figure 1-9. They operate similarly to a brushless motor except that the BLDC (brushless direct current motor) changes its speed through variations in the PWM RC signal, while the servo changes its position.

They also require their respective power stage. Additionally, they are not as fast at changing position as a brushless motor. Due to this fact, there is a risk of breaking or burning a servomotor with a sudden change of the PWM signal. A PWM signal used for servos must be slower than a PWM signal used for a BLDC.

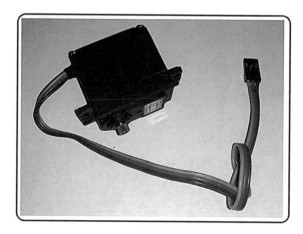

Figure 1-9. *Servomotor*

Propellers

It is difficult for a motor to act directly on the environment. An interaction like this requires objects, such as wheels or propellers (as shown in Figure 1-10), depending on whether it is a watercraft, an aircraft, or a ground vehicle. For safety purposes, the vehicle should be tested without them until you obtain a desired behavior. A motor has two types of performances. The first is known as a full-load operation, which occurs when the propellers are placed, and the second is free performance, which implies that the motor does not have a propeller or some other object attached to its structure. Both cases represent extreme situations. In the case of the free performance, which is common for initial tests, it is recommended to use pieces of paper instead of the propellers as a safety load (weight). During the full-load mode, it is recommended not to reach the maximum load value (weight) recommended by the manufacturer.

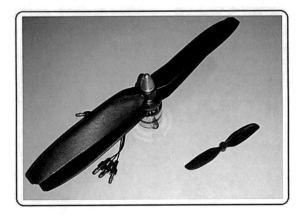

Figure 1-10. *Propellers*

Structure Components

The following sections discuss the components that give shape and support to the vehicle.

Frame

The frame is simply the chassis or vehicle's body (Figure 1-11) on which the other components are mounted.

Figure 1-11. *Frame with propellers*

Vibration-Damping Mounts

Vibration-damping mounts are structures designed for absorbing or reducing the noise that induces the vibration of the vehicle on the sensors or the processor and thus avoids incorrect measurements or computational errors.

Mechanical Connector

It is evident that the components must be fixed, either permanently or long-term (screws) or in a replaceable way or short-term (Velcro, straps).

Measurement Components

The following sections discuss the components that allow the vehicle to know where it is placed.

Miscellaneous Sensors

A multicopter requires motion and speed sensors on the XY plane and for the altitude, as well as three-dimensional rotational speed and angular sensors. They can be analog sensors, digital or serial ones, even on-board and external sensors. The most common are barometers, IMUs, gyroscopes, accelerometers, LIDARs, cameras, and motion tracking systems. (See the Appendix to learn more about them).

GPS

Although it is a three-dimensional motion and speed sensor system (translational), GPS gets its own section because it is widely used by makers and scientists, especially in open terrain applications. It is basically a satellite triangulation system that is affected by the environment; therefore it is only recommended for open space operations.

Command Components

The following sections discuss the components that allow the vehicle to act and be commanded.

Autopilot

Autopilot is the specialized processing unit for unmanned vehicles (see Figure 1-12). Also, there are some microcontrollers or development boards adapted to function as autopilots. They have closed and open architectures (see the section about the ways to program a drone in Chapter 5).

Figure 1-12. *Autopilot*

Telemetry Modules

Telemetry modules are units for wireless and remote transmission of information (see Figure 1-13). They have a limited operating range. Telemetry modules can be used to intercommunicate two or more vehicles with each other, or a fixed base with one or more drones. They can be used to transmit positions taken with a motion capture system to the vehicle. They are generally bidirectional modules.

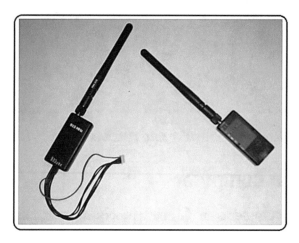

Figure 1-13. *Telemetry modules*

RC Modules

Unlike telemetry modules, RC modules allow for manual control of the drone by sticks and buttons. They have a wide operating range and some of them allow video transmission. They are usually unidirectional, which means that they have a transmitter module and a receiver device. See Figure 1-14.

21

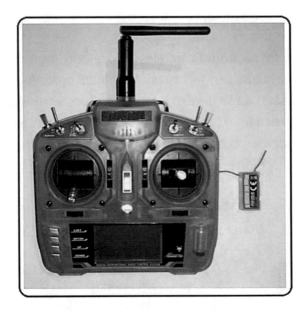

Figure 1-14. *Remote controller and receiver*

Companion Computer

A companion computer is an on-board processing unit that is used to carry out demanding tasks which usually go beyond the scope of the autopilot (such as making artificial vision or SLAM). Examples are the Raspberry Pi single-board computer, a microcontroller, a microprocessor, or FPGA. Basically the autopilot is directly used for the flight control and the companion computer is used for indirect tasks for that flight.

Power Components

The following sections discuss the components that energize the vehicle.

Battery/Tethered Supplies

The use of batteries or tethered supplies to energize the system is evident. Although most drones currently employ LIPO-type batteries (see Figure 1-15 vto the right) for long-term applications, there are available power converters or power supplies, which implies a vehicle anchored to an electrical extension. Obviously, such an extension entails special use conditions and mobility restrictions. The ideal conditions for these power supplies is that they have reduced voltage and current ripples, or spikes, at a level that the supplied values are as constant as possible. As the batteries have extensive documentation, we are going to talk a little more about wired or tethered supplies.

There are four types of tethered supplies:

- **By power supplies**: In this case, the biggest impediment is the cost, since a multicopter drone based on brushless motors consumes much more current than voltage (a small vehicle easily consumes approximately 12V/60A). In such a way, while having a power source that provides said voltage and current, you must consider that the cables and wires must be able to deal with these parameters, including the fact that a cable that consumes so much current must be physically heavy and bulky, and thus not suited for use for high altitudes. Therefore, this option is recommended if your application is at laboratory level where the drone barely exceeds one and a half meters of elevation.

- **By car batteries**: The same thing happens as in the previous case, but the cost is slightly reduced considering that car batteries are very commercial units. However, a car battery is usually heavy and requires special care for transportation and electric charging.

- **By power converters**: In this case, it is required to provide medium voltage and low current, 400V/3A for example, in order to supply a power converter capable of transforming said input into 12V/100A. These power converters are available through some manufacturers (VICOR, for example). They usually weigh 200g including heat sinks and are a viable option for these tethered applications.

- **By solar cells**: The restrictions are similar to the previous cases, with the implications that such cells have (such as size and power density).

You could possibly argue that there are fuel-based options because they have decades of use in standard helicopters; however, for electric multicopters they still have research challenges (with the exception of fuel generators, where a fuel-based engine is used as the power source for an electrical plant).

Battery Indicator

If a battery is used, it is important to have a device that alerts us when said battery is about to run out, so the aircraft does not collapse and get damaged. Basically they are small voltmeters with light or sound indicators.

Power Distributor

A power distributor is a device designed to use multiple motors with a single power supply. They are basically current dividers either in a harness presentation (they consume more space but they are easier to manipulate) or as electronic circuit boards (they are reduced in space but they are difficult to manipulate). See Figure 1-15 in the middle.

Power Module

A power module is a device that enables the autopilot to be powered from the main battery. See Figure 1-15 to the left.

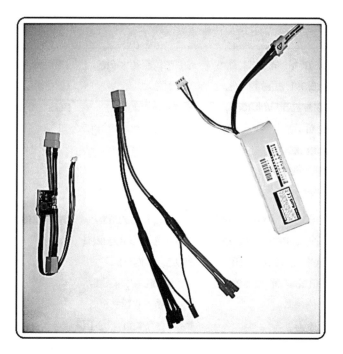

Figure 1-15. *Power module, power distributor, and battery*

Electrical Connector

Electrical connectors are a way to interconnect various electrical or electronic devices. There are versions designed for power or data. Power connectors can handle large amounts of voltage and/or current. Data connectors are used exclusively to send and receive information that generally consumes very low current or voltage.

Tables 1-2 through 1-4 display more information about the previous components and are presented in three categories: power components, mechanical components, and control components.

Table 1-2. *Power Components and Characteristics*

Power component	Main characteristics	Frequent procedures	Types
Battery	Number of cells, size, weight, amp hours, operating voltages, C or discharge rate, connectors, accessories required for their use (a charger)	Charge, discharge, storage, transportation, connector soldering, parallelization or serialization	There are many but LIPO batteries are the most abundant.
Power supply	Power, current, voltage, ripple, frequency, input voltage (110/220), number of phases	Filtering if required, phase joint if required, amplification or reduction, regulation, discharge protection, transformation (AC-DC)	Switched and linear
Battery indicator	Number of cells allowed, light or sound indicators	Pin verification	On board or external

(continued)

Table 1-2. (*continued*)

Power component	Main characteristics	Frequent procedures	Types
Power module	Maximum current supported, maximum voltage supported, electromagnetic shield, maximum current measured, type of connectors	Electromagnetic shielding if required, adding current or voltage sensors if required, parallelization if required	For low and high current
Power distributor	Maximum current supported, maximum voltage supported, number of motors to be powered, BEC, size, weight, type electromagnetic shield	Terminal soldering, serialization or parallelization, electromagnetic shielding	Hub (harness) or board (circuit)
Power connectors	Maximum current supported, maximum voltage supported, compatibility with the components, thermal resistance, flexibility, plug/unplug capacities	Terminal soldering, replacement	Each application has its own set of connectors.
Power stages and ESCs	Maximum size, weight, current and voltage, reversibility, BEC or optocoupling	Configuration (usually via a software interface)	Reversible or non-reversible, PWM-RC or PWM duty cycle, standard or optocoupled, for brushless or brushed motors

Table 1-3. *Control Components and Characteristics*

Control component	Main characteristics	Frequent procedures	Types
Autopilot	Size, weight, number of motors, connectors, available ports, architecture, programming language, processor, required power	Programming	Open and closed architectures
Sensors	Resolution, size, weight, type, linearity, power required, kind of connector, range, and operating conditions	Soldering, signal coupling, filtering	Analog, digital, and serial
Telemetry modules	Size, operating voltages and currents, required accessories, connectors compatibility, maximum distance, legality of operation frequencies	Binding and labeling, data speed configuration	American and European standards
Remote controller	Maximum distance, support for LIPO batteries, legality of operation frequencies, number of channels, binding mode, type of auxiliary channels, sensitivity, transmission modes, screen or not, presence or not of a PPM channel in the receiver	Binding the receiver with the transmitter, sticks and buttons configuration	By number of channels and additional features as a screen

(continued)

Table 1-3. (*continued*)

Control component	Main characteristics	Frequent procedures	Types
Memory card	Memory size, type, adapters, accessibility for plugging, number of work cycles	Write, erase, external or on board use, format conversion	Usually by their memory size and commercial type
Companion computer	The same that an autopilot has plus additional processing features and compatibilities with hardware and software	Programming	By level of code abstraction (natural language vs. machine language), also by their hardware performance
Stop button	Accessibility to the user, size, colors, mechanical suppression	Level of accessibility, programming	Push buttons, sticks, based on time or based on events
Data connectors	Standard to use and compatibilities, tools to use them, speed, electromagnetic shields, market availability, number of pins, sealed or not, standard or special versions, maximum voltage and current, easy or rigid plugging	Soldering, replacing, programming	It depends on each application.

Table 1-4. *Mechanial Components and Characteristics*

Mechanical component	Main characteristics	Frequent procedures	Types
Frame	Material, hardness, lightness, holes, levels, accessories, size and weight, landing gear, anti-shock systems, folding or not, electromagnetic shielding	Component connection, balancing, restoration	Common classifications are by size, materials, and folding ability
Motors	kv, weight and dimensions, maximum current and voltage, maximum thrust and torque	Getting the start value and proportionality gains of torque and thrust with respect to their speed and the propeller, PWM binding (with the remote control)	Brushed and brushless, speed or position, kind of control signal (DC, BLDC, servo, stepper, AC, PWM RC or PWM duty cycle, etc.)
Propellers	Pitch, diameter, edge, number of blades, flexibility, hardness, sense of rotation	Balancing, edge cutting	Usual classifications are based on the material, the flexibility, and the number of blades.
Fasteners	Material, hardness, lightness, accessories, size and weight, fast or slow change	Each mechanical connection is a case of analysis and depends on the application.	Fast change or permanent connection
Anti-vibration mounts	Size, frame compatibility, mobility, kind of suppression	Balancing	For motors, for autopilots, for sensors

Now that you know the introductory concepts about drone components, let's see how to choose them.

Component Selection

This process is divided, as a recommended design, into three sub-processes (the analysis is carried out considering brushless motors since they are the most employed with quadcopters).

Vehicle Selection

Vehicle selection is an iterative process that consists of

1. Choosing motors. Motors are chosen according to the weight and the speed that you want to operate the vehicle. Therefore you must consult two important parameters in datasheets: the maximum weight that each motor can lift and its maximum value of RPMs (in brushless motors this is called kv and it must not be confused with the electromechanical constants of the motor).

2. According to the above (the load capacity and the speed of the vehicle), the propellers are chosen.

3. Once the motors and propellers are selected, the ESCs are chosen. Again, in the datasheet of the brushless motors you can find the current and voltage required by these operating conditions. This allows selecting the ESCs. It is recommended that ESCs consume 30% more current compared to that consumed by their respective motors in order to overcome power loss.

4. With the previous point and the inclusion of other components such as the autopilot and auxiliary motors, an adequate battery or power source is chosen.

5. Considering the dimensions of all the components and the final weight (which can be calculated by using individual datasheets for each element of the vehicle), the frame is selected.

6. Considering the final weight, you must return to the step 1 and verify that the motors still satisfy your requirements. If not, you must repeat the design process.

Remote Control Selection

The remote control is the direct link with the pilot, assuming that you want a manual intervention or at least a human-controlled emergency stop. The selection process is as follows:

1. The minimum number of channels to fly a quadcopter are four (X, Y, Z, and yaw angle). In other vehicles, for example a car, they are only two (moving forward and turning). However, you must take into account if you also require an emergency stop, a button that could be used to open and close a clamp. Each one of these tasks needs at least their own auxiliary channel. Hence, six, eight, or ten channel radio controls are employed. These additional channels can be sticks, buttons, or knobs, and they can be used through combinatorial logics and activation states (to learn more about state machines, see my book on Ardupilot and other references included in the Appendix).

2. Once you know how many channels you require, the
    next thing is to determine the maximum distance
    that the remote control will allow from the human
    operator to the vehicle. This will determine the
    operation area in which the vehicle will have human
    interaction, and this will affect whether or not the
    drone would be recoverable in an emergency.

3. The following are subjective details of operation,
    and consist in asking yourself about whether or
    not a camera monitor on the remote control is
    necessary, whether you want to operate more than
    one vehicle with the same RC, and so on.

4. The next step is to find out how long you need to
    use the vehicle because this will affect the durability
    of the batteries in the remote control. This way
    remote controls with LIPO battery connectors are
    recommended for long periods of working time.

5. Finally, you must verify that the autopilot and the
    remote control receiver have PPM ports. Otherwise,
    you must buy the corresponding adapters.

Autopilot Selection

The autopilot selection will depend on your programming skills and also
on the degree of immersion you want to have with the vehicle.

1. If you do not need to program specialized tasks, it is
    enough to buy a generic drone.

2. If more specialized tasks are required but you do not know how to program, it is recommended that you buy an autopilot that allows you to use a GUI, such as Mission Planner. A recommended autopilot here is the Pixhawk.

3. If you know how to program and you want to design your own tasks without concentrating on the design of the vehicle, it is recommended that you use a simplified SDK such as Dronekit. This SDK requires that you know how to program in the Python language but allows the vehicle to be used as a particle that moves in X, Y, Z, and rotates on its own axis. The Pixhawk is also recommended here.

4. If you (in addition to the previous point) just want to design or test control laws in predesigned vehicles, then it is necessary to use an extended SDK. This kind of SDK allows operating a vehicle in particle mode but through force and torque interaction instead of just defining trajectories. An example is the Bebop Autonomy SDK or the Simulink libraries for the Pixhawk autopilot.

5. If you, in addition to point 4, are designing an experimental vehicle or a vehicle that is out of the standard models that are compatible with the extended SDKs, then you require an autopilot compatible with a full SDK. Examples of this type of SDK are the Ardupilot libraries and the PX4 libraries. Again, the Pixhawk autopilot can be used here.

6. If, in addition to what is described in point 5, you must carry out other specialized tasks, such as the use of artificial vision, it is highly recommended that you employ a companion computer together with the autopilot. For example, you can use a Raspberry Pi, an Odroid, or a laptop with ROS to perform the artificial vision algorithm, in combination with the Pixhawk executing the flight algorithm. Or, even better, you can use an embedded unit that combines the autopilot and the companion computer such as NavIO cards or the ErleBrain.

Notice that moving forward through the selection process also involves moving from a hobbyist user to a scientific one, requiring a deeper understanding of programming, control, and mathematical modeling, but in return you will have the capacity for a total design and not only the restrictions of selecting a few parameters.

You learned about the components and how to select them. It's time that you learn how to assemble them.

Component Connection

This section illustrates the way to connect the components of a drone. This can help you avoid very common assembly mistakes at the mechanical, electrical, and control levels.

Mechanical Connection

The main element of the mechanical connection is the frame, to which the rest of the components are attached. See Figure 1-16.

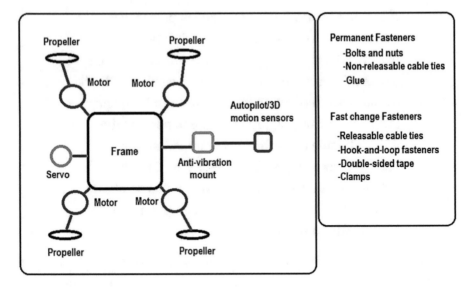

Figure 1-16. *Mechanical connection*

Electrical Connection

The central element here is the battery or power supply. Notice that the motors are not directly plugged to this power supply. See Figure 1-17.

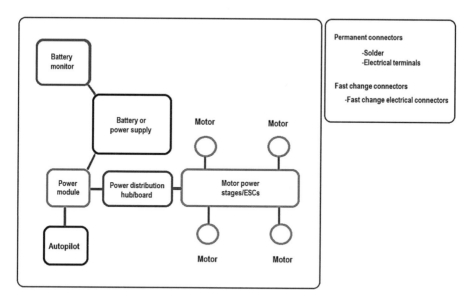

Figure 1-17. *Electrical connection*

Control Connection

The central element here is the autopilot. In this level is also placed the user interface or the interface with an auxiliary computer located on the ground. See Figure 1-18.

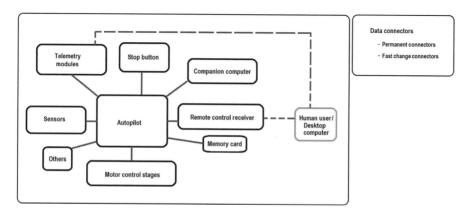

Figure 1-18. *Control connection*

Summary

In this chapter, you learned about the components for designing drones with a particular focus on quadcopters but extendable to other types of aircraft, including their historical context, etymologies, and the most common search results in order to choose the name of your work. You also learned about the type of drones that are useful for your activities, some generic security measures, as well as the most widely used international standard for modeling and design of a drone and its components. Regarding the components, you learned some useful classifications, their most frequent characteristics and procedures, and their connections and selection. You are invited to take a look at the Appendix for a selected bibliography to complete your knowledge in the indicated topics. In the next chapter, you will learn about drone modeling, which is also useful for many types of aerial vehicles.

CHAPTER 2

Modeling

This chapter focuses on the modeling of drones. You will learn about frames of reference, kinematics, dynamics, models of propulsion or allocation, and linear modeling considerations. As a result, you will be able to model a drone and extend this knowledge to other types of vehicles and aircraft.

Regarding aerodynamics, we won't cover these topics because the design of the vehicles analyzed in this book are mostly vertical takeoff and have low speeds, light weights, and/or small size areas in their operation with respect to other types of vehicles (airplanes and manned aircraft, for example). See Figure 2-1.

You may notice that a multicopter requires thrust components to achieve its motion (this is called thrust vectoring). For this reason, we separate the aerodynamic analysis into two useful sections in the Appendix. One of them is about the calculation of the maximum drone speeds and could serve for the design of racing drones. The other is about how to extend the knowledge of this book to other types of aircraft. In these sections, you will use the knowledge acquired in this chapter and you will expand it by introducing aerodynamic effects.

The elements that have high aerodynamic effects due to their rotation speeds are the propellers. However, they will not be considered here because it is assumed that you will not manufacture your own propellers but rather you will buy them (but if necessary, you can read more about their design in the references section of the Appendix). It is also assumed that you will fly your aircraft most of the time at a considerable distance

© Julio Alberto Mendoza-Mendoza, Victor Javier Gonzalez-Villela,
Carlos Fernando Aguilar-Ibañez, Leonardo Fonseca-Ruiz 2021
J. A. Mendoza-Mendoza et al., *Drones to Go*, https://doi.org/10.1007/978-1-4842-6788-2_2

from the floor or walls or even other objects and vehicles; otherwise, you can read related information about restrictions in the Appendix.

Let's start with a description of the frames of modeling.

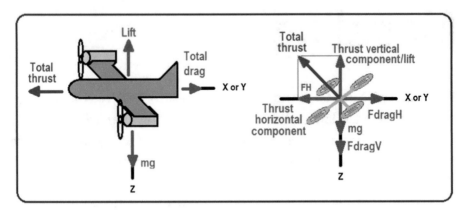

Figure 2-1. *Generic forces acting on a plane and a quadcopter equivalent*

Frames of Modeling

There are three frames of modeling associated with a quadcopter, as you will soon see. The modeling of said vehicle is developed in mixed frames and is done at the convenience of the sensors and mathematical operations. These frames are the world frame, the vehicle frame, and the motor frame, and they are illustrated in Figure 2-2.

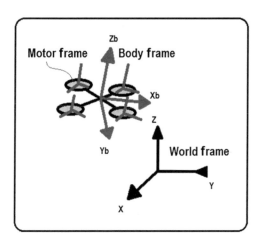

Figure 2-2. *Frames of modeling*

- The world frame (or base, or fixed frame, or inertial frame) indicates a fixed coordinate system. The vehicle moves with respect to this fixed reference. This can be a global geographical reference such as an Earth pole, a simple corner, or the center of a room.

- The vehicle frame (or body frame, or mobile, or non-inertial frame) indicates the coordinate system that is usually placed at a point of interest on board the vehicle (the geometric center, or the mass center, or the gravitational or buoyancy centers, among many others). It is with respect to this frame and the fixed frame that translations and rotations are measured.

- Finally, the frame of the motors (or propulsion frame, or actuator, or allocation frame) is each one of the frames placed on each motor. They have the function of distributing the force and torque of each motor to the vehicle's reference frame.

Notice that in order to facilitate the calculations, as far as possible, the Z axes corresponding to the world and the vehicle frames, respectively, are usually placed in parallel. This is because the quadcopter design allows it and, as you will see later, because smooth flight considerations are made (this simplification in the selection of said axes is not possible in vehicles with more advanced mobility, for example those of the omnidirectional type).

It's time to move on to the kinematics of the drone. First we will consider translational kinematics.

Translational Kinematics

Let's assume that we want to associate the world frame with the vehicle frame. Although this seems simple at first sight, it is necessary to remember that all association of concepts should be carried out in an impartial space.

To do this, imagine that students in a classroom are asked to indicate the position of an insect walking on the whiteboard with respect to their positions, as indicated in Figure 2-3.

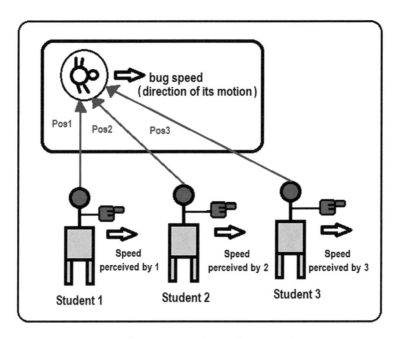

Figure 2-3. *Motion and position of an object with respect to external observers*

As you can see, everyone will have a different notion of the insect and they will give a result that depends on the location where they are placed.

However, everyone, no matter their position, can indicate that the insect is moving in the indicated direction.

In this way, an impartial element for the people in that classroom is the motion of the insect, and this motion is related to its speed.

This suggests that if the world frame is placed in different positions with respect to the vehicle, as you can see in Figure 2-4, the invariant relationship between frames would not be at the position level but at the speed level (as a vector), and this is valid for an observer or sensor placed in each world frame.

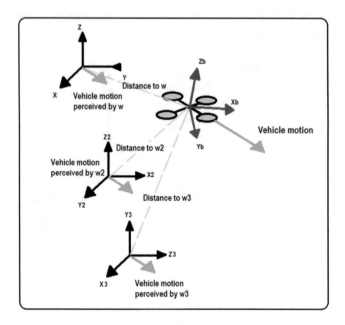

Figure 2-4. *Motion and position of a drone with respect to different world frames*

From the previous figures, you can see that the perception of the vehicle motion in each frame is not modified by the distance between the frames. However, by superimposing two of them as in Figure 2-5, it may be noticed that there is an influence of the orientation in their respective axes. Therefore, in order to relate them, it is necessary to find a trigonometric projection between the respective axes of the coordinate frames. This in a three-dimensional mode is reduced to finding rotation matrices (note the use of Newton's notation, which is a letter or symbol adorned with a dot; this implies a first order derivative, and in our case indicates that this is a relationship between velocity frames or speed, as was previously stated).

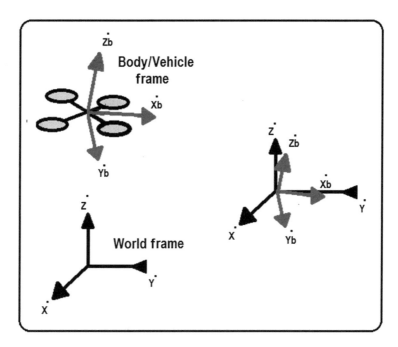

Figure 2-5. *Body and world frames overlapped*

Among the family of rotation matrices, and for accomplishing the ISO 1151–2: 1985 standard, this text will use the Euler angle sequence of roll, pitch, and yaw, known as Tait-Bryan. This is

$$R = R_{z_\psi} R_{x_\phi} R_{y_\theta}$$

$$R = \begin{bmatrix} c\psi c\theta - s\phi s\psi s\theta & -c\phi s\psi & c\psi s\theta + s\phi s\psi c\theta \\ s\psi c\theta + s\phi c\psi s\theta & c\phi c\psi & s\psi s\theta - s\phi c\psi c\theta \\ -c\phi s\theta & s\phi & c\phi c\theta \end{bmatrix}$$

$$\begin{bmatrix} \dot{x} \\ \dot{y} \\ \dot{z} \end{bmatrix} = R \begin{bmatrix} \dot{x}_b \\ \dot{y}_b \\ \dot{z}_b \end{bmatrix}$$

Remember that individual rotations are defined as (note that the pivot is the axis of rotation)

$$R_{x_\phi} = \begin{bmatrix} 1 & 0 & 0 \\ 0 & \cos\phi & -\sin\phi \\ 0 & \sin\phi & \cos\phi \end{bmatrix} \qquad R_{z_\psi} = \begin{bmatrix} \cos\psi & -\sin\psi & 0 \\ \sin\psi & \cos\psi & 0 \\ 0 & 0 & 1 \end{bmatrix}$$

$$R_{y_\theta} = \begin{bmatrix} \cos\theta & 0 & \sin\theta \\ 0 & 1 & 0 \\ -\sin\theta & 0 & \cos\theta \end{bmatrix}$$

A good question here is, Why is this sequence of rotations a multiplication and not a sum? And the answer at least from the viewpoint of the mathematical congruence is simple. Each rotation matrix must be orthonormal because each one of its columns represents unit vectors whose components vary between 0 and 1 and describe perpendicular axes (to verify this property, consult the recommended texts on linear algebra and rotation matrices), so if we add them, there is a risk that the resulting elements will exceed unit values, while if we multiply them, as they are fractional numbers, zeros, or ones, the result will continue to be fractional numbers, zeros, or ones. Therefore, the composition of a successive sequence of rotation matrices must be multiplicative.

Notice that the set of equations that we use are valid at the speed level and also at the force level. This statement will be used later, and its demonstration and foundation for the most demanding readers can be found in a large number of texts as an application of D'Alembert's principle and the principle of the virtual work, also known as the principle of least action.

Now you will learn about the rotational kinematics of the drone.

Rotational Kinematics

Obtaining the translational kinematics was relatively easy, considering the existence of reference frames directly linked through rotations. However, this is not the case for rotational variables (notice that we have angular information regarding the world frame given by Euler's angles, but we do not have angular information directly in the body or vehicle frame). For deducing the kinematics, it becomes necessary to use the mathematical properties of a rotation matrix.

Rotation matrices must fulfil the principle of orthonormality. This implies the following:

$$RR^T = I$$

As indicated, the most objective analysis to establish a relationship between frames is at the speed level. The velocities and consequently the speed are obtained from positional derivatives, so a first intuition is to derive the previous equation. Note that this is a derivative with respect to the time, so if the rotation matrix depends on the Euler angles when deriving, the angular rates of said Euler angles will appear (chain rule). Also notice that the following result is obtained with the rules of the derivative of a product (a matrix product) and the derivative of a constant (an identity matrix):

$$\dot{R}R^T + R\dot{R}^T = 0$$

Using the following property of the transposed matrices in the second term of the previous equation

$$(AB)^T = B^T A^T$$
$$(\dot{R}R^T)^T = R\dot{R}^T$$

and replacing this property, we get

$$\dot{R}R^T + R\dot{R}^T = \dot{R}R^T + (\dot{R}R^T)^T = 0$$

From this result a special type of matrices called antisymmetric or skew-symmetric are invoked. They satisfy the following:

$$S + S^T = 0$$

Therefore, it is true that the following term is a skew-symmetric matrix:

$$S = \dot{R}R^T$$

And what is this useful for?

A skew-symmetric matrix is associated with a representation of the cross product. Suppose we have two vectors:

$$a = \begin{bmatrix} a_x & a_y & a_z \end{bmatrix}$$
$$b = \begin{bmatrix} b_x & b_y & b_z \end{bmatrix}$$

$$a \times b = \begin{bmatrix} 0 & -a_z & a_y \\ a_z & 0 & -a_x \\ -a_y & a_x & 0 \end{bmatrix} \begin{bmatrix} b_x \\ b_y \\ b_z \end{bmatrix} = S(a)b$$

In this way, an antisymmetric matrix (in this case the one associated with the vector a) contains information of a vector distributed in its elements in the indicated way.

The question about the equation's usefulness remains open and it will be answered now. Just keep in mind the concept of skew-symmetric matrix and its relationship with the cross product.

Suppose that the car in Figure 2-6 only rotates around its Zb axis with angular velocity equal to the theta derivative. Note that the Z axis of the world frame and the body frame (Zb) are parallel (both of them point towards you).

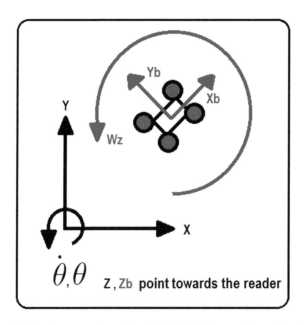

Figure 2-6. *Body frame of a wheeled vehicle and its relationship with the world frame*

It is obvious for this example that the angular velocity in the Z axis of the body frame is equal to the derivative of theta measured in the fixed frame (again, because they are parallel axes).

$$\omega_z = \dot{\theta}$$

So we can reach the same result with the skew-symmetric equation:

$$R_z(\theta) = \begin{bmatrix} \cos\theta & -\sin\theta & 0 \\ \sin\theta & \cos\theta & 0 \\ 0 & 0 & 1 \end{bmatrix}$$

$$S = \dot{R}R^T = \begin{bmatrix} -\dot{\theta}\sin\theta & -\dot{\theta}\cos\theta & 0 \\ \dot{\theta}\cos\theta & -\dot{\theta}\sin\theta & 0 \\ 0 & 0 & 0 \end{bmatrix} \begin{bmatrix} \cos\theta & \sin\theta & 0 \\ -\sin\theta & \cos\theta & 0 \\ 0 & 0 & 1 \end{bmatrix} = \begin{bmatrix} 0 & -\dot{\theta} & 0 \\ \dot{\theta} & 0 & 0 \\ 0 & 0 & 0 \end{bmatrix}$$

We can conclude from the definition of the elements of a skew-symmetric matrix that

$$S(\omega) = \begin{bmatrix} 0 & -\omega_z & \omega_y \\ \omega_z & 0 & -\omega_x \\ -\omega_y & \omega_x & 0 \end{bmatrix} = \dot{R}R^T$$

Then, by using Euler's compound rotation matrix and by doing the previous procedure, as well as the corresponding simplifications, the following is obtained (it is an interesting exercise that you develop the full sequence of these equations; remember that the rotation matrix derivative is with respect to the time, and also remember the total differential concept):

$$R = R_{z_\psi} R_{x_\phi} R_{y_\theta}$$

$$R = \begin{bmatrix} c\psi c\theta - s\phi s\psi s\theta & -c\phi s\psi & c\psi s\theta + s\phi s\psi c\theta \\ s\psi c\theta + s\phi c\psi s\theta & c\phi c\psi & s\psi s\theta - s\phi c\psi c\theta \\ -c\phi s\theta & s\phi & c\phi c\theta \end{bmatrix}$$

$$\omega = \begin{bmatrix} \omega_{xB} \\ \omega_{yB} \\ \omega_{zB} \end{bmatrix} = \begin{bmatrix} c\theta & 0 & -c\phi s\theta \\ 0 & 1 & s\phi \\ s\theta & 0 & c\phi c\theta \end{bmatrix} \begin{bmatrix} \dot{\phi} \\ \dot{\theta} \\ \dot{\psi} \end{bmatrix} = \begin{bmatrix} p \\ q \\ r \end{bmatrix}$$

where

$$\dot{R} = \frac{dR}{d\theta}\dot{\theta} + \frac{dR}{d\phi}\dot{\phi} + \frac{dR}{d\psi}\dot{\psi}$$

This relates the body frame angular velocities with the fixed frame angular velocities. Remember that the fixed frame is expressed in Euler's angles.

For those who prefer geometry to developing equations, there is also an understandable and visual deduction for obtaining this relationship between velocities in Beedford's book indicated in the Appendix.

Note also that the imposition of said angular orthonormality constraints gives to the drones what is known as a non-holonomic property (this is unnoticeable in smooth or linear flight modes, as you will see soon).

Finally, observe that the (p q r) nomenclature was introduced. This is frequently used with aircraft and of course multicopters.

Now that you have the kinematics of the drone, it's time to look at the dynamics, but before that, we provide you with a brief on the forces acting on a drone and its propellers.

Forces Acting on a Multicopter and Its Propellers

Before developing the dynamic equations, it is convenient to deduce the basic forces that act on a multicopter. Aerodynamic effects could be added, but since they vary between outdoor and indoor operations, even at near or far distances from the ground, they are considered as non-generic material that can be consulted in other works or briefly in the Appendix (see drone maximum velocities).

The most obvious force acting on a drone is gravity. Let's consider that the vehicle is well balanced, and that said force is located directly at the center of gravity or the center of geometry, which for this kind of vehicle is desirable to coincide. See Figure 2-7.

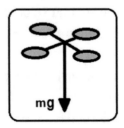

Figure 2-7. *Gravity force actuating on a drone*

Forces Acting on a Propeller

The next step is to analyze the forces on a single propeller. Note that this analysis is performed for two-bladed propellers but is expandable for more blades with the corresponding trigonometric projections.

The first thing that is considered is that the thrust force on each blade can be equivalent to a force placed on a point of said blade. In Figure 2-8, they are labeled FL (or left) and FR (or right). The second thing that is considered is that the propeller is well balanced, which implies that the distance between the center of the propeller to the analysis point on each blade is the same (a radius r).

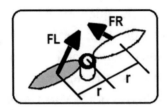

Figure 2-8. *Forces actuating on the blades of a propeller and their lever arms*

Also, we will use the propeller frame shown in Figure 2-9.

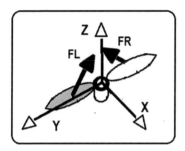

Figure 2-9. *A propeller frame for analysis*

The following step is to decompose the forces on each blade into their vertical and horizontal components (Z and H labels). See Figure 2-10.

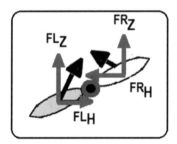

Figure 2-10. *Components of the forces acting on each blade*

Next, we perform the sum of forces and torques in the three respective axes (X, Y, and Z). As symmetry and balancing assumptions are made in each blade, it is possible to perform the following equalities:

$$FR = FL$$

$$FR_Z = FL_Z = F_Z$$

$$FR_H = FL_H = F_H$$

From the previous figure, the vertical analysis of forces is simple. Notice the fact that using more blades increases the vehicle's load capacity (as expected, each blade acts as a support axle).

$$\sum F_z = FL_z + FR_z = 2F_z$$

The analysis in X Y is the same, and for this we will take advantage of the radial symmetry of the propeller (this analysis using odd blades becomes very interesting since it requires trigonometric projections, but the final result must be the same).

Suppose that the propeller is positioned for a moment on the X or Y axis, as indicated in Figure 2-11.

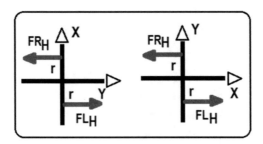

Figure 2-11. *Top view of the forces acting on each blade. The Z axis points towards you*

$$\sum F_X = \sum F_Y = FL_H + FR_H = F_H - F_H = 0$$

Therefore, it is shown that as long as the propeller is adequately balanced, the horizontal forces that each blade generates will be canceled. However, as you have noticed, there is also the presence of the radii of action and consequently torques. This is analyzed as follows.

Let's go back to the previous figure, and adding the fact that the Z axis points towards you, the torque around this axis is as shown in Figure 2-12.

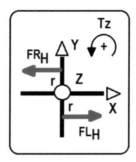

Figure 2-12.   *Top view of the forces acting on each blade for analyzing the equivalent torque. The Z axis points towards you*

$$\sum \tau_Z = r(FR_H + FL_H) = 2rF_H$$

Note that increasing the blade number also increases the propeller torque capacity (each blade acts as a lever arm).

And finally we will determine the horizontal torque (around the X or Y axes; there is no difference). See Figure 2-13.

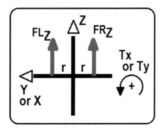

Figure 2-13.   *Lateral view of the forces acting on each blade for analyzing the horizontal torque. The Y or X axis points towards you*

$$\sum \tau_X = \sum \tau_Y = r(FR_Z + FL_Z) = r(F_Z - F_Z) = 0$$

The most important conclusion of the previous analysis is the next. While the propellers are well balanced, they can only generate a vertical thrust force on their axis of action and a torque around the same axis. See Figure 2-14.

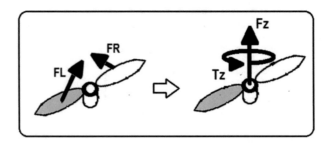

Figure 2-14. *Equivalent force and torque of the propeller with respect to its center*

An interesting exercise for you is to deduce the same effect for a propeller with three blades distributed at 120 degrees each. The final result must be the same.

Forces Acting on the Vehicle

Based on the previous conclusion, we will transfer the forces of each propeller to the center of the vehicle. See Figure 2-15.

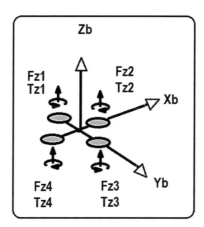

Figure 2-15. *Forces and torques generated by each propeller with respect to the center of a quadcopter, and the corresponding vehicle frame for this analysis*

For this example and for the expected results, we will do it as in the case of Figure 2-15. Pay attention to the fact that the labeling and the direction of the Cartesian axes, as well as the numbering of the motors, and their sense of rotation, and even their geometric distribution, influence what we will see and is known as allocation or propulsion matrix. Also notice that half of the motors rotate clockwise with respect to the other half, in order to prevent autorotation (which implies that the vehicle rotates in an undesired way around its main axis). This could happen if all the motors or most of them rotate in one sense (clockwise or counterclockwise).

Analyzing the forces on the Zb axis, we have

$$\sum F_{ZB} = F_{Z1} + F_{Z2} + F_{Z3} + F_{Z4}$$

Considering a well-balanced vehicle with well-balanced propellers, in the Yb and Xb axes there are no forces acting directly on them, just torques, therefore,

$$\sum F_{XB} = \sum F_{YB} = 0$$

Notice that there are conditions where these forces are present and they cannot be canceled out from the model. However, these effects usually appear in large aircraft and they can be simplified by means of mathematical transformations or control compensation. See Reza-Olfati's article in the Appendix.

Let's continue with the torques. The first thing to do is to establish a positive sense of rotation, as illustrated in Figure 2-16.

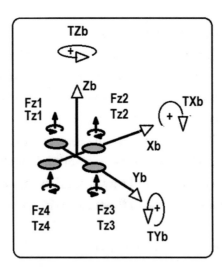

Figure 2-16. *Forces and torques generated by each propeller with respect to the center of a quadcopter, and a sense of positive rotation for this analysis*

Observe that in the case of the torque around the Zb axis, this is directly induced by the individual torques of each motor. See Figure 2-17.

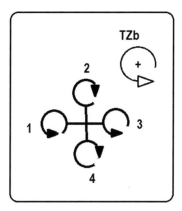

Figure 2-17. *Drone's top view for the analysis of torque around the Zbody axis, which points towards you*

$$\sum T_{ZB} = T_{Z1} - T_{Z2} + T_{Z3} - T_{Z4}$$

In the case of the Yb and Xb axes, torques are induced as a lever arm effect given by the thrust forces and their respective radii. See Figure 2-18 and Figure 2-19. Note that the vehicle must be well balanced to ensure identical or highly similar radii or lever arms.

$$\sum T_{YB} = r(F_{Z2} - F_{Z4})$$

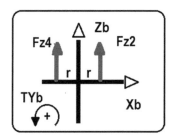

Figure 2-18. *Drone's lateral view for the analysis of torque around the Y axis, which points towards you*

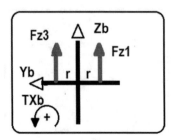

Figure 2-19. *Drone's lateral view for the analysis of torque around the X axis, which points towards you*

$$\sum T_{XB} = r(F_{Z1} - F_{Z3})$$

The important conclusion here is that a quadcopter has at its center of gravity, coincident by design with the geometric center, one thrust and three torques generated by its motors and the action of the force of gravity. See Figure 2-20. Notice that the force of gravity is always perpendicular to the ground or world frame, but this is not the case for FZb (drone thrust), because FZb is perpendicular to the body of the drone or the vehicle frame. Soon we will use the appropriate relationships between these frames.

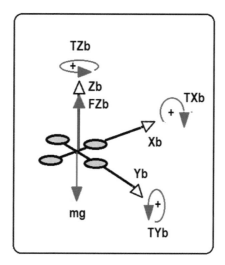

Figure 2-20. *Equivalent forces and torques acting on the center of the drone, generated by its motors and the gravity*

Having learned about the forces acting on the vehicle, it is time to study its dynamics.

Translational Dynamics

Having established the motion or kinematic relationships between frames, and the forces acting on a quadcopter, we will deduce the equations that produce these motions. In this case, we will start with the translational dynamics.

For this, it is convenient to ask ourselves where and why to do this analysis.

The translational dynamics is generally deducted in the fixed frame. Why? Just for mathematical simplification and for compatibility with the sensors (most of the translational sensors indicate the position of the drone with respect to a fixed frame like a GPS).

The procedure is as follows:

1. Symmetry and point mass assumptions are done (a quadcopter type drone is designed in a way that is balanced and generally its center of gravity coincides with its geometric center or at least is located as close as possible).

2. Newton's second law equation is used for the aircraft as it was a particle with three-dimensional motion (that is the purpose of the step 1 assumptions).

$$\vec{a} = \begin{bmatrix} a_x \\ a_y \\ a_z \end{bmatrix}$$

$$\vec{F} = m\vec{a}$$

3. Since we are interested in controlling the aircraft motion (modeled as a particle), we rewrite the previous equation with respect to the position (acceleration is defined as the second derivative of the position).

$$\vec{a} = \begin{bmatrix} \ddot{x} \\ \ddot{y} \\ \ddot{z} \end{bmatrix} \qquad \vec{F} = m \begin{bmatrix} \ddot{x} \\ \ddot{y} \\ \ddot{z} \end{bmatrix}$$

4. We add the free-fall effect (gravity).

$$\vec{F} + m \begin{bmatrix} 0 \\ 0 \\ -g \end{bmatrix} = m \begin{bmatrix} \ddot{x} \\ \ddot{y} \\ \ddot{z} \end{bmatrix}$$

5. Since we want to model the drone in the fixed frame and the thrust force of the drone acts on the body frame, we must relate them, so see Figure 2-21. In this case, as an extension of D'Alembert's principle, it is valid to indicate the following. Remember that the matrix of rotation is the composition given by the Tait-Bryan rotations.

$$\vec{F} = R \begin{bmatrix} 0 \\ 0 \\ F_{BZ} \end{bmatrix}$$

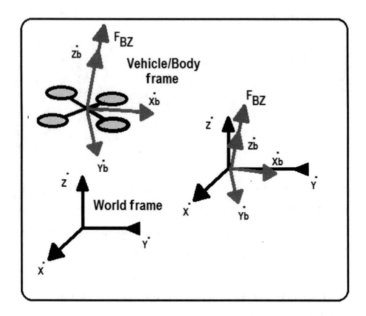

Figure 2-21. *Thrust force of a quadcopter overlapped between the body and the world frames*

6. So, the system of equations that model the translational dynamics is

$$
R \begin{bmatrix} 0 \\ 0 \\ F_{BZ} \end{bmatrix} + m \begin{bmatrix} 0 \\ 0 \\ -g \end{bmatrix} = m \begin{bmatrix} \ddot{x} \\ \ddot{y} \\ \ddot{z} \end{bmatrix}
$$

Note that this is the simplified model, but you can add effects such as air friction, turbulence, and more, depending on the needs of your work.

Now that you know about the translational dynamics, let's move to rotational dynamics.

Rotational Dynamics

In this part, we use Euler's equations for rotational motion. They are the equivalent of Newton's second law for rotational motion.

Unlike the translational dynamics, this analysis is expressed in the body frame. The reasons are again simplification of equations and compatibility with the sensors, which generally provide on-board rotation measurements.

The procedure is as follows:

1. We use the rotational equivalent of Newton's second law or Euler's equations. Note that unlike the previous case, J is not a constant like mass but is a 3x3 matrix which, when multiplied by angular accelerations, produces a 3x1 vector.

$$\vec{F} = m\vec{a} \qquad \vec{\tau} = J\vec{\alpha}$$
$$\vec{F}_{3\times1} = m_{1\times1}\vec{a}_{3\times1}$$
$$\vec{\tau}_{3\times1} = J_{3\times3}\vec{\alpha}_{3\times1}$$

2. We rewrite in terms of something known or measurable such as the onboard angular velocity (note that the translational analysis is expressed in terms of the second derivative of the position). In this case, it helps that the sensors generally allow measuring on-board angular velocities. Observe that the acceleration is also the first derivative of the velocity.

$$\vec{\tau} = J\vec{\alpha} = J \begin{bmatrix} \dot{\omega}_x \\ \dot{\omega}_y \\ \dot{\omega}_z \end{bmatrix}$$

3. Rigid and symmetrical body assumptions are made to consider that the inertia matrix only has components on its diagonal, which means that everything that is not on the diagonal is negligible.

$$J = \begin{bmatrix} J_x & 0 & 0 \\ 0 & J_y & 0 \\ 0 & 0 & J_z \end{bmatrix}$$

$$\vec{\tau} = \begin{bmatrix} J_x \dot{\omega}_x \\ J_y \dot{\omega}_y \\ J_z \dot{\omega}_z \end{bmatrix}$$

4. The gravitational effect is omitted because when considering that the drone is symmetrical, rigid, and well balanced with respect to its center, the torques created by the force of gravity are canceled (lever arm radii tend to zero). You should consider that this does not happen with an unbalanced vehicle or a drone with large dimensions (for example, a drone transporting something placed on the edge of its frame like a robotic arm).

However, the effects of centrifugal accelerations are usually important (in the smooth flight simplification, you will notice that these accelerations are omitted due to the reduced angular velocities).

$$\vec{\tau} = \begin{bmatrix} J_x\dot{\omega}_x \\ J_y\dot{\omega}_y \\ J_z\dot{\omega}_z \end{bmatrix} + \begin{bmatrix} \omega_x \\ \omega_y \\ \omega_z \end{bmatrix} \times \begin{bmatrix} J_x\omega_x \\ J_y\omega_y \\ J_z\omega_z \end{bmatrix}$$

Why are these centrifugal effects omitted during translational analysis? Because the thrust force position is almost zero with respect to the vehicle's analysis center, and therefore they are negligible (but not for large vehicles, where something similar happens to the rotational effect of gravity). As you can see, in rotational motion, they are considered because they do not depend on the action radii but they depend on angular velocities.

5. Developing the equations (cross product), the rotational dynamics become

$$\begin{bmatrix} \tau_{BX} \\ \tau_{BY} \\ \tau_{BZ} \end{bmatrix} = \begin{bmatrix} J_x\dot{\omega}_x \\ J_y\dot{\omega}_y \\ J_z\dot{\omega}_z \end{bmatrix} + \begin{bmatrix} \omega_y\omega_z J_z - \omega_y\omega_z J_y \\ \omega_x\omega_z J_x - \omega_x\omega_z J_z \\ \omega_x\omega_y J_y - \omega_x\omega_y J_x \end{bmatrix}$$

This dynamics will be simplified later with the smooth flight conditions. However, they will be employed again in the geometric control section.

You have learned about kinematics and dynamics. In order to close our modeling, let's talk about the allocation model.

Allocation Model

The propulsion or allocation model establishes the relationship between the motors and the vehicle's center of analysis (the gravity center, for example). It is the link between theory (modeling, simulation, and control) and practice (design and programming).

Steps for Obtaining the Allocation Model

The procedure for obtaining this model is really similar to the one carried out in the section where the torques and forces acting on the quadcopter are demonstrated. However, it is repeated in a systematic way.

In general, the following relationship is expected (assuming, of course, a linear behavior of the motors):

$$
\begin{bmatrix}
F_{XB} \\
F_{YB} \\
F_{ZB} \\
\tau_{XB} \\
\tau_{YB} \\
\tau_{ZB}
\end{bmatrix}_{6 \times 1}
= [A]_{6 \times m}
\begin{bmatrix}
\omega_1 \\
\omega_2 \\
\vdots \\
\omega_m
\end{bmatrix}_{m \times 1}
$$

where w, with index from 1 to m, represents the speed of each one of the m motors of the vehicle and A is an allocation matrix that indicates how each motor influences the behavior of the three possible torques and three possible forces in the Cartesian space. This Cartesian space is associated with the center of analysis of said aircraft (the gravity one, for example). In most of the multicopters, the A matrix has constant elements, but they can vary if, for example, each motor has a system of servos that alter its position and orientation.

Note that the result of this modeling process changes for each drone configuration, but the process described is generic and is as follows:

1. The first thing to do is to establish an axes convention, including positive directions of motion. This includes defining both translations and rotations; see Figure 2-22. In practice, this is done according to the remote control sticks, which are frequently based on the aforementioned ISO standard (see the design section of this book).

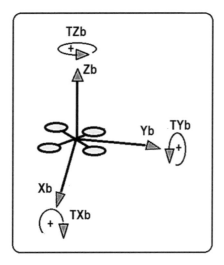

Figure 2-22. *Axes convention for step 1*

2. The next step is to attach a label to the motors. This involves their sense of rotation and their geometric distribution with respect to the other motors.

In this case, and to give a concrete example, we are using a flat geometry called X configuration, with the indicated senses of rotation, the following labels, and also with radial symmetry, as shown in Figure 2-23.

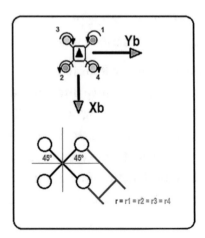

Figure 2-23. *Motor labeling for step 2*

Note that this is usually done with respect to the autopilot reference (generally a little arrow).

3.   Now we must relate the motions established in step 1 with the effects of torque and thrust of each motor; see Figure 2-24. Remember that there are torques created by the action of individual torques and torques generated by the lever arms.

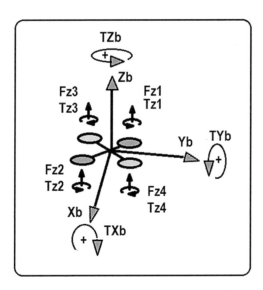

Figure 2-24. *Motor forces and torques acting on the selected frame for step 3*

The Allocation Model for a Quadcopter

By carrying out a similar procedure to the one in the previous section about the forces acting on a quadcopter, the following is obtained (remember that each aircraft configuration is different, but it can be analyzed following this example as a starting point):

$$F_{ZB} = F_{Z1} + F_{Z2} + F_{Z3} + F_{Z4}$$
$$F_{XB} = F_{YB} = 0$$
$$\tau_{ZB} = \tau_{Z1} + \tau_{Z2} - \tau_{Z3} - \tau_{Z4}$$
$$\tau_{XB} = (F_{Z2} + F_{Z3})r\cos(45) - (F_{Z1} + F_{Z4})r\cos(45)$$
$$\tau_{YB} = (F_{Z1} + F_{Z3})r\sin(45) - (F_{Z2} + F_{Z4})r\sin(45)$$

Notice that the torques around the body frame Z axis are directly produced by other torques (those of the motors), while the torques around the body frame X and Y axes are caused by the action of the lever arms, as illustrated in Figure 2-25.

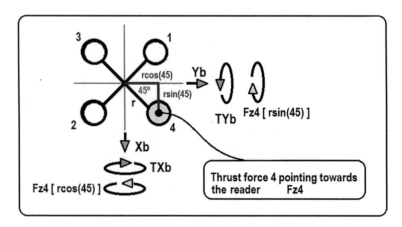

Figure 2-25. *Motor lever arm components for calculating torques (exemplified for motor 4)*

For simplicity, this is illustrated only for motor 4, but you can deduce the remaining components. Observe the direction of the lever arms with respect to the coordinate axes and consequently their components. Also, keep in mind the rotation caused by each motor with respect to the reference axis in order to determine the appropriate signs. In this case, both components in X and Y are negative and this is reflected in the equations, because the rotations that thrust 4 produces are opposite to the reference of positive rotation previously set.

Next, a series of assumptions will be made to simplify the above equations as much as possible. You must evaluate whether such assumptions are feasible or not in your own designs.

The following relationships between forces and torques with the rotation speed of each motor are assumed (these assumptions are more or less adequate since motor manufacturers usually ensure this degree of linear proportion). Observe the proportionality constants that relate the torque and thrust force with the speed of the motor.

$$\tau = \kappa_T \omega$$
$$F = \kappa_F \omega$$

Therefore and also assuming that all of the motors are the same (if the motors are the same model, the proportionality constants, according to the manufacturer, will be similar or approximately the same),

$$F_{ZB} = \kappa_F(\omega_1 + \omega_2 + \omega_3 + \omega_4)$$
$$F_{XB} = F_{YB} = 0$$
$$\tau_{ZB} = \kappa_\tau(\omega_1 + \omega_2 - \omega_3 - \omega_4)$$
$$\tau_{XB} = r\cos(45)\kappa_F(-\omega_1 + \omega_2 + \omega_3 - \omega_4)$$
$$\tau_{YB} = r\sin(45)\kappa_F(\omega_1 - \omega_2 + \omega_3 - \omega_4)$$

The next assumption is that the terms kf, kt, rcos (45) kf, and rsin (45) kf are constant gains and as they are present in all the terms that contain an angular velocity w, they can be factorized and absorbed by compensation for Fzb, Tzb, Txb, and Tyb.

In this way, it is common to find this simplified representation. Note that said compensation considers symmetries, and if the angles of the arms or their distances were different (an asymmetric drone), these terms should be taken into account and not omitted:

$$F_{ZB} = \omega_1 + \omega_2 + \omega_3 + \omega_4$$
$$F_{XB} = F_{YB} = 0$$
$$\tau_{ZB} = \omega_1 + \omega_2 - \omega_3 - \omega_4$$
$$\tau_{XB} = -\omega_1 + \omega_2 + \omega_3 - \omega_4$$
$$\tau_{YB} = \omega_1 - \omega_2 + \omega_3 - \omega_4$$

These equations are simpler than the original ones and admit this vectorial representation:

$$
\begin{bmatrix} F_{XB} \\ F_{YB} \\ F_{ZB} \\ \tau_{XB} \\ \tau_{YB} \\ \tau_{ZB} \end{bmatrix} = \begin{bmatrix} 0 & 0 & 0 & 0 \\ 0 & 0 & 0 & 0 \\ 1 & 1 & 1 & 1 \\ -1 & 1 & 1 & -1 \\ 1 & -1 & 1 & -1 \\ 1 & 1 & -1 & -1 \end{bmatrix} \begin{bmatrix} \omega_1 \\ \omega_2 \\ \omega_3 \\ \omega_4 \end{bmatrix}
$$

And thus the following reduction (to simplify matrix operations):

$$
\begin{bmatrix} F_{ZB} \\ \tau_{XB} \\ \tau_{YB} \\ \tau_{ZB} \end{bmatrix} = \begin{bmatrix} 1 & 1 & 1 & 1 \\ -1 & 1 & 1 & -1 \\ 1 & -1 & 1 & -1 \\ 1 & 1 & -1 & -1 \end{bmatrix} \begin{bmatrix} \omega_1 \\ \omega_2 \\ \omega_3 \\ \omega_4 \end{bmatrix}
$$

For those who wonder how X and Y motions are controlled, this will be seen later in the control section of this book, but it is anticipated that it is due to their dependence on angular variables (nested control).

Note that for hexarotors or tricopters, we will inevitably have non-square matrices and it will be necessary to use pseudoinverses or numerical optimization algorithms.

Continuing our analysis, once we design the control values of this vector,

$$
\begin{bmatrix} F_{ZB} \\ \tau_{XB} \\ \tau_{YB} \\ \tau_{ZB} \end{bmatrix}
$$

its distribution to the motors is done as follows:

$$
\begin{bmatrix} \omega_1 \\ \omega_2 \\ \omega_3 \\ \omega_4 \end{bmatrix} = \begin{bmatrix} 1 & 1 & 1 & 1 \\ -1 & 1 & 1 & -1 \\ 1 & -1 & 1 & -1 \\ 1 & 1 & -1 & -1 \end{bmatrix}^{-1} \begin{bmatrix} F_{ZB} \\ \tau_{XB} \\ \tau_{YB} \\ \tau_{ZB} \end{bmatrix}
$$

In order to reduce processing and avoid calculating said inverse and matrix multiplication over and over again, this is programmed in a developed way, that is

$$
\begin{bmatrix} 1 & 1 & 1 & 1 \\ -1 & 1 & 1 & -1 \\ 1 & -1 & 1 & -1 \\ 1 & 1 & -1 & -1 \end{bmatrix}^{-1} = \begin{bmatrix} \frac{1}{4} & -\frac{1}{4} & \frac{1}{4} & \frac{1}{4} \\ \frac{1}{4} & \frac{1}{4} & -\frac{1}{4} & \frac{1}{4} \\ \frac{1}{4} & \frac{1}{4} & \frac{1}{4} & -\frac{1}{4} \\ \frac{1}{4} & -\frac{1}{4} & -\frac{1}{4} & -\frac{1}{4} \end{bmatrix}
$$

which, under the same argument of constant-values absorption done by the control of torques and forces, is equivalent in action to (this is the allocation matrix)

$$
\begin{bmatrix} 1 & 1 & 1 & 1 \\ -1 & 1 & 1 & -1 \\ 1 & -1 & 1 & -1 \\ 1 & 1 & -1 & -1 \end{bmatrix}^{-1} \approx \begin{bmatrix} 1 & -1 & 1 & 1 \\ 1 & 1 & -1 & 1 \\ 1 & 1 & 1 & -1 \\ 1 & -1 & -1 & -1 \end{bmatrix}
$$

and finally

$$
\begin{bmatrix} \omega_1 \\ \omega_2 \\ \omega_3 \\ \omega_4 \end{bmatrix} = \begin{bmatrix} 1 & -1 & 1 & 1 \\ 1 & 1 & -1 & 1 \\ 1 & 1 & 1 & -1 \\ 1 & -1 & -1 & -1 \end{bmatrix} \begin{bmatrix} F_{ZB} \\ \tau_{XB} \\ \tau_{YB} \\ \tau_{ZB} \end{bmatrix} = \begin{bmatrix} F_{ZB} - \tau_{XB} + \tau_{YB} + \tau_{ZB} \\ F_{ZB} + \tau_{XB} - \tau_{YB} + \tau_{ZB} \\ F_{ZB} + \tau_{XB} + \tau_{YB} - \tau_{ZB} \\ F_{ZB} - \tau_{XB} - \tau_{YB} - \tau_{ZB} \end{bmatrix}
$$

This format must be incorporated both into automatic controls (designed and introduced by control theory, as will be seen in the corresponding section) and into manual controls (from a remote control, for example). When using a remote control, the vector to be incorporated into the motors is this:

$$\begin{bmatrix} Throttle \\ Roll \\ Pitch \\ Rudder \end{bmatrix}$$

A semiautomatic design (with manual and automatic operations) could be as follows (this sum of vectors must be multiplied by the allocation matrix to inject its effect into each motor):

$$\begin{bmatrix} F_{ZB} \\ \tau_{XB} \\ \tau_{YB} \\ \tau_{ZB} \end{bmatrix} + \begin{bmatrix} Throttle \\ Roll \\ Pitch \\ Rudder \end{bmatrix}$$

A natural question is if the previous equations have a simpler way to be used. The answer is affirmative but it also implies certain operating conditions. Let's see what happens.

Linear Simplifications

Before making a second set of simplifications, let's remember those already made, keeping in mind that you should reconsider using them with your mathematical models.

- Small size vehicles, which implies inertial simplifications

- Well-balanced vehicles with respect to their center of gravity, which implies simplifications of torques and forces

- Alignment of the center of gravity with the geometric center, which implies radial simplifications, or lever arms tending to zero

- Well-balanced propellers, which implies that each propeller provides only a thrust and a torque

- Symmetry of the vehicles, in order to impose simplifications on the inertia matrix, and that also implies the reduction of centrifugal equations

- Basic modeling that does not consider friction, turbulence, or other aerodynamic modeling effects. This provides a highly simplified model which is subject to be performed in almost any dynamic simulation software.

Having said that, let's proceed with the task simplifications.

A smooth flight mode implies here that the roll and pitch angles tend to zero, while the yaw angle can take any value for redirecting the aircraft, as the steering wheel in a car.

A smooth flight mode also involves smooth angular speeds. This implies that

- Roll and pitch angles will follow these approximations when they tend to zero:

$$\sin(x) \approx x$$
$$\sin(x) \approx 0$$
$$\cos(x) \approx 1$$

Pay attention to the sine approximations; both are used according to the most convenient of them. The one that equals to zero is a limit, and the one that is equal to the straight line is a linear approximation (for example, the first element of a Taylor series). These approaches do not contradict each other and they are complementary. Also, they are equally useful (in fact, they can appear simultaneously in the same problem).

- Slow angular velocities, when multiplied among them, produce a smaller result which tends to zero.

$$\omega_x \omega_y = \omega_y \omega_z = \omega_x \omega_z \approx 0$$

This will also affect the dynamic behavior of the vehicle in the following way.

If we develop the translational dynamic model,

$$R \begin{bmatrix} 0 \\ 0 \\ F_{BZ} \end{bmatrix} + m \begin{bmatrix} 0 \\ 0 \\ -g \end{bmatrix} = m \begin{bmatrix} \ddot{x} \\ \ddot{y} \\ \ddot{z} \end{bmatrix}$$

and we remember that

$$R = R_{z_\psi} R_{x_\phi} R_{y_\theta}$$

$$R = \begin{bmatrix} c\psi c\theta - s\phi s\psi s\theta & -c\phi s\psi & c\psi s\theta + s\phi s\psi c\theta \\ s\psi c\theta + s\phi c\psi s\theta & c\phi c\psi & s\psi s\theta - s\phi c\psi c\theta \\ -c\phi s\theta & s\phi & c\phi c\theta \end{bmatrix}$$

we will have

$$\begin{bmatrix} F_{BZ} \left(\sin\theta \cos\psi + \sin\phi \cos\theta \sin\psi \right) \\ F_{BZ} \left(\sin\theta \sin\psi - \sin\phi \cos\theta \cos\psi \right) \\ F_{BZ} \cos\phi \cos\theta \end{bmatrix} + m \begin{bmatrix} 0 \\ 0 \\ -g \end{bmatrix} = m \begin{bmatrix} \ddot{x} \\ \ddot{y} \\ \ddot{z} \end{bmatrix}$$

Applying the smooth flight conditions, translational dynamics is simplified in this way (note that a simplification of the translational kinematics is implicit). Observe that this smooth flight only applies to roll and pitch angles, while the yaw angle can be commanded arbitrary and obeys a desired value.

$$F_{BZ} \begin{bmatrix} \theta \cos \psi_d + \phi \sin \psi_d \\ \theta \sin \psi_d - \phi \cos \psi_d \\ 1 \end{bmatrix} + m \begin{bmatrix} 0 \\ 0 \\ -g \end{bmatrix} = m \begin{bmatrix} \ddot{x} \\ \ddot{y} \\ \ddot{z} \end{bmatrix}$$

Note that these sine simplifications for small angles were applied for convenience. If we used the other simplification, we would only have zeros and there would be no equations to interact with.

$$\sin(x) \approx x$$

At rotational level, we have the following dynamic model:

$$\begin{bmatrix} \tau_{BX} \\ \tau_{BY} \\ \tau_{BZ} \end{bmatrix} = \begin{bmatrix} J_x \dot{\omega}_x \\ J_y \dot{\omega}_y \\ J_z \dot{\omega}_z \end{bmatrix} + \begin{bmatrix} \omega_y \omega_z J_z - \omega_y \omega_z J_y \\ \omega_x \omega_z J_x - \omega_x \omega_z J_z \\ \omega_x \omega_y J_y - \omega_x \omega_y J_x \end{bmatrix}$$

And because of the smooth flight, slow angular velocities is simplified in this way:

$$\begin{bmatrix} \tau_{BX} \\ \tau_{BY} \\ \tau_{BZ} \end{bmatrix} = \begin{bmatrix} J_x \dot{\omega}_x \\ J_y \dot{\omega}_y \\ J_z \dot{\omega}_z \end{bmatrix}$$

It is worth analyzing whether it is feasible to express this equation directly in the fixed frame or not. For this, it is necessary to project torques and angular velocities from the vehicle frame to the fixed frame. We will use the kinematic relationship previously deduced:

$$\omega = \begin{bmatrix} \omega_{xB} \\ \omega_{yB} \\ \omega_{zB} \end{bmatrix} = \begin{bmatrix} c\theta & 0 & -c\phi s\theta \\ 0 & 1 & s\phi \\ s\theta & 0 & c\phi c\theta \end{bmatrix} \begin{bmatrix} \dot{\phi} \\ \dot{\theta} \\ \dot{\psi} \end{bmatrix}$$

This is simplified as follows:

$$\begin{bmatrix} \omega_{xB} \\ \omega_{yB} \\ \omega_{zB} \end{bmatrix} = \begin{bmatrix} 1 & 0 & 0 \\ 0 & 1 & 0 \\ 0 & 0 & 1 \end{bmatrix} \begin{bmatrix} \dot{\phi} \\ \dot{\theta} \\ \dot{\psi} \end{bmatrix}$$

Here these approximations for small angles were used for convenience:

$$\sin(x) \approx 0$$

This is because what is desired here is to disappear terms and not keep them for further analysis.

Returning to the dynamic rotational model developed in the frame of the vehicle, we do the following to bring it to the fixed frame:

$$\begin{bmatrix} T_{\dot{\phi}} \\ T_{\theta} \\ T_{\dot{\psi}} \end{bmatrix} = J_w \begin{bmatrix} TBX \\ TBY \\ TBZ \end{bmatrix} = \begin{bmatrix} J_x \dot{\omega}_x \\ J_y \dot{\omega}_y \\ J_z \dot{\omega}_z \end{bmatrix}$$

$$J_w = \begin{bmatrix} c\theta & 0 & -c\phi s\theta \\ 0 & 1 & s\phi \\ s\theta & 0 & c\phi c\theta \end{bmatrix}$$

For the angular velocities, we must carry out the following operations:

$$\omega = J_w \dot{\Theta} \qquad \dot{\Theta} = \begin{bmatrix} \dot{\phi} \\ \dot{\theta} \\ \dot{\psi} \end{bmatrix}$$

$$\dot{\omega} = J_w \ddot{\Theta} + \dot{J}_w \dot{\Theta}$$

But remember that (and remember that the inverse of an identity matrix is also an identity matrix):

$$J_w = \begin{bmatrix} c\theta & 0 & -c\phi s\theta \\ 0 & 1 & s\phi \\ s\theta & 0 & c\phi c\theta \end{bmatrix} \approx \begin{bmatrix} 1 & 0 & 0 \\ 0 & 1 & 0 \\ 0 & 0 & 1 \end{bmatrix}$$

Therefore,

$$\dot{J}_w \approx \begin{bmatrix} 0 & 0 & 0 \\ 0 & 0 & 0 \\ 0 & 0 & 0 \end{bmatrix} \qquad \dot{\omega} \approx J_w \ddot{\Theta} \approx \begin{bmatrix} \ddot{\phi} \\ \ddot{\theta} \\ \ddot{\psi} \end{bmatrix}$$

In this way, the rotational dynamics in the vehicle frame become the same as in the fixed frame.

$$\begin{bmatrix} \tau_\phi \\ \tau_\theta \\ \tau_\psi \end{bmatrix} = J_w \begin{bmatrix} \tau_{BX} \\ \tau_{BY} \\ \tau_{BZ} \end{bmatrix} = \begin{bmatrix} J_x \dot{\omega}_x \\ J_y \dot{\omega}_y \\ J_z \dot{\omega}_z \end{bmatrix}$$

$$\begin{bmatrix} \tau_\phi \\ \tau_\theta \\ \tau_\psi \end{bmatrix} \approx \begin{bmatrix} \tau_{BX} \\ \tau_{BY} \\ \tau_{BZ} \end{bmatrix} \approx \begin{bmatrix} J_x \ddot{\phi} \\ J_y \ddot{\theta} \\ J_z \ddot{\psi} \end{bmatrix}$$

In short, the smooth flight simplification altered the original set of equations as indicated in Figures 2-26, 2-27, and 2-28.

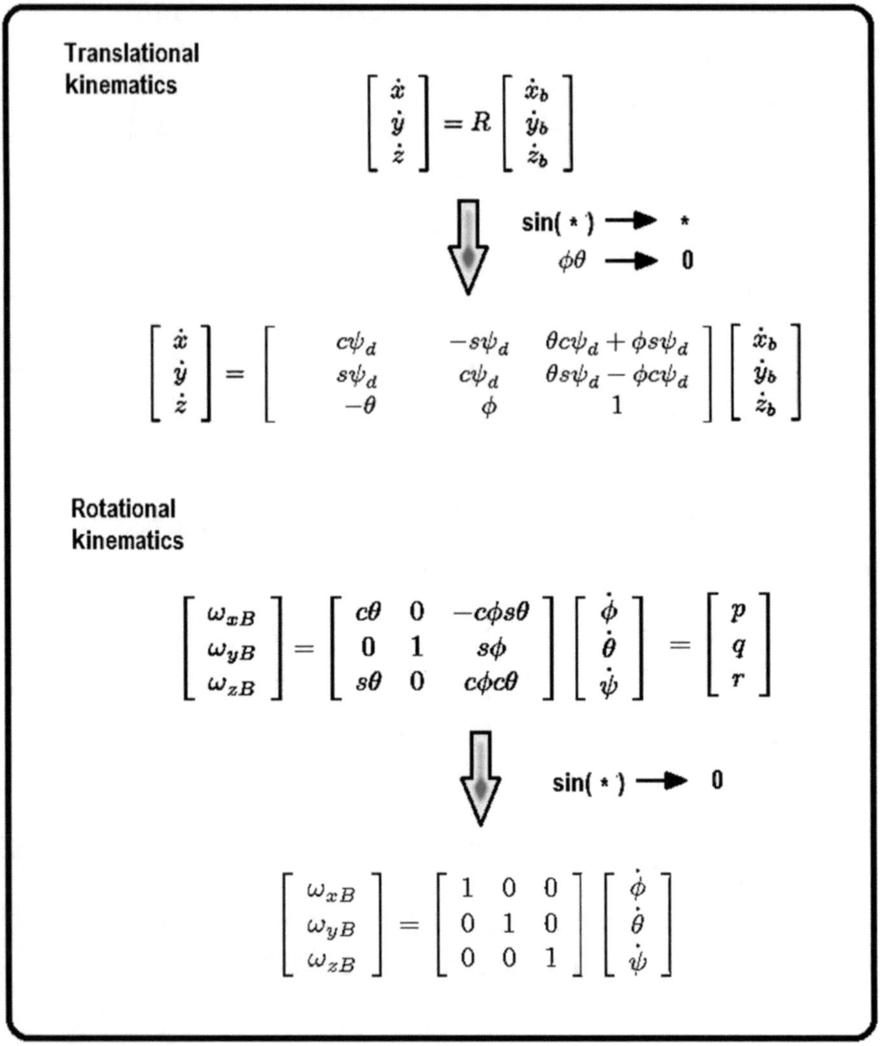

Translational kinematics

$$\begin{bmatrix} \dot{x} \\ \dot{y} \\ \dot{z} \end{bmatrix} = R \begin{bmatrix} \dot{x}_b \\ \dot{y}_b \\ \dot{z}_b \end{bmatrix}$$

$$\sin(*) \longrightarrow * \\ \phi\theta \longrightarrow 0$$

$$\begin{bmatrix} \dot{x} \\ \dot{y} \\ \dot{z} \end{bmatrix} = \begin{bmatrix} c\psi_d & -s\psi_d & \theta c\psi_d + \phi s\psi_d \\ s\psi_d & c\psi_d & \theta s\psi_d - \phi c\psi_d \\ -\theta & \phi & 1 \end{bmatrix} \begin{bmatrix} \dot{x}_b \\ \dot{y}_b \\ \dot{z}_b \end{bmatrix}$$

Rotational kinematics

$$\begin{bmatrix} \omega_{xB} \\ \omega_{yB} \\ \omega_{zB} \end{bmatrix} = \begin{bmatrix} c\theta & 0 & -c\phi s\theta \\ 0 & 1 & s\phi \\ s\theta & 0 & c\phi c\theta \end{bmatrix} \begin{bmatrix} \dot{\phi} \\ \dot{\theta} \\ \dot{\psi} \end{bmatrix} = \begin{bmatrix} p \\ q \\ r \end{bmatrix}$$

$$\sin(*) \longrightarrow 0$$

$$\begin{bmatrix} \omega_{xB} \\ \omega_{yB} \\ \omega_{zB} \end{bmatrix} = \begin{bmatrix} 1 & 0 & 0 \\ 0 & 1 & 0 \\ 0 & 0 & 1 \end{bmatrix} \begin{bmatrix} \dot{\phi} \\ \dot{\theta} \\ \dot{\psi} \end{bmatrix}$$

Figure 2-26. *Linear simplifications for kinematics*

Translational dynamics

$$R \begin{bmatrix} 0 \\ 0 \\ F_{BZ} \end{bmatrix} + m \begin{bmatrix} 0 \\ 0 \\ -g \end{bmatrix} = m \begin{bmatrix} \ddot{x} \\ \ddot{y} \\ \ddot{z} \end{bmatrix}$$

$$\sin(*) \longrightarrow *$$
$$\phi\theta \longrightarrow 0$$

$$F_{BZ} \begin{bmatrix} \theta \cos \psi_d + \phi \sin \psi_d \\ \theta \sin \psi_d - \phi \cos \psi_d \\ 1 \end{bmatrix} + m \begin{bmatrix} 0 \\ 0 \\ -g \end{bmatrix} = m \begin{bmatrix} \ddot{x} \\ \ddot{y} \\ \ddot{z} \end{bmatrix}$$

Rotational dynamics

$$\begin{bmatrix} \tau_{BX} \\ \tau_{BY} \\ \tau_{BZ} \end{bmatrix} = \begin{bmatrix} J_x \dot{\omega}_x \\ J_y \dot{\omega}_y \\ J_z \dot{\omega}_z \end{bmatrix} + \begin{bmatrix} \omega_x \\ \omega_y \\ \omega_z \end{bmatrix} \times \begin{bmatrix} J_x \omega_x \\ J_y \omega_y \\ J_z \omega_z \end{bmatrix}$$

$$\sin(*) \longrightarrow 0$$

$$\begin{bmatrix} \tau_\phi \\ \tau_\theta \\ \tau_\psi \end{bmatrix} \approx \begin{bmatrix} \tau_{BX} \\ \tau_{BY} \\ \tau_{BZ} \end{bmatrix} \approx \begin{bmatrix} J_x \ddot{\phi} \\ J_y \ddot{\theta} \\ J_z \ddot{\psi} \end{bmatrix}$$

Figure 2-27. *Linear simplifications for dynamics*

Note that the changes were done in the kinematic relationships and of course in the dynamics, but the propulsion equations remain the same (keep in mind that if your vehicle has a thrust vectoring system, the allocation matrix will also change).

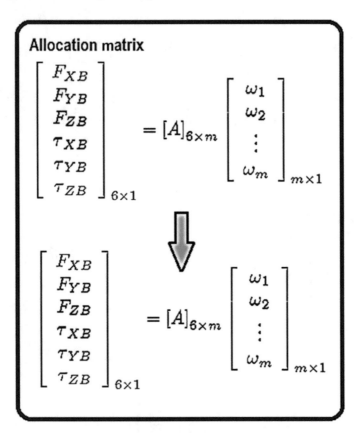

Figure 2-28. *Linear simplifications for the allocation matrix (in this example, the equations remain the same)*

Summary

In this chapter, you learned the generic model of drones with a particular but not exclusive approach to quadcopters. The chapter explained the frames of modeling, the kinematic and dynamic equations of rotational and translational types, the generic modeling of a propeller, the allocation or propulsion model, and finally some linear simplifications that will be useful in the next chapter. These topics are very common in different books and articles about drones. Again, you are invited to explore the Appendix if you want to deepen your knowledge on the topics learned. In the next chapter, you will see topics related to the design of controllers seen as two types of families: vehicle mode (or first-person view or on-board control mode) and robot mode (or third-person view or external control mode).

CHAPTER 3

Control of Drones

In this chapter with scientific impact, you will learn about four of the most employed drone controllers based on two classifications, one that visualizes the aircraft as a vehicle and the other as a robot. This chapter will also show you some control concepts and basic notions of Lyapunov's theory of stability. Finally, a section on the trajectory planning is included. As a result, you will be able to understand and implement most of the drone controllers available, including the powerful geometric control. With this in mind, you can extend this knowledge to other types of vehicles and aircraft.

Remember that in order to inject the controllers that we will study into the vehicle's motors (and in general any other controller), you must do it by using the allocation or propulsion matrix calculated for your respective vehicles. The allocation matrix for the particular case that was analyzed in the previous chapter was

$$
\begin{bmatrix} \omega_1 \\ \omega_2 \\ \omega_3 \\ \omega_4 \end{bmatrix} = \begin{bmatrix} 1 & -1 & 1 & 1 \\ 1 & 1 & -1 & 1 \\ 1 & 1 & 1 & -1 \\ 1 & -1 & -1 & -1 \end{bmatrix} \begin{bmatrix} F_{ZB} \\ \tau_{XB} \\ \tau_{YB} \\ \tau_{ZB} \end{bmatrix} = \begin{bmatrix} F_{ZB} - \tau_{XB} + \tau_{YB} + \tau_{ZB} \\ F_{ZB} + \tau_{XB} - \tau_{YB} + \tau_{ZB} \\ F_{ZB} + \tau_{XB} + \tau_{YB} - \tau_{ZB} \\ F_{ZB} - \tau_{XB} - \tau_{YB} - \tau_{ZB} \end{bmatrix}
$$

Thus, the objective of this chapter consists of learning the most generic methods to design the FZB force and the remaining three torques.

Note also that this is valid if a SDK type 3 is used, as indicated in the section on the ways to program a drone in Chapter 5. In the case of using a SDK type 2, said force and torques will be injected directly into the vehicle without requiring the allocation matrix. Finally, in the case of using a SDK

© Julio Alberto Mendoza-Mendoza, Victor Javier Gonzalez-Villela,
Carlos Fernando Aguilar-Ibañez, Leonardo Fonseca-Ruiz 2021
J. A. Mendoza-Mendoza et al., *Drones to Go*, https://doi.org/10.1007/978-1-4842-6788-2_3

type 1 or a GUI, you will only be able to define trajectory profiles (you will not be able to design your own controllers; you can just modify preloaded controls gains and paths).

You will see that a quadcopter, like any other unmanned vehicle, can be analyzed and viewed as a robot or as a vehicle, and in both cases the control may or may not be automatic.

Before talking about these controllers, let's talk about the useful zero concept.

Useful Zero Concept

The control objective is the introduction of useful zeros in order to develop a task.

In control theory, it is usual to find three types of zero: the zero by definition, the zero by domination, and the zero by approximation. Do not confuse these concepts with those of poles and zeros of linear control theory.

- The zero by definition is an ideal and a constant value to which it is intended to bring an error or estimation. It is also a static or dynamic balance that ensures a force or motion equilibrium.

- The zero by domination is when a term within an equation is too large with respect to the other terms such that the equation simply behaves like the dominant term without giving importance to the effects of the rest of the terms. These nullified terms are considered as a zero by domination. This type of zero is very common in electrical and electronic circuit analysis and also in control theory. Figure 3-1 shows a graph of a function in which the domination effect can

be considered approximately equal to 4. Observe that
the dominated sine component can be considered as a
zero in proportion to the 4.

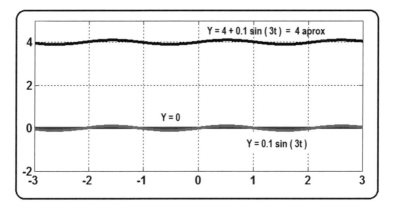

Figure 3-1. *An example of zero by domination*

On the other hand, what here is called a useful
zero is the one that is obtained by time behavior.
Mathematically it will be any function that tends to
zero as the time increases.

A function widely used in control theory as a useful zero is the negative
exponential. This useful zero can be observed behaving like a zero as
the time evolves. Note the fact that there is no negative time. This is just
plotted as an expanded view:

$$y = Ae^{-Bt}$$

This function will always have the behavior shown in Figure 3-2 as long
as B has a positive value.

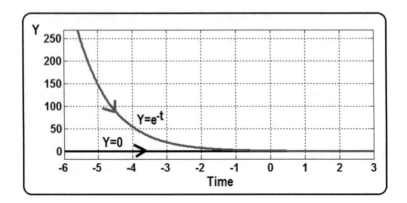

Figure 3-2. *An example of zero by approximation*

Note that a useful zero is a way to force something to become as a constant zero. This function is also the solution and behavior associated with this differential equation:

$$\frac{dy}{dt} = -y$$

$$\int \frac{dy}{y} = \int -dt \implies \ln(y) = -t \implies y = e^{-t}$$

Using Newton's notation, it is equal to

$$\dot{y} = -y$$

In a more generic way, this family of differential equations always results in a decreasing exponential function, which tends to zero as long as B and K are positive values:

$$B\dot{y} = -Ky$$

If we make the following variable changes, we obtain an equation known as PD controller:

$$B\dot{y} + Ky = K_d\dot{E} + K_pE$$

which implies that the value E associated with the error to be controlled will tend to zero, and as E is defined like

$$E = v_d - v$$

In other words, the desired value minus the actual value of a variable, for example a position or an orientation:

$$E \to 0$$
$$v_d - v \to 0$$
$$v \to v_d$$

The desired value will tend to be the real value and therefore we will have accomplished our task!

We will use this useful zero concept and its PD application later.

Keep in mind that the first-order differential equation, and consequently the PD, has a physical equivalent called a massless damped harmonic oscillator or a spring damper system. Therefore, the proportional term can be interpreted as an induced spring and the differential term as an induced damper; see Figure 3-3. Said induced spring serves to pull the real system towards the desired value, and the induced damper serves to stop the real system at said value. If it were just the induced spring and not the induced damper, the real system would not stop and it would remain oscillating around the desired value (the zero value of the error).

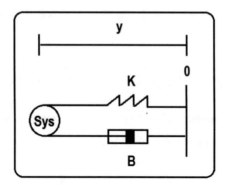

Figure 3-3. *The physical analogy of a PD controller*

Another useful zero is the second order differential equation or mass spring damper system, also called a damped harmonic oscillator, as long as the terms M, B, and K are positive. The deduction is a little less intuitive and is a matter of linear control and differential equations books. However, for the purposes of this book and under the given conditions, we will just assume that this system is also a useful zero.

$$M\ddot{y} + B\dot{y} + Ky = 0$$

For control purposes, it is highlighted that the PID control behaves like said mass spring damper system (at least mathematically, since there are physical considerations during the implementation as the effect of using differentiators instead of integrators).

$$\frac{d\left(K_d\dot{E} + K_pE + K_i \int E\right)}{dt} = K_d\ddot{E} + K_p\dot{E} + K_iE$$

Having learned about the useful zero concept, let's continue with the controllers. We will start with the robot mode controllers.

Robot Mode Control

If the drone is analyzed as a robot, the control design will involve seeing it as if it was controlled by a third person or as an external view. For these purposes, the control objective will be to move a reference point of the quadcopter to a given three-dimensional location with or without a regulated orientation. See Figure 3-4.

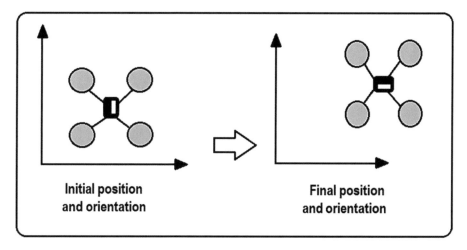

Initial position and orientation

Final position and orientation

Figure 3-4. *Robot mode control of a drone seen as a third person task*

It's time to explain the robot mode control called linear Cartesian control with no yaw variation.

Fully Linear Cartesian Control with No Yaw Variation

This is a simple and very basic controller that allows an operation like the one shown in Figure 3-5, which simply consists of following a path without altering the orientation of the drone. This is useful, for example, in

planting or in house-painting patterns. Let's describe its independent and
dependent dynamics modules.

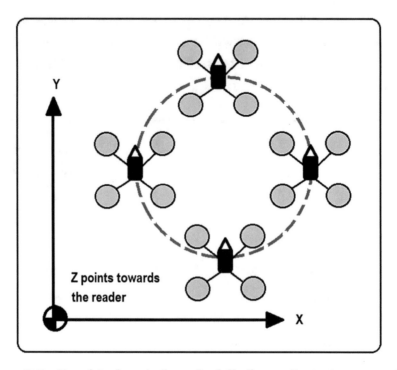

Figure 3-5. *Graphic description of a fully linear Cartesian control*
with no yaw variation

Control of the Independent Dynamics

Let's return to the linearized dynamic model of a drone by separating the
dynamics that have no dependence on the other variables (observe that
this is done with respect to the motion variables in which you can identify
three positions and three orientations). So we have

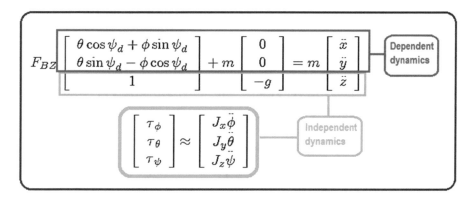

Note that the dependence on the X and Y dynamics is with respect to the dynamics of the theta and phi angles. Therefore we isolate the equations that do not have an interaction with other equations, that is, those of psi and Z. Note that psi differs from the desired psi due to the fact that the latter one is a constant value or a trajectory, and in the case of our example the desired psi will be equal to zero.

$$F_{BZ} \begin{bmatrix} \theta \cos \psi_d + \phi \sin \psi_d \\ \theta \sin \psi_d - \phi \cos \psi_d \end{bmatrix} = m \begin{bmatrix} \ddot{x} \\ \ddot{y} \end{bmatrix}$$

$$\begin{bmatrix} \tau_\phi \\ \tau_\theta \end{bmatrix} \approx \begin{bmatrix} J_x \ddot{\phi} \\ J_y \ddot{\theta} \end{bmatrix}$$

$$\psi_d \approx 0$$

$$F_{BZ} - mg = m\ddot{z}$$

$$\tau_\psi \approx J_z \ddot{\psi}$$

⇨

$$\frac{F_{BZ}}{m} \begin{bmatrix} \theta \\ -\phi \end{bmatrix} = \begin{bmatrix} \ddot{x} \\ \ddot{y} \end{bmatrix}$$

$$\begin{bmatrix} \tau_\phi / J_x \\ \tau_\theta / J_y \end{bmatrix} \approx \begin{bmatrix} \ddot{\phi} \\ \ddot{\theta} \end{bmatrix}$$

$$F_{BZ} - mg = m\ddot{z}$$

$$\tau_\psi \approx J_z \ddot{\psi}$$

If the thrust force in Z is proposed as follows

$$F_{BZ} = m(g + PD_z + \ddot{z}_d)$$

where

$$PD_z = K_{PZ}(z_d - z) + K_{DZ}(\dot{z}_d - \dot{z})$$

when replacing it into the dynamic model and particularly into the Z equation, we will have the following:

$$m(g + PD_z + \ddot{z}_d) - mg = m\ddot{z}$$
$$m(PD_z + (\ddot{z}_d - \ddot{z})) = 0$$
$$K_{PZ}(z_d - z) + K_{DZ}(\dot{z}_d - \dot{z}) + (\ddot{z}_d - \ddot{z}) = 0$$

This becomes a useful zero or damped harmonic oscillator.

$$E_z = z_d - z$$
$$K_{PZ}(E_z) + K_{DZ}(\dot{E}_z) + (\ddot{E}_z) = 0$$

And as long as the gains satisfy at least being positive along other criteria found in linear control books, we know that

$$E_z \rightarrow 0$$
$$z \rightarrow z_d$$
$$\dot{z} \rightarrow \dot{z}_d$$
$$\ddot{z} \rightarrow \ddot{z}_d$$

Furthermore, it is demonstrated by control theory that if the desired value is a constant or a function whose maximum absolute value can be limited by a constant (a sine or a cosine for example),

$$z_d = K$$
$$z \rightarrow K$$
$$\dot{z} \rightarrow \dot{z}_d \rightarrow 0$$
$$\ddot{z} \rightarrow \ddot{z}_d \rightarrow 0$$

a similar reasoning can be applied with a PID controller. You can develop the demonstration on your own as an exercise.

This also implies that

$$F_{BZ} = m(g + PD_z + \ddot{z}_d) \to mg$$

and consequently

$$\frac{F_{BZ}}{m}\begin{bmatrix} \theta \\ -\phi \end{bmatrix} = \begin{bmatrix} \ddot{x} \\ \ddot{y} \end{bmatrix} \quad \to \quad g\begin{bmatrix} \theta \\ -\phi \end{bmatrix} = \begin{bmatrix} \ddot{x} \\ \ddot{y} \end{bmatrix}$$

We will use this result soon.

On the other hand, in practice and simulation, there are people who simplify the proposed thrust control as follows:

$$F_{BZ} = mg + PD_z$$

And it will work if the differential and proportional gains are big enough, by the following considerations:

1. If the flight accelerations are small (which comes from the assumption that we made about smooth flight).

$$F_{BZ} = mg + mPD_z + m\ddot{z}_d$$

$$mg + mPD_z \gg m\ddot{z}_d$$
$$F_{BZ} \approx mg + mPD_z$$

2. If the mass is constant or bounded by a constant, it can be absorbed by the proportional and differential gains (one constant multiplied by other constant produces another constant):

$$mPD_z = mK_{PZ}(z_d - z) + mK_{DZ}(\dot{z}_d - \dot{z})$$

$$mK_{PZ}(z_d - z) + mK_{DZ}(\dot{z}_d - \dot{z}) \approx K_{PZ}(z_d - z) + K_{DZ}(\dot{z}_d - \dot{z})$$
$$F_{BZ} \approx mg + PD_z$$

Let's continue with the equation related to psi (yaw variable).

In this case, the control value can be defined as

$$\tau_\psi = J_z(PD_\psi + \ddot{\psi}_d)$$

When this control is replaced into the yaw model, it leads to the following:

$$J_z(PD_\psi + \ddot{\psi}_d) = J_z\ddot{\psi}$$
$$K_{P\psi}(\psi_d - \psi) + K_{D\psi}(\dot{\psi}_d - \dot{\psi}) + (\ddot{\psi}_d - \ddot{\psi}) = 0$$
$$K_{P\psi}(E_\psi) + K_{D\psi}(\dot{E}_\psi) + (\ddot{E}_\psi) = 0$$

Again, if the controller gains are at least positive and satisfy the other guidelines described in automatic control textbooks, we will have a useful zero or a mass spring damper system, which implies that

$$E_\psi = \psi_d - \psi$$
$$E_\psi \rightarrow 0$$
$$\psi \rightarrow \psi_d$$
$$\dot{\psi} \rightarrow \dot{\psi}_d$$
$$\ddot{\psi} \rightarrow \ddot{\psi}_d$$

considering again the smooth flight conditions (small accelerations) and the constant values absorption. As deduced for the variable Z, we will have the following:

$$\psi_d = K$$
$$\psi \rightarrow K$$
$$\dot{\psi} \rightarrow \dot{\psi}_d \rightarrow 0$$
$$\ddot{\psi} \rightarrow \ddot{\psi}_d \rightarrow 0$$

$$J_z(PD_\psi + \ddot{\psi}_d) \approx PD_\psi \approx \tau_\psi$$

Now, we proceed to control the dependent dynamics.

Control of the Dependent Dynamics

From the previous simplifications, we can note that the remaining system is

$$\begin{bmatrix} \tau_\phi / J_x \\ \tau_\theta / J_y \end{bmatrix} \approx \begin{bmatrix} \ddot{\phi} \\ \ddot{\theta} \end{bmatrix}$$

$$g \begin{bmatrix} \theta \\ -\phi \end{bmatrix} = \begin{bmatrix} \ddot{x} \\ \ddot{y} \end{bmatrix}$$

The subsystems that do not have dependencies on other variables are the rotational ones, while the translational ones depend on those rotational variables.

For this reason, it is reasonable to start designing the controllers of the rotational dynamics. Under a similar argument to the one presented for the yaw variable, and for the reasons already explained about smooth flight (small accelerations) and constant absorption, these controllers for roll and pitch are proposed:

$$\tau_\phi = J_x(PD_\phi + \ddot{\phi}_d) \approx PD_\phi$$
$$\tau_\theta = J_y(PD_\theta + \ddot{\theta}_d) \approx PD_\theta$$

This implies in a similar way to the previously analyzed variables that

$$
\begin{array}{cc}
E_\phi \to 0 & E_\theta \to 0 \\
\phi \to \phi_d & \theta \to \theta_d \\
\dot{\phi} \to \dot{\phi}_d & \dot{\theta} \to \dot{\theta}_d \\
\ddot{\phi} \to \ddot{\phi}_d & \ddot{\theta} \to \ddot{\theta}_d
\end{array}
$$

As a consequence, the dependent dynamics can be controlled through the desired values of the angles on which they depend. This is logical, since a quadcopter is able to move in X and Y through roll and pitch tilting.

$$\begin{bmatrix} \ddot{x} \\ \ddot{y} \end{bmatrix} = g \begin{bmatrix} \theta \\ -\phi \end{bmatrix} \approx g \begin{bmatrix} \theta_d \\ -\phi_d \end{bmatrix}$$

Then the desired values of theta and phi are selected in this way (this is known as external control loop or nested control):

$$\theta_d = \frac{1}{g}(PD_x + \ddot{x}_d)$$

$$\phi_d = -\frac{1}{g}(PD_y + \ddot{y}_d)$$

This feedback on the translational X and Y dynamics has as a consequence

$$E_{x,y} \to 0$$
$$x, y \to x_d, y_d$$
$$\dot{x}, \dot{y} \to \dot{x}_d, \dot{y}_d$$
$$\ddot{x}, \ddot{y} \to \ddot{x}_d, \ddot{y}_d$$

Under the premises of smooth flight, bounded trajectories with small accelerations, and absorption of constants previously used, the auxiliary controllers can be simply

$$\theta_d = PD_x$$
$$\phi_d = -PD_y$$

In summary, the control to be injected is as follows (see the simulation in the next chapter to observe its performance):

$$F_{BZ} = mg + PD_z$$
$$\tau_\psi = PD_\psi$$

$$\theta_d = PD_x$$
$$\phi_d = -PD_y$$
$$\tau_\phi = PD_\phi$$
$$\tau_\theta = PD_\theta$$

which is expanded in the following way:

$$F_{BZ} = mg + K_{Pz}(z_d - z) + K_{Dz}(\dot{z}_d - \dot{z})$$
$$\tau_\psi = K_{P\psi}(\psi_d - \psi) + K_{D\psi}(\dot{\psi}_d - \dot{\psi})$$

$$\theta_d = K_{Px}(x_d - x) + K_{Dx}(\dot{x}_d - \dot{x})$$
$$\phi_d = -[K_{Py}(y_d - y) + K_{Dy}(\dot{y}_d - \dot{y})]$$
$$\tau_\phi = K_{P\phi}(\phi_d - \phi) + K_{D\phi}(\dot{\phi}_d - \dot{\phi})$$
$$\tau_\theta = K_{P\theta}(\theta_d - \theta) + K_{D\theta}(\dot{\theta}_d - \dot{\theta})$$

Remember the introduction to the ISO 1151–2: 1985 standard, and note that the theta measurement is made with respect to the Y axis but its variation influences the X motion. Likewise, the phi measurement is made around the X axis, but its variation influences the motion on Y.

Finally, given that

$$\ddot{\psi}_d = 0$$
$$\dot{\psi}_d = 0$$
$$\lim_{x \to x_d} \theta_d = 0$$
$$\dot{\theta}_d \approx 0$$
$$\lim_{y \to y_d} \phi_d = 0$$
$$\dot{\phi}_d \approx 0$$

$$\tau_\psi = -K_{P\psi}\psi - K_{D\psi}\dot{\psi}$$
$$\tau_\phi = K_{P\phi}(\phi_d - \phi) + K_{D\phi}(\dot{\phi}_d - \dot{\phi}) \approx K_{P\phi}(\phi_d - \phi) - K_{D\phi}\dot{\phi}$$
$$\tau_\theta = K_{P\theta}(\theta_d - \theta) + K_{D\theta}(\dot{\theta}_d - \dot{\theta}) \approx K_{P\theta}(\theta_d - \theta) - K_{D\theta}\dot{\theta}$$

you should notice that the desired speeds of theta and fi are not zero, and that they should be the corresponding derivatives of the translational PDs. However, zero is a good approximation considering the smooth flight approximation and the variable convergence described above.

Concerning to this smooth flight approximation, let's see what happens in this flightmode to the controllers.

Linear Decoupling of the Controllers

Another important consideration is the fact that in this type of smooth flight with fixed yaw equal to zero, the controllers are decoupled (at least the linear controllers like PD, PID, etc.), so the planar translations and the roll and pitch rotations seem to have an independent behavior, for example

$$\tau_\theta \approx K_{P\theta}(\theta_d - \theta) - K_{D\theta}\dot\theta = K_{P\theta}\theta_d - K_{P\theta}\theta - K_{D\theta}\dot\theta$$
$$\theta_d = K_{Px}(x_d - x) + K_{Dx}(\dot x_d - \dot x)$$

$$\Downarrow$$

$$\tau_\theta \approx K_{P\theta}[K_{Px}(x_d - x) + K_{Dx}(\dot x_d - \dot x)] - K_{P\theta}\theta - K_{D\theta}\dot\theta$$

making the previous assumptions of constant absorption

$$K_{P\theta}K_{Px} \approx K_{Px}$$
$$K_{P\theta}K_{Dx} \approx K_{Dx}$$

The following is obtained:

$$\tau_\theta \approx K_{Px}(x_d - x) + K_{Dx}(\dot x_d - \dot x) + K_{P\theta}(0 - \theta) + K_{D\theta}(0 - \dot\theta) \approx PD_x + PD_\theta$$

A similar result is obtained for the variable phi. Do this as an exercise. Before ending this section, let's talk about some remarks.

Remarks and Graphical Interpretations

Graphically, the implementation of this control has the sequence shown in Figure 3-6.

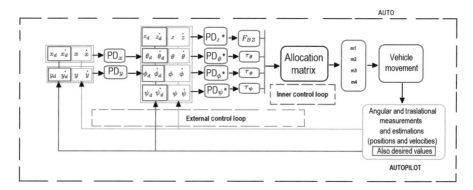

Figure 3-6. *Graphic sequence of a fully linear Cartesian control with no yaw variation*

Two versions with remote control (semi-automatic or guided manual mode) are as follows.

In this first version, the remote control only alters the desired values; see Figure 3-7.

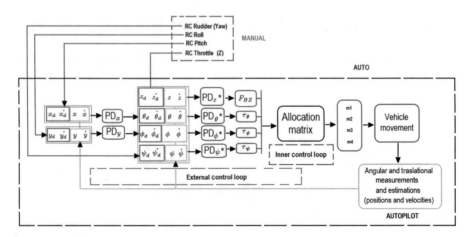

Figure 3-7. *Graphic sequence of a fully linear Cartesian control with no yaw variation and with manual radio control command at the desired values*

In the second version, the remote control, modifies the torques and forces; see Figure 3-8.

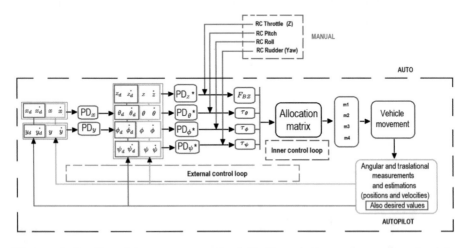

Figure 3-8. *Graphic sequence of a fully linear Cartesian control with no yaw variation and with manual radio control command at the force and torque control*

Notice that there are as many combinations of manual modes as you want. In the examples described, the second one could be dangerous because you directly affect the controllers, but the risk is reduced if you introduce small and bounded values.

You learned about the robot mode control without yaw variation. Let's move to the one with variable yaw.

Fully Linear Cartesian Control with Yaw Variation

This type of controller is a modification of the previous one. Now the drone is able to follow a trajectory, and it can also modify its yaw angle; see Figure 3-9. This operation is useful for recording an object, person, or building located inside the path, as in the case of surveillance operations.

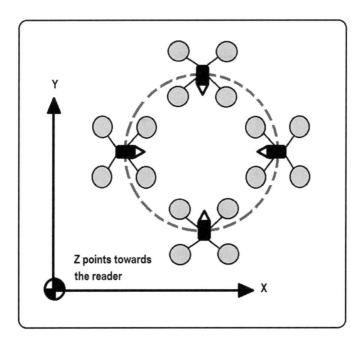

Figure 3-9. *Graphic representation of a fully linear Cartesian control with yaw variation*

In the case of this flight mode, the thrust and torque controls are identical to the previous section:

$$F_{BZ} = mg + PD_z$$
$$T_\psi = PD_\psi$$
$$T_\phi = PD_\phi$$
$$T_\theta = PD_\theta$$

What changes is the design of the desired theta and phi auxiliary controllers, as follows.

The XY dynamic systems cannot be simplified since psi does not have a zero value:

$$\frac{F_{BZ}}{m} \begin{bmatrix} \theta \cos \psi_d + \phi \sin \psi_d \\ \theta \sin \psi_d - \phi \cos \psi_d \end{bmatrix} = \begin{bmatrix} \ddot{x} \\ \ddot{y} \end{bmatrix} \rightarrow g \begin{bmatrix} \theta \cos \psi_d + \phi \sin \psi_d \\ \theta \sin \psi_d - \phi \cos \psi_d \end{bmatrix}$$

But you can rewrite them in matrix form like this:

$$\begin{bmatrix} \ddot{x} \\ \ddot{y} \end{bmatrix} = g \begin{bmatrix} \cos \psi_d & \sin \psi_d \\ \sin \psi_d & -\cos \psi_d \end{bmatrix} \begin{bmatrix} \theta \\ \phi \end{bmatrix}$$

From the roll and pitch controllers, remember that

$$\theta \rightarrow \theta_d$$
$$\phi \rightarrow \phi_d$$
$$\begin{bmatrix} \ddot{x} \\ \ddot{y} \end{bmatrix} = g \begin{bmatrix} \cos \psi_d & \sin \psi_d \\ \sin \psi_d & -\cos \psi_d \end{bmatrix} \begin{bmatrix} \theta_d \\ \phi_d \end{bmatrix}$$

The following auxiliary controllers can be proposed:

$$\begin{bmatrix} \theta_d \\ \phi_d \end{bmatrix} = \frac{1}{g} \begin{bmatrix} \cos \psi_d & \sin \psi_d \\ \sin \psi_d & -\cos \psi_d \end{bmatrix}^{-1} \begin{bmatrix} PDx + \ddot{x}_d \\ PDy + \ddot{y}_d \end{bmatrix} = \frac{1}{g} \begin{bmatrix} \cos \psi_d & \sin \psi_d \\ \sin \psi_d & -\cos \psi_d \end{bmatrix} \begin{bmatrix} PDx + \ddot{x}_d \\ PDy + \ddot{y}_d \end{bmatrix}$$

Substituting the auxiliary controllers into the given dynamic model:

$$\begin{bmatrix} \ddot{x} \\ \ddot{y} \end{bmatrix} = g \begin{bmatrix} \cos\psi_d & \sin\psi_d \\ \sin\psi_d & -\cos\psi_d \end{bmatrix} \frac{1}{g} \begin{bmatrix} \cos\psi_d & \sin\psi_d \\ \sin\psi_d & -\cos\psi_d \end{bmatrix} \begin{bmatrix} PDx + \ddot{x}_d \\ PDy + \ddot{y}_d \end{bmatrix}$$

Simplifying:

$$\begin{bmatrix} \ddot{x} \\ \ddot{y} \end{bmatrix} = \begin{bmatrix} PDx + \ddot{x}_d \\ PDy + \ddot{y}_d \end{bmatrix}$$

$$\begin{bmatrix} 0 \\ 0 \end{bmatrix} = \begin{bmatrix} PDx + (\ddot{x}_d - \ddot{x}) \\ PDy + (\ddot{y}_d - \ddot{y}) \end{bmatrix}$$

And this implies that

$$E_x = x_d - x \to 0$$
$$x \to x_d$$

$$E_y = y_d - y \to 0$$
$$y \to y_d$$

Rewriting the proposed matrix form to an equivalent but programmable one (which avoids making a lot of matrix multiplications to a computer), we obtain a known equation found in drone research:

$$\begin{bmatrix} \theta_d \\ \phi_d \end{bmatrix} \approx \begin{bmatrix} \cos\psi_d & \sin\psi_d \\ \sin\psi_d & -\cos\psi_d \end{bmatrix} \begin{bmatrix} PDx \\ PDy \end{bmatrix} = \begin{bmatrix} PD_x \cos\psi_d + PD_y \sin\psi_d \\ PD_x \sin\psi_d - PD_y \cos\psi_d \end{bmatrix}$$

Finally, note that the matrix depending on psi desired is a rotation matrix (this will be very useful for the interpretation of the geometric control in the upcoming section).

There are two ways to verify that this is a rotation matrix:

1. Turning the matrix into a known rotation matrix by using transformations:

$$\begin{bmatrix} \cos(x) & \sin x \\ \sin x & -\cos x \end{bmatrix} \quad x = \pi/2 - a$$

$$\begin{bmatrix} \cos(\pi/2 - a) & \sin(\pi/2 - a) \\ \sin(\pi/2 - a) & -\cos(\pi/2 - a) \end{bmatrix} = \begin{bmatrix} \sin a & \cos a \\ \cos a & -\sin a \end{bmatrix}$$

$$\begin{bmatrix} \sin a & \cos a \\ \cos a & -\sin a \end{bmatrix} \begin{bmatrix} 0 & 1 \\ 1 & 0 \end{bmatrix} = \begin{bmatrix} \cos a & \sin a \\ -\sin a & \cos a \end{bmatrix} = R_y(a)$$

2. Using a property of the rotation matrices previously employed in this book:

$$R^T R = I$$

$$\begin{bmatrix} \cos \psi_d & \sin \psi_d \\ \sin \psi_d & -\cos \psi_d \end{bmatrix}^T \begin{bmatrix} \cos \psi_d & \sin \psi_d \\ \sin \psi_d & -\cos \psi_d \end{bmatrix} = \begin{bmatrix} 1 & 0 \\ 0 & 1 \end{bmatrix}$$

In summary, the controller proposed in this section is as follows (see the simulation section to observe the performance of this control):

$$F_{BZ} = mg + PD_z$$
$$T_\psi = PD_\psi$$
$$T_\phi = PD_\phi$$
$$T_\theta = PD_\theta$$

$$\begin{bmatrix} \theta_d \\ \phi_d \end{bmatrix} \approx \begin{bmatrix} PD_x \cos \psi_d + PD_y \sin \psi_d \\ PD_x \sin \psi_d - PD_y \cos \psi_d \end{bmatrix}$$

The graphic sequence of these controllers is displayed in Figure 3-10.

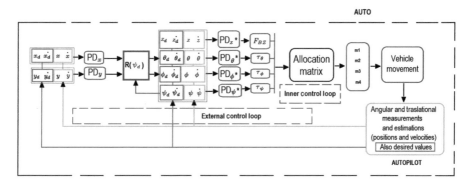

Figure 3-10. *Graphic sequence of a fully linear Cartesian control with yaw variation*

For the remote control variants, they can be adapted considering two ways; see Figure 3-11.

- The first is to include the yaw action over the corresponding remote controls for roll and pitch (through yaw compensation as in the previous control). In this way, the manual behavior of the vehicle will be as in the left side of the figure.

- The second is not to include such variation and the manual behavior of the vehicle will be as in the right side of the same figure.

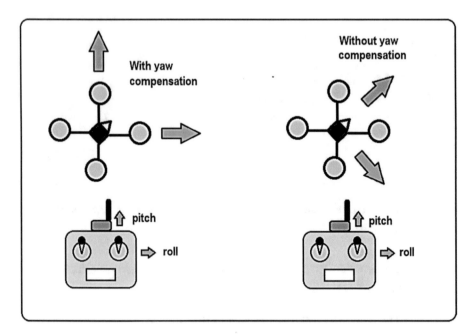

Figure 3-11. *Remote control variants when a fully linear Cartesian control with yaw variation is used*

At this point, you have learned about the robot mode control, which allows a smooth flight. Now it's time to see the vehicle mode control, which allows higher degrees of mobility and acrobatic or aggressive motion.

Vehicle Mode Control

In the case of being analyzed as a vehicle, the control design of the drone implies seeing it as if it were a first person mode, an on-board experience, or in the "cockpit." See Figure 3-12. For the purposes of this, the line of sight of the aircraft, also known as the guide vector (the vector that would have a pilot on board), should be regulated by means of "rudders" or "thrusters." Unlike the robot mode or third person mode, the coupling between rotational and translational controllers and dynamics is bigger or even totally dependent. This is a mathematical drawback, but it also represents an advantage in versatility and usage for aggressive or acrobatic operations.

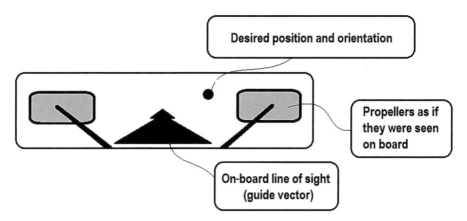

Figure 3-12. *Graphic representation of the vehicle mode control (as a first person view)*

Let's start with the spherical control (based on rudders) and then the geometric one (based on thrusters).

Spherical Control (Rudders and Guide Vector)

The following is a basic vehicle mode control. Note that this type of controller is widely used with wheeled robots. See Figure 3-13.

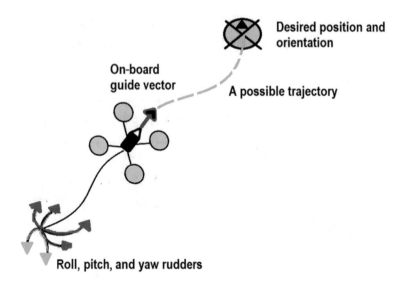

Figure 3-13. *Graphic representation of the spherical control*

In this type of control, it is convenient to change from the linear Cartesian space to one based on spherical coordinates, where the guide vector is associated with the resultant of the Cartesian components and the rudders are associated with the angular motion of said sphere. These angles are tangential projections of the Cartesian components.

Step 1. Define the resultant (guide vector) and the rudder angles.

Let's remember that the dynamic model is given by

$$
\begin{bmatrix}
F_{BZ} \left(\sin\theta \cos\psi + \sin\phi \cos\theta \sin\psi \right) \\
F_{BZ} \left(\sin\theta \sin\psi - \sin\phi \cos\theta \cos\psi \right) \\
F_{BZ} \cos\phi \cos\theta
\end{bmatrix}
+ m
\begin{bmatrix}
0 \\
0 \\
-g
\end{bmatrix}
= m
\begin{bmatrix}
\ddot{x} \\
\ddot{y} \\
\ddot{z}
\end{bmatrix}
$$

$$
\begin{bmatrix}
\tau_\phi \\
\tau_\theta \\
\tau_\psi
\end{bmatrix}
\approx
\begin{bmatrix}
J_x \ddot{\phi} \\
J_y \ddot{\theta} \\
J_z \ddot{\psi}
\end{bmatrix}
$$

Notice that for our purposes, this model will not be simplified to the smooth flight conditions (linearization).

From previous sections, note that there are six controllers: four of them are physical or force-torque commanded, and the remaining two are auxiliary or trajectory dependent:

$$\begin{bmatrix} F_{BZ} \\ \tau_\theta \\ \tau_\phi \\ \tau_\psi \\ \theta_d \\ \phi_d \end{bmatrix}.$$

In the case of this new design, the torque controllers in roll, pitch, and yaw will be left as in the preceding sections:

$$\tau_\psi = PD_\psi$$
$$\tau_\phi = PD_\phi$$
$$\tau_\theta = PD_\theta$$

This implies that

$$\theta \rightarrow \theta_d$$
$$\phi \rightarrow \phi_d$$
$$\psi \rightarrow \psi_d$$

The remaining three controllers to be defined:

$$\begin{bmatrix} F_{BZ} \\ \theta_d \\ \phi_d \end{bmatrix}$$

Since the thrust force is related to a Cartesian vector, we are going to associate the guide vector to it. With regard to the auxiliary controllers of roll and pitch (which are needed to move the vehicle on the plane), we will associate them with the rudders that will determine the direction of the guide vector.

Step 2. Find the value of the guide vector and the rudders.

We rewrite the translational or dependent dynamic equations in terms of the controllers to be defined. Note that the only independent variable is psi:

$$
\begin{bmatrix} F_{BZ}\left(\sin\theta_d\cos\psi_d + \sin\phi_d\cos\theta_d\sin\psi_d\right) \\ F_{BZ}\left(\sin\theta_d\sin\psi_d - \sin\phi_d\cos\theta_d\cos\psi_d\right) \\ F_{BZ}\cos\phi_d\cos\theta_d \end{bmatrix} + m \begin{bmatrix} 0 \\ 0 \\ -g \end{bmatrix} = m \begin{bmatrix} \ddot{x}_d \\ \ddot{y}_d \\ \ddot{z}_d \end{bmatrix}
$$

As you can see, FBZ, as well as the desired values of theta and phi, are available through the entire system of equations (three unknowns and three equations). Notice also that the main objective of our controllers is that both the translational variables and their derivatives converge to their desired values. This is

$$
x \rightarrow x_d
$$
$$
y \rightarrow y_d
$$
$$
z \rightarrow z_d
$$

Solving these equations for the desired rudders and guide vector is not simple. This way we proceed step by step by using projective and resultant relationships. Initially, it is convenient to obtain FBZ by using the scalar equivalent of these vector equations (the vector norm).

The translational dynamic equations are rewritten in this way. Note that the rudders and guide vector variables were separated from the independent variable psi:

$$
\begin{bmatrix} \cos\psi_d & \sin\psi_d & 0 \\ \sin\psi_d & -\cos\psi_d & 0 \\ 0 & 0 & 1 \end{bmatrix} \begin{bmatrix} F_{BZ}\sin\theta_d \\ F_{BZ}\sin\phi_d\cos\theta_d \\ F_{BZ}\cos\phi_d\cos\theta_d \end{bmatrix} = m \begin{bmatrix} \ddot{x}_d \\ \ddot{y}_d \\ \ddot{z}_d + g \end{bmatrix}
$$

We solve for the rudders and the guide vector:

$$
\begin{bmatrix} F_{BZ}\sin\theta_d \\ F_{BZ}\sin\phi_d\cos\theta_d \\ F_{BZ}\cos\phi_d\cos\theta_d \end{bmatrix} = m \begin{bmatrix} \cos\psi_d & \sin\psi_d & 0 \\ \sin\psi_d & -\cos\psi_d & 0 \\ 0 & 0 & 1 \end{bmatrix}^{-1} \begin{bmatrix} \ddot{x}_d \\ \ddot{y}_d \\ \ddot{z}_d + g \end{bmatrix} = \begin{bmatrix} m\ddot{x}_d\cos\psi_d + m\ddot{y}_d\sin\psi_d \\ m\ddot{x}_d\sin\psi_d - m\ddot{y}_d\cos\psi_d \\ m\left(g + \ddot{z}_d\right) \end{bmatrix}
$$

One way to get a scalar from a vector is with the dot product:

$$\begin{bmatrix} F_{BZ} \sin \theta_d \\ F_{BZ} \sin \phi_d \cos \theta_d \\ F_{BZ} \cos \phi_d \cos \theta_d \end{bmatrix}^T \begin{bmatrix} F_{BZ} \sin \theta_d \\ F_{BZ} \sin \phi_d \cos \theta_d \\ F_{BZ} \cos \phi_d \cos \theta_d \end{bmatrix}$$

$$= \left(\cos^2 \theta_d \cos^2 \phi_d\right) F_{BZ}^2 + \left(\cos^2 \theta_d \sin^2 \phi_d\right) F_{BZ}^2 + \left(\sin^2 \theta_d\right) F_{BZ}^2 = F_{BZ}^2$$

$$\begin{bmatrix} m\ddot{x}_d \cos \psi_d + m\ddot{y}_d \sin \psi_d \\ m\ddot{x}_d \sin \psi_d - m\ddot{y}_d \cos \psi_d \\ m\left(g + \ddot{z}_d\right) \end{bmatrix}^T \begin{bmatrix} m\ddot{x}_d \cos \psi_d + m\ddot{y}_d \sin \psi_d \\ m\ddot{x}_d \sin \psi_d - m\ddot{y}_d \cos \psi_d \\ m\left(g + \ddot{z}_d\right) \end{bmatrix}$$

$$= m^2 \left(g + \ddot{z}_d\right)^2 + \left(m\ddot{x}_d \cos \psi_d + m\ddot{y}_d \sin \psi_d\right)^2 + \left(m\ddot{x}_d \sin \psi_d - m\ddot{y}_d \cos \psi_d\right)^2 = m^2\left([\ddot{z}_d+g]^2 + \ddot{y}_d^2 + \ddot{x}_d^2\right)$$

Thus

$$F_{BZ} = m\sqrt{([\ddot{z}_d + g]^2 + \ddot{y}_d^2 + \ddot{x}_d^2)}$$

Note that FBZ is a scalar that contains information from our guide vector (its distance).

The rudders must be presented in arctangent mode (in order to be compatible with spherical coordinates). They are obtained from the following equations. Notice that the yaw angle is an independent rudder.

$$\begin{bmatrix} F_{BZ} \sin \theta_d \\ F_{BZ} \sin \phi_d \cos \theta_d \\ F_{BZ} \cos \phi_d \cos \theta_d \end{bmatrix} = \begin{bmatrix} m\ddot{x}_d \cos \psi_d + m\ddot{y}_d \sin \psi_d \\ m\ddot{x}_d \sin \psi_d - m\ddot{y}_d \cos \psi_d \\ m\left(g + \ddot{z}_d\right) \end{bmatrix}$$

$$\frac{F_{BZ} \sin \phi_d \cos \theta_d}{F_{BZ} \cos \phi_d \cos \theta_d} = \tan \phi_d = \frac{\ddot{x}_d \sin \psi_d - \ddot{y}_d \cos \psi_d}{g + \ddot{z}_d}$$

$$\phi_d = \arctan\left(\frac{\ddot{x}_d \sin \psi_d - \ddot{y}_d \cos \psi_d}{g + \ddot{z}_d}\right)$$

$$(F_{BZ} \sin \phi_d \cos \theta_d)^2 + (F_{BZ} \cos \phi_d \cos \theta_d)^2 = F_{BZ}^2 \cos^2 \theta_d$$
$$= m^2 \left([\ddot{x}_d \sin \psi_d - \ddot{y}_d \cos \psi_d]^2 + [g + \ddot{z}_d]^2 \right)$$

$$F_{BZ} \cos \theta_d = m\sqrt{\left([\ddot{x}_d \sin \psi_d - \ddot{y}_d \cos \psi_d]^2 + [g + \ddot{z}_d]^2 \right)}$$

$$\frac{F_{BZ} \sin \theta_d}{F_{BZ} \cos \theta_d} = \tan \theta_d = \frac{\ddot{x}_d \cos \psi_d + \ddot{y}_d \sin \psi_d}{\sqrt{([\ddot{x}_d \sin \psi_d - \ddot{y}_d \cos \psi_d]^2 + [g + \ddot{z}_d]^2)}}$$

$$\theta_d = \arctan \left(\frac{\ddot{x}_d \cos \psi_d + \ddot{y}_d \sin \psi_d}{\sqrt{([\ddot{x}_d \sin \psi_d - \ddot{y}_d \cos \psi_d]^2 + [g + \ddot{z}_d]^2)}} \right)$$

The form of these equations implies spherical coordinates expressed in the Cartesian framework where the radius is the guide vector magnitude FBZ and the spherical angles are determined by the rudders (roll, pitch, and yaw desired values).

Step 3. Inject the controller.

This is done by replacing the found values of the guide vector magnitude and the rudders in the original translational dynamics with the following trigonometric identities:

$$\cos(\arctan(A)) = \frac{1}{\sqrt{A^2 + 1}}$$

$$\sin(\arctan(A)) = \frac{A}{\sqrt{A^2 + 1}}$$

$$\begin{bmatrix} F_{BZ} \left(\sin \theta_d \cos \psi_d + \sin \phi_d \cos \theta_d \sin \psi_d \right) \\ F_{BZ} \left(\sin \theta_d \sin \psi_d - \sin \phi_d \cos \theta_d \cos \psi_d \right) \\ F_{BZ} \cos \phi_d \cos \theta_d \end{bmatrix} + m \begin{bmatrix} 0 \\ 0 \\ -g \end{bmatrix} = m \begin{bmatrix} \ddot{x} \\ \ddot{y} \\ \ddot{z} \end{bmatrix}$$

The following is obtained:

$$\begin{bmatrix} \ddot{x} \\ \ddot{y} \\ \ddot{z} \end{bmatrix} = \begin{bmatrix} \ddot{x}_d \\ \ddot{y}_d \\ \ddot{z}_d \end{bmatrix}$$

For example (this is a tedious but necessary example that can be developed with the help of a numerical computing program, like MATLAB),

$$m\sqrt{\ddot{x}_d^2 + \ddot{y}_d^2 + (\ddot{z}_d + g)^2}\,\frac{1}{\sqrt{1+(\frac{\ddot{x}_d \sin \psi - \ddot{y}_d \cos \psi}{\ddot{z}_d + g})^2}}\,\frac{1}{\sqrt{1+(\frac{\ddot{x}_d \cos \psi + \ddot{y}_d \sin \psi}{\sqrt{(\ddot{x}_d \sin \psi - \ddot{y}_d \cos \psi)^2 + (\ddot{z}_d + g)^2}})^2}}$$

$$= \; F_{BZ}\cos\theta_d \cos\phi_d$$

$$\frac{1}{1+\frac{\ddot{x}_d^2 \sin^2 \psi + \ddot{y}_d^2 \cos^2 \psi - 2\ddot{x}_d \ddot{y}_d \sin \psi \cos \psi}{(\ddot{z}_d + g)^2}}\,\frac{1}{1+\frac{\ddot{x}_d^2 \cos^2 \psi + \ddot{y}_d^2 \sin^2 \psi + 2\ddot{x}_d \ddot{y}_d \sin \psi \cos \psi}{(\ddot{x}_d \sin \psi - \ddot{y}_d \cos \psi)^2 + (\ddot{z}_d + g)^2}} = \cos^2 \theta_d \cos^2 \phi_d$$

$$= \frac{(g+\ddot{z}_d)^2}{g^2 + 2g\ddot{z}_d + \ddot{x}_d^2 + \ddot{y}_d^2 + \ddot{z}_d^2}$$

$$F_{BZ}^2 \cos^2 \theta_d \cos^2 \phi_d = \frac{(g+\ddot{z}_d)^2}{g^2 + 2g\ddot{z}_d + \ddot{x}_d^2 + \ddot{y}_d^2 + \ddot{z}_d^2} m^2(\ddot{x}_d^2 + \ddot{y}_d^2 + (\ddot{z}_d + g)^2) = m^2 (g + \ddot{z}_d)^2$$

$$F_{BZ}\cos\theta_d \cos\phi_d = m(\ddot{z}_d + g)$$

Consequentially,

$$m(\ddot{z}_d + g) - mg = m\ddot{z}$$
$$\ddot{z} = \ddot{z}_d$$

In the same way, the results for X and Y dynamics can be obtained. This implies that the following can be proposed:

$$\begin{bmatrix} \ddot{x}_d \\ \ddot{y}_d \\ \ddot{z}_d \end{bmatrix} = \begin{bmatrix} PD_x + \ddot{x}_d \\ PD_y + \ddot{y}_d \\ PD_z + \ddot{z}_d \end{bmatrix}$$

with this

$$\begin{bmatrix} \ddot{x} \\ \ddot{y} \\ \ddot{z} \end{bmatrix} = \begin{bmatrix} PD_x + \ddot{x}_d \\ PD_y + \ddot{y}_d \\ PD_z + \ddot{z}_d \end{bmatrix}$$

$$\begin{bmatrix} 0 \\ 0 \\ 0 \end{bmatrix} = \begin{bmatrix} PDx + (\ddot{x}_d - \ddot{x}) \\ PDy + (\ddot{y}_d - \ddot{y}) \\ PDz + (\ddot{z}_d - \ddot{z}) \end{bmatrix} = \begin{bmatrix} K_{Px}(x_d - x) + K_{Dx}(\dot{x}_d - \dot{x}) + (\ddot{x}_d - \ddot{x}) \\ K_{Py}(y_d - y) + K_{Dy}(\dot{y}_d - \dot{y}) + (\ddot{y}_d - \ddot{y}) \\ K_{Pz}(z_d - z) + K_{Dz}(\dot{z}_d - \dot{z}) + (\ddot{z}_d - \ddot{z}) \end{bmatrix}$$

$$x \rightarrow x_d$$
$$y \rightarrow y_d$$
$$z \rightarrow z_d$$

In practice and under the previously described smooth flight conditions, we can simply say that

$$
\begin{bmatrix} \ddot{x}_d \\ \ddot{y}_d \\ \ddot{z}_d \end{bmatrix} = \begin{bmatrix} PD_x \\ PD_y \\ PD_z \end{bmatrix}
$$

In summary, the guide vector and rudders are injected as follows:

$$
\begin{bmatrix} \ddot{x}_d \\ \ddot{y}_d \\ \ddot{z}_d \end{bmatrix} = \begin{bmatrix} PD_x \\ PD_y \\ PD_z \end{bmatrix}
$$

$$
\phi_d = \arctan\left(\frac{\ddot{x}_d \sin\psi_d - \ddot{y}_d \cos\psi_d}{g + \ddot{z}_d} \right)
$$

$$
\theta_d = \arctan\left(\frac{\ddot{x}_d \cos\psi_d + \ddot{y}_d \sin\psi_d}{\sqrt{([\ddot{x}_d \sin\psi_d - \ddot{y}_d \cos\psi_d]^2 + [g + \ddot{z}_d]^2)}} \right)
$$

$$
F_{BZ} = m\sqrt{([\ddot{z}_d + g]^2 + \ddot{y}_d^2 + \ddot{x}_d^2)}
$$

$$
\tau_\psi = PD_\psi
$$
$$
\tau_\phi = PD_\phi
$$
$$
\tau_\theta = PD_\theta
$$

We say that this is a vehicle mode control, or a first person mode control, or an on-board mode control because this is how a pilot into the cockpit would behave. Additionally, this type of control has decades of use in wheeled robots.

Figure 3-14 illustrates this controller seen as a scheme (remember that the controls proposed here can be any other than the PD, but the structure is the same in general).

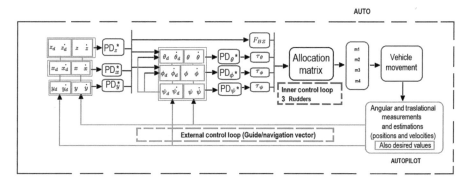

Figure 3-14. *Graphic sequence of the spherical control*

The incorporation of a remote controller can be done as stated in the previous sections.

You learned about the spherical control for drones. Now we will teach you one of the most powerful controllers available, the geometric one.

Introduction to Geometric Control for Drones (Thrusters and Guide Vector)

The previous case was based on trigonometric considerations. A more advanced controller based on rotation-matrix theory is explained in this section.

This time, the vehicle will not have a guide vector and three rudders (as in the previous case, psi counted as an independent rudder, and also phi and theta). In the case in this section, the vehicle will have a guide vector and three thrusters; see Figure 3-15. Imagine that we changed the onboard "steering wheels" or "rudders" by commands that activate a kind of forward-backward, up-down, and left-right "thrusters." This is also widely used in robotics and is associated with **noa** vectors for correcting or describing the orientation of a body by means of three orthogonal vectors; two of them are designable and only one is independent on the others.

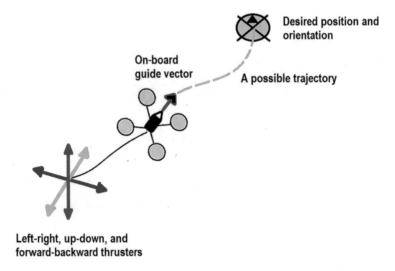

Figure 3-15. *Graphic representation of the geometric control*

Notice that the **noa** vectors have these names because of their use in robotics of manipulators, and specifically in a gripper or robotic hand, where **a** is a unit vector that represents the gripper approach, **n** is a normal vector with respect to **a**, and **o** is also a normal vector to **a** and **n**, which is used to orientate the gripper. See Figure 3-16.

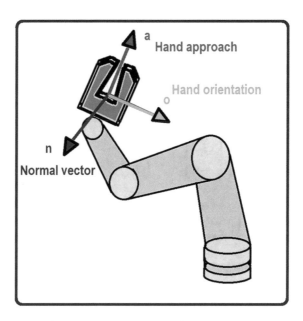

Figure 3-16. *Graphic representation of the noa vectors in a robotic manipulator*

This section requires that you possess a good knowledge about the following tools (all the useful properties are indicated as they are used, but you should read a little more about them): norms and distances in metric spaces (absolute value, quadratic distance, etc.); matrix invariants (trace, determinant, etc.); rotation matrices and their properties including their derivative properties; the transpose of a matrix and its properties; the trace of a matrix; and the equivalent matrix product of the cross product known as hat product and its inverse operation called vee product.

Let's begin with the translational part.

Translational Control

This control uses the alternative kinematic representation based on rotation matrices and also uses the nonlinearized general dynamic model. This is

$$
R \begin{bmatrix} 0 \\ 0 \\ F_{Bz} \end{bmatrix} + m \begin{bmatrix} 0 \\ 0 \\ -g \end{bmatrix} = m \begin{bmatrix} \ddot{x} \\ \ddot{y} \\ \ddot{z} \end{bmatrix}
$$

$$
\begin{bmatrix} \tau_{BX} \\ \tau_{BY} \\ \tau_{BZ} \end{bmatrix} = \begin{bmatrix} J_x \dot{\omega}_x \\ J_y \dot{\omega}_y \\ J_z \dot{\omega}_z \end{bmatrix} + \begin{bmatrix} \omega_y \omega_z J_z - \omega_y \omega_z J_y \\ \omega_x \omega_z J_x - \omega_x \omega_z J_z \\ \omega_x \omega_y J_y - \omega_x \omega_y J_x \end{bmatrix}
$$

$$
\omega = \begin{bmatrix} \omega_{xB} \\ \omega_{yB} \\ \omega_{zB} \end{bmatrix} = \begin{bmatrix} c\theta & 0 & -c\phi s\theta \\ 0 & 1 & s\phi \\ s\theta & 0 & c\phi c\theta \end{bmatrix} \begin{bmatrix} \dot{\phi} \\ \dot{\theta} \\ \dot{\psi} \end{bmatrix} \quad \Rightarrow \quad \dot{R} = RS
$$

Instead of using a Tait-Bryan angular kinematics (in that case, the control was based on trigonometry), now the kinematic model is based on rotation matrices and the control is based on the properties of these matrices.

The equivalence is really simple. Just remember that from the S matrix, you can obtain the elements of the angular velocity in the body frame and their relationship with the roll, pitch, and yaw angular velocities in the world frame (this was demonstrated in the previous chapter):

$$
S(\omega) = \begin{bmatrix} 0 & -\omega_z & \omega_y \\ \omega_z & 0 & -\omega_x \\ -\omega_y & \omega_x & 0 \end{bmatrix} = \dot{R} R^T
$$

You may wonder about the advantages of changing the model from an operation based on rudders to one based on thrusters, and we will anticipate you that it is extremely useful in cases where the body angles are not small (this is opposite to the consideration of the smooth flight mode that we have been supposing in all our previous designs). In other words, it is useful for aggressive and acrobatic movements.

According to the previous paragraph, note that we cannot work with Euler's angles in a direct way, but indirectly by using their equivalent rotation matrix.

The control of the translational dynamics uses a concept known in control theory as annihilator. Note that in Tae Young Lee's articles (see these articles in the Appendix) from which we based our analysis, the axes have an opposite sense with respect to the positive values that we are considering here. Keep in mind these inverted axes for the correlation between this text and the aforementioned articles.

A thrust controller, which contains the guide vector information, is as follows:

$$
\begin{aligned}
F_{BZ} &= \left(\begin{bmatrix} K_{Px}(x_d - x) + K_{Dx}(\dot{x}_d - \dot{x}) + m\ddot{x}_d \\ K_{Py}(y_d - y) + K_{Dy}(\dot{y}_d - \dot{y}) + m\ddot{y}_d \\ K_{Pz}(z_d - z) + K_{Dz}(\dot{z}_d - \dot{z}) + m\ddot{z}_d \end{bmatrix} + \begin{bmatrix} 0 \\ 0 \\ mg \end{bmatrix} \right) \cdot \left[R \begin{bmatrix} 0 \\ 0 \\ 1 \end{bmatrix} \right] \\
&= C_{xyz} \cdot \left(R \begin{bmatrix} 0 \\ 0 \\ 1 \end{bmatrix} \right)
\end{aligned}
$$

Observe the presence of a dot product since FBZ is a scalar quantity. Also observe the presence of the unit vector [0 0 1]. This is where FBZ is located at the drone frame.

A constraint for the previous rotation matrix is

$$ R \rightarrow R_d $$

$$ R_d = \begin{bmatrix} b_{1d} & b_{2d} & b_{3d} \end{bmatrix} = \begin{bmatrix} b_{1dx} & b_{2dx} & b_{3dx} \\ b_{1dy} & b_{2dy} & b_{3dy} \\ b_{1dz} & b_{2dz} & b_{3dz} \end{bmatrix} $$

Later you will see that these b-vectors, which are the components of the desired rotation matrix, are used as a type of **noa** vector where b3 is equivalent to the vector **a**, b2 to **o**, and b1 to **n**. See Figure 3-17.

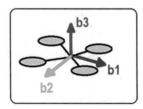

Figure 3-17. *b vectors that compose the desired rotation matrix*

Notice that

$$b_{3d} = R_d \begin{bmatrix} 0 \\ 0 \\ 1 \end{bmatrix} = \begin{bmatrix} b_{1dx} & b_{2dx} & b_{3dx} \\ b_{1dy} & b_{2dy} & b_{3dy} \\ b_{1dz} & b_{2dz} & b_{3dz} \end{bmatrix} \begin{bmatrix} 0 \\ 0 \\ 1 \end{bmatrix}$$

where our first design restriction is as follows:

$$b_3 = R \begin{bmatrix} 0 \\ 0 \\ 1 \end{bmatrix} = \frac{C_{xyz}}{|C_{xyz}|}$$

This implies three things:

- The first is that it is necessary to design a control for the rotation matrix such that it behaves as the desired rotation matrix. This will be done later in this section.

- The second is that the vehicle's guide vector is linked to the thrust, which is associated with the vehicle's Z axis or b3.

- The third is that vector b3 is normalized in order not to exceed the maximum values allowed in a rotation matrix (orthonormality).

They happen at the same time, as follows.

Taking advantage of the fact that FBZ is a scalar, we rewrite our dynamic model as follows:

$$
m \begin{bmatrix} \ddot{x} \\ \ddot{y} \\ \ddot{z} \end{bmatrix} = R \begin{bmatrix} 0 \\ 0 \\ F_{BZ} \end{bmatrix} + m \begin{bmatrix} 0 \\ 0 \\ -g \end{bmatrix} = \boxed{F_{BZ}} R \begin{bmatrix} 0 \\ 0 \\ 1 \end{bmatrix} + m \begin{bmatrix} 0 \\ 0 \\ -g \end{bmatrix}
$$

We substitute the thrust that contains the guide vector in our translational dynamics:

$$
m \begin{bmatrix} \ddot{x} \\ \ddot{y} \\ \ddot{z} \end{bmatrix} = C_{xyz} \cdot \left(R \begin{bmatrix} 0 \\ 0 \\ 1 \end{bmatrix} \right) R \begin{bmatrix} 0 \\ 0 \\ 1 \end{bmatrix} + m \begin{bmatrix} 0 \\ 0 \\ -g \end{bmatrix}
$$

This would seem to have an irrelevant behavior, but now we divide by 1 the term that contains the rotation matrix.

Where 1 is equal to (remember that the inverse of a rotation matrix multiplied by said rotation matrix is an identity matrix)

$$
\begin{bmatrix} 0 \\ 0 \\ 1 \end{bmatrix}^T R^T R \begin{bmatrix} 0 \\ 0 \\ 1 \end{bmatrix} = 1
$$

This way

$$
C_{xyz} \cdot \left(R \begin{bmatrix} 0 \\ 0 \\ 1 \end{bmatrix} \right) R \begin{bmatrix} 0 \\ 0 \\ 1 \end{bmatrix} = \frac{C_{xyz} \cdot \left(R \begin{bmatrix} 0 \\ 0 \\ 1 \end{bmatrix} \right) R \begin{bmatrix} 0 \\ 0 \\ 1 \end{bmatrix}}{\begin{bmatrix} 0 \\ 0 \\ 1 \end{bmatrix}^T R^T R \begin{bmatrix} 0 \\ 0 \\ 1 \end{bmatrix}}
$$

Then, rewriting (remember our first restriction)

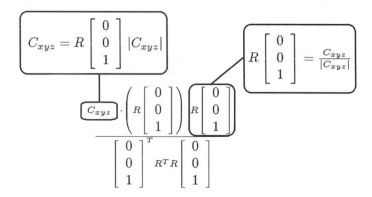

And finally (here we use the relationship between the dot product and the transpose operator)

$$\frac{R\begin{bmatrix}0\\0\\1\end{bmatrix}|C_{xyz}|\cdot\left(R\begin{bmatrix}0\\0\\1\end{bmatrix}\right)}{\begin{bmatrix}0\\0\\1\end{bmatrix}^T R^T R\begin{bmatrix}0\\0\\1\end{bmatrix}}\frac{C_{xyz}}{|C_{xyz}|}=\frac{\left(\begin{bmatrix}0\\0\\1\end{bmatrix}^T R^T\right)|C_{xyz}|\left(R\begin{bmatrix}0\\0\\1\end{bmatrix}\right)}{\begin{bmatrix}0\\0\\1\end{bmatrix}^T R^T R\begin{bmatrix}0\\0\\1\end{bmatrix}}\frac{C_{xyz}}{|C_{xyz}|}=C_{xyz}$$

So, the closed-loop equation of the translational dynamic system becomes

$$m\begin{bmatrix}\ddot{x}\\\ddot{y}\\\ddot{z}\end{bmatrix}=C_{xyz}\cdot\left(R\begin{bmatrix}0\\0\\1\end{bmatrix}\right)R\begin{bmatrix}0\\0\\1\end{bmatrix}+m\begin{bmatrix}0\\0\\-g\end{bmatrix}=C_{xyz}+m\begin{bmatrix}0\\0\\-g\end{bmatrix}$$

$$m\begin{bmatrix}\ddot{x}\\\ddot{y}\\\ddot{z}\end{bmatrix}=\begin{bmatrix}K_{Px}(x_d-x)+K_{Dx}(\dot{x}_d-\dot{x})+m\ddot{x}_d\\K_{Py}(y_d-y)+K_{Dy}(\dot{y}_d-\dot{y})+m\ddot{y}_d\\K_{Pz}(z_d-z)+K_{Dz}(\dot{z}_d-\dot{z})+m\ddot{z}_d\end{bmatrix}+\begin{bmatrix}0\\0\\mg\end{bmatrix}+m\begin{bmatrix}0\\0\\-g\end{bmatrix}$$

This leads to three mass spring damper systems, and choosing the proportional and differential values appropriately implies that (the extensive and formal proof is in Tae Young Lee's articles that you can consult in the Appendix)

$$\begin{bmatrix} 0 \\ 0 \\ 0 \end{bmatrix} = \begin{bmatrix} K_{Px}(x_d - x) + K_{Dx}(\dot{x}_d - \dot{x}) + m(\ddot{x}_d - \ddot{x}) \\ K_{Py}(y_d - y) + K_{Dy}(\dot{y}_d - \dot{y}) + m(\ddot{y}_d - \ddot{y}) \\ K_{Pz}(z_d - z) + K_{Dz}(\dot{z}_d - \dot{z}) + m(\ddot{z}_d - \ddot{z}) \end{bmatrix}$$

$$x \longrightarrow x_d$$
$$y \longrightarrow y_d$$
$$z \longrightarrow z_d$$

Now, let's continue with the rotational part.

Rotational Control

It is time for the most difficult part of this controller: the design of the orientation control by regulating the rotation matrix. For this, we consider that all the closed loop controllers are based on an error. An error is a distance between a desired value and a measured value. With scalar quantities, this distance is simply a subtraction. In a similar way, we are going to define the concept of distance between two rotation matrices (the measured and the desired one).

To begin with, we already know that the matrix R is defined by Euler's angles as

$$R = R_{z_\psi} R_{x_\phi} R_{y_\theta}$$

$$R = \begin{bmatrix} c\psi c\theta - s\phi s\psi s\theta & -c\phi s\psi & c\psi s\theta + s\phi s\psi c\theta \\ s\psi c\theta + s\phi c\psi s\theta & c\phi c\psi & s\psi s\theta - s\phi c\psi c\theta \\ -c\phi s\theta & s\phi & c\phi c\theta \end{bmatrix}$$

and the fact that the desired matrix contains the three "thrusters." This is because in a rotation matrix, each one of its columns represents the behavior of a Cartesian axis. Also, as mentioned, each column is a unit vector that satisfies the normal vector condition, and the orthogonal condition is satisfied with the following definitions:

$$R_d = \begin{bmatrix} b_{1d} & b_{2d} & b_{3d} \end{bmatrix}$$

$$b_{1d} = b_{2d} \times b_{3d}$$
$$b_{2d} = \frac{b_{3d} \times B_{des}}{|b_{3d} \times B_{des}|}$$
$$b_{3d} = \frac{C_{xyz}}{|C_{xyz}|}$$

As mentioned, these vectors are **noa** type vectors, and for their definition it is very important that they are orthonormal to each other. This explains the presence of the cross products and the normalized quantities. Finally, in the case of b1d since it is the cross product of two normalized or unitary vectors, it is also normalized or unitary.

Notice that the only independent vectors are Bdes and b3d, and the only one that can be designed is Bdes, since b3d must satisfy our constraint condition to regulate FBZ. In the case of b1d, it is forced to fulfill the orthonormality with the two remaining vectors.

An example of Bdes can be

$$B_{des} = \begin{bmatrix} \cos \psi_d & \sin \psi_d & 0 \end{bmatrix}$$

This vector is linked to b1d and b2d, and allows for example the rotation around the ZB axis (a forced but functional yaw regulation, not entirely carried out, because of the interaction in b1d and b2d, with b3d).

Having defined the measured rotation matrix and the desired rotation matrix, let's remember some concepts about distance. The distance between two scalars is a subtraction. The distance between two vectors is, among many others, a quadratic vector norm (the square root of the sum of its scalar subtractions at the second power). For matrices, there are also several definitions of distance. Here we will use the Frobenius norm because of its invariant properties (the trace and the determinant are invariant values in a matrix and the Frobenius norm is based on traces).

As you can see, all distances are either a scalar or a scalar function. If a and b are scalar values, the distance is

$$a, b = C, C_d$$
$$d_{ab} = |a - b| = |C - C_d|$$

If they are vectors, a very common type of distance is

$$a = [a_x, a_y, a_n] = [C_x, C_y, C_n]$$
$$b = [b_x, b_y, b_n] = [C_{dx}, C_{dy}, C_{dn}]$$
$$d_{ab} = \sqrt{(C_x - C_{dx})^2 + (C_y - C_{dy})^2 + (C_z - C_{dz})^2} = \sqrt{(a-b)^T(a-b)}$$

And the vector components (individual subtractions) can be obtained in this way (it is useful to know these components in order to design a three-dimensional control):

$$\nabla f(d_{ab}) \rightarrow \nabla(\tfrac{d_{ab}^2}{2}) = \begin{bmatrix} C_x - C_{dx} & , & C_y - C_{dy} & , & C_z - C_{dz} \end{bmatrix}$$

where the operator used here (the inverted triangle also known as nabla or del) is known as the gradient and is a type of directional derivative that obtains the vector components from a scalar function dependent on several variables (in this case, a function of the distance, which is already a scalar dependent on several variables).

If a and b are matrices, the Frobenius distance is

$$a = R$$
$$b = R_d$$
$$d_{ab} = Frob(R - R_d) = \sqrt{trace\left[(R - R_d)^T(R - R_d)\right]}$$

Note that the sequence of the subtractions is dimensionally extended.

Doing the following operations (valid for rotation matrices and using trace product properties)

$$trace((R^T - R_d^T)(R - R_d)) = trace(R_d^T R_d + R^T R - R_d^T R - R^T R_d)$$
$$= trace(2(I - R_d^T R)) = 2trace(I - R_d^T R)$$

is obtained

$$d_{ab} = \sqrt{2trace(I - R_d^T R)}$$

In this case, since we have a scalar and we need to design a three-dimensional orientation control, we need a way to obtain a three-dimensional vector from said distance definition. Remember that having defined the distance between our measured matrix and the desired matrix, we must generate three errors from it in order to generate the three torques of the vehicle.

One way is by applying the concept of directional derivative (here we will use a type of directional derivative called a trivialized right derivative) and considering that our distance is a scalar function of several variables, when we derive directionally we will obtain a vector expression in a similar way as when we applied the gradient (nabla) to the distance between two vectors.

The trivialized right derivative is widely used in this type of controller, but given its complexity of interpretation, we will only use it as a tool. For more information about it, see the documents of Bullo and Taeyoung Lee in the Appendix. It should be noted that the value of 1/4 is used here for convenience in a way such that the final result is expressed in terms of 1/2 and this is particularly useful in nonlinear control to eliminate constant values through matrix properties or derivatives. However, you can use any other multiplier. The result only alters the values to be dragged during the procedure.

$$D_R f(d_{ab}) = D_R \left[\frac{1}{4}d_{ab}^2\right] = D_R \left[\frac{1}{2}trace(I - R_d^T R)\right] = -\frac{1}{2}trace(R_d^T D_R R)$$
$$= -\frac{1}{2}trace(R_d^T R S(n))$$

Observe three things:

- In the case of the trace, because it is a linear operation, the derivative of the trace is the trace of the derivative.

- Also, we use the fact that the generic derivative of a rotation matrix produces the rotation matrix multiplied by a skew-symmetric matrix (S). However, note that said antisymmetric matrix is not the same as the previous one described in Chapter 2. This is because that was a derivative with respect to the time and this is a derivative with respect to the direction of change. However, an antisymmetric matrix dependent on the rate of change (n) is generated.

- Finally, note that the derivative of the identity matrix is zero, and that the remaining derivative only affects the term of the rotation matrices, where Rd is considered as a "constant" because it is independent of R (this derivative is done with respect to R).

In summary, the following properties were used:

$$D(trace\,[M]) = trace(D\,[M])$$
$$\dot{R} = RS(w) \neq D_R R = RS(n)$$

The term S(n) is a representation that indicates the presence of a vector n that is transformed to a skew matrix in order to avoid the use of cross products and to allow the use of matrix products.

From now on, we will use the notations hat and vee. A notation equivalent to S(n) is the hat operator, which implies obtaining a skew matrix from a vector.

$$n = \begin{bmatrix} n_x \\ n_y \\ n_z \end{bmatrix} \qquad S(n) = \begin{bmatrix} 0 & -n_z & n_y \\ n_z & 0 & -n_x \\ -n_y & n_x & 0 \end{bmatrix}$$

$$S(n) = \hat{n}$$
$$D_R f(d_{ab}) = -\tfrac{1}{2} trace(R_d^T R S(n)) = -\tfrac{1}{2} trace(R_d^T R \hat{n})$$

If you look carefully, you can see that we do not yet have a vector that we can use, since the trace is a scalar and even the product on which the trace is being applied is a matrix.

However, there are three useful facts.

The first is that the following identity exists:

$$trace\,[\hat{r}\hat{c}] = trace\left(\begin{bmatrix} 0 & -r_z & r_y \\ r_z & 0 & -r_x \\ -r_y & r_x & 0 \end{bmatrix} \begin{bmatrix} 0 & -c_z & c_y \\ c_z & 0 & -c_x \\ -c_y & c_x & 0 \end{bmatrix} \right)$$

$$= trace \begin{bmatrix} -c_y r_y - c_z r_z & c_x r_y & c_x r_z \\ c_y r_x & -c_x r_x - c_z r_z & c_y r_z \\ c_z r_x & c_z r_y & -c_x r_x - c_y r_y \end{bmatrix}$$

$$= -2c_x r_x - 2c_y r_y - 2c_z r_z$$

$$= -2(\breve{c} \cdot \breve{r}) = -2\breve{c}^T \breve{r}$$

For this, we use the operator vee, which is the inverse of the operator hat and implies obtaining a vector from a skew matrix:

$$\breve{S}(n) = n = \breve{\hat{n}}$$

The second is that the following matrix and in general any other matrix can be decomposed as the sum of a skew part and a symmetric part as follows:

$$R_d^T R = \frac{R_d^T R - (R_d^T R)^T}{2} + \frac{R_d^T R + (R_d^T R)^T}{2}$$

In this way

$$-\tfrac{1}{2}trace(R_d^T R \hat{n}) = -\tfrac{1}{2}trace(\frac{R_d^T R - (R_d^T R)^T}{2}\hat{n} + \frac{R_d^T R + (R_d^T R)^T}{2}\hat{n})$$

The third fact is that the trace of the product of a symmetric matrix by a skew symmetric one is zero, so only the trace of the product of the skew matrices survives:

$$-\tfrac{1}{2}trace(\frac{R_d^T R - (R_d^T R)^T}{2}\hat{n} + \frac{R_d^T R + (R_d^T R)^T}{2}\hat{n}) = -\tfrac{1}{4}trace([R_d^T R - (R_d^T R)^T]\hat{n})$$

Using the equality that relates the trace of the product of two antisymmetric matrices to the dot product of their equivalent vee vectors, we have that

$$-\tfrac{1}{4}trace([R_d^T R - (R_d^T R)^T]\hat{n}) = \frac{(R_d^T R - R^T R_d)\check{\cdot}n}{2}$$

Finally, the error vector that we are looking for is this:

$$e_R = \frac{(R_d^T R - R^T R_d)\check{}}{2}$$

To formulate our attitude control (also known as orientation control), in addition to the orientation error component (in this case given by rotation matrices, which serves to incorporate a proportional part), an angular velocity component is required (for incorporate a derivative part). This is done in the following way.

A first attempt is to propose

$$e_\omega = \omega - \omega_d$$

Simple logic indicates that these angular velocities (the measured one and the reference one) are vectors, and what is explained in this equation could be directly applied:

$$\nabla f(d_{ab}) \rightarrow \nabla\left(\tfrac{d_{ab}^2}{2}\right) = \left[\ \ C_x - C_{dx} \ , \ \ C_y - C_{dy} \ , \ \ C_z - C_{dz}\ \right]$$

However, the desired angular velocity and the measured one cannot be directly subtracted since they lie within different spaces. In this way, we will use a deduction based on the derivatives of the rotation matrix. See Figure 3-18.

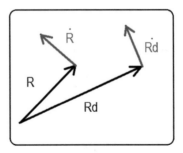

Figure 3-18. *Graphic representation of the spaces where the desired and real rotation matrices derivatives lie*

In a simplified way, we indicate that the speed of a rotation matrix is tangential to itself. Note that neither the rotation matrix nor its derivative are vectors but matrices, although we can use their eigenvectors in order to imagine and represent them graphically. A mathematical proof of the perpendicularity of the derivative of a rotation matrix with respect to its rotation matrix is given by the equation of the derivative of a rotation matrix in which appears a skew-symmetric matrix depending on the angular velocity, and because this antisymmetric matrix is the equivalent of a cross product, the result is an orthogonal matrix.

From the fact that the desired rotation matrix does not lie within the same space as the measured rotation matrix, it is necessary to do the process shown in Figure 3-19.

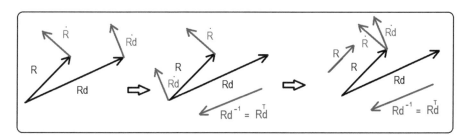

Figure 3-19. *Graphic sequence for homologating the rotation matrices derivatives*

The result of this graphic sequence produces the following equation:

$$\dot{R} - \dot{R}_d(R_d^T R)$$

Since it is required a difference between angular velocities, we need to rewrite the previous equation in this way:

$$\dot{R} - \dot{R}_d(R_d^T R) = RS(\omega) - R_d S(\omega_d) R_d^T R$$

If the second term is multiplied by the identity matrix (remember that this is equivalent to multiply by 1),

$$RR^T = I$$

$$RS(\omega) - R_d S(\omega_d) R_d^T R = RS(\omega) - RR^T R_d S(\omega_d) R_d^T R$$

The equation is rewritten in terms of R:

$$\dot{R} - \dot{R}_d(R_d^T R) = R\left[S(\omega) - R^T R_d S(\omega_d) R_d^T R\right]$$

This can be rewritten as follows (the property of the transpose of a product):

$$R\left[S(\omega) - R^T R_d S(\omega_d) R_d^T R\right] = R\left[S(\omega) - R^T R_d S(\omega_d)\left(R^T R_d\right)^T\right]$$

There are two useful identities. Observe that for avoiding the use of an enormous hat symbol, this has been placed at the end of the parentheses and this just implies that it must be applied to the result of the operations inside the parentheses:

$$R(x \times y) = Rx \times Ry = RS(x)y$$
$$R\hat{x}R^T = RS(x)R^T = R(x \times R^T) = Rx \times I = S(Rx)I = S(Rx) = \widehat{(Rx)}$$

Using these identities in the equation that we are developing (specifically in its second term), we have

$$R\left[S(\omega) - R^T R_d S(\omega_d)\left(R^T R_d\right)^T\right] = R\left[\hat{\omega} - \widehat{(R^T R_d \omega_d)}\right]$$

Since the sum of two antisymmetric matrices is another skew-symmetric matrix

$$R\left[\hat{\omega} - \widehat{(R^T R_d \omega_d)}\right] = R\widehat{(\omega - R^T R_d \omega_d)}$$

the angular velocity error that we are looking for is simply the vector

$$e_\omega = \omega - R^T R_d \omega_d$$

Note that wd is not an arbitrary value and must be obtained as a dependency on Rd as follows:

$$S(\omega_d) = R_d^T \dot{R}_d$$

Note that in the model of our rotational dynamics we have the term

$$\dot{\omega}$$

Its indirect use (this will be compensated soon) is obtained in this way:

$$e_\omega = \omega - R^T R_d \omega_d$$
$$\dot{e}_\omega = \dot{\omega} - \dot{R}^T R_d \omega_d - R^T \dot{R}_d \omega_d - R^T R_d \dot{\omega}_d$$
$$\dot{e}_\omega = \dot{\omega} - (RS(\omega))^T R_d \omega_d - R^T R_d S(\omega_d)\omega_d - R^T R_d \dot{\omega}_d$$

It must be noticed that

$$S(\omega_d)\omega_d = \omega_d \times \omega_d = 0$$

This way

$$\dot{e}_\omega = \dot{\omega} - (RS(\omega))^T R_d \omega_d - R^T R_d \dot{\omega}_d$$
$$\dot{e}_\omega = \dot{\omega} - (S^T(\omega)R^T) R_d \omega_d - R^T R_d \dot{\omega}_d$$

Applying the definition of a skew-symmetric matrix:

$$S^T = -S$$
$$\dot{e}_\omega = \dot{\omega} + S(\omega)R^T R_d \omega_d - R^T R_d \dot{\omega}_d$$

We will use this result soon.

Returning to our original rotational dynamics, it can be rewritten as follows:

$$\begin{bmatrix} \tau_{BX} \\ \tau_{BY} \\ \tau_{BZ} \end{bmatrix} = \begin{bmatrix} J_x \dot{\omega}_x \\ J_y \dot{\omega}_y \\ J_z \dot{\omega}_z \end{bmatrix} + \begin{bmatrix} \omega_y \omega_z J_z - \omega_y \omega_z J_y \\ \omega_x \omega_z J_x - \omega_x \omega_z J_z \\ \omega_x \omega_y J_y - \omega_x \omega_y J_x \end{bmatrix}$$

$$\tau = J\dot{\omega} + \omega \times J\omega$$

By using the definitions of the rotation error and the angular velocity error that we deduced previously, we can propose the following control:

$$\tau = -K_R e_R - K_\omega e_\omega + \omega \times J\omega$$

where KR and Kw are scalar (the idea is to scale the corresponding error vectors identically to preserve their orthonormal proportions).

If we replace this controller into the original equation, we have

$$-K_R e_R - K_\omega e_\omega + \omega \times J\omega = J\dot{\omega} + \omega \times J\omega$$
$$-K_R e_R - K_\omega e_\omega = \boxed{J\dot{\omega}}$$

This equation requires the dynamic compensation of the term enclosed. We will teach you how to do this in the next section.

Dynamics Compensation and Additional Remarks

As can be seen, the derivative term of the angular velocity remains in the equation. As we have previously done, the PD can be made large enough to overcome this term, or it can be compensated. For this, remember that we deduced this equation:

$$\dot{e}_\omega = \dot{\omega} + S(\omega)R^T R_d \omega_d - R^T R_d \dot{\omega}_d$$

Thus, we can modify the proposed control to incorporate the following:

$$\tau = -K_R e_R - K_\omega e_\omega + \omega \times J\omega - J(S(\omega)R^T R_d \omega_d - R^T R_d \dot{\omega}_d)$$

Substituting the modified control into the rotational dynamics we have

$$\tau = J\dot{\omega} + \omega \times J\omega$$
$$-K_R e_R - K_\omega e_\omega + \omega \times J\omega - J(S(\omega)R^T R_d \omega_d - R^T R_d \dot{\omega}_d) = J\dot{\omega} + \omega \times J\omega$$
$$-K_R e_R - K_\omega e_\omega - J(\dot{\omega} + S(\omega)R^T R_d \omega_d - R^T R_d \dot{\omega}_d) = 0$$
$$-K_R e_R - K_\omega e_\omega - J\dot{e}_\omega = 0$$

This system is not exactly a mass spring damper system, but its similarity, along with the necessary conditions which are developed with the Lyapunov method used by Lee, Leok, and McClamroch in *Control of Complex Maneuvers for a Quadrotor UAV using Geometric Methods on SE (3)* and in *Geometric Tracking Control of a Quadrotor UAV on SE (3)* by the same authors, which you can consult in the Appendix, implies that

$$e_R \rightarrow 0$$
$$R \rightarrow R_d$$
$$e_\omega \rightarrow 0$$
$$\omega \rightarrow \omega_d$$

Here we omit these deductions, since they are even longer to carry out step by step than the explanation made for the definition of the errors and their interaction with the dynamics made in this section. A first step is to find a relationship between the rotation error and the angular velocity error, which is also developed by the aforementioned authors. The second step is to continue with the following section.

In summary, the non-linear system associated with the drone in non-smooth flight is controlled as follows:

$$F_{BZ} = \left(\left[\begin{array}{c} K_{Px}(x_d - x) + K_{Dx}(\dot{x}_d - \dot{x}) + m\ddot{x}_d \\ K_{Py}(y_d - y) + K_{Dy}(\dot{y}_d - \dot{y}) + m\ddot{y}_d \\ K_{Pz}(z_d - z) + K_{Dz}(\dot{z}_d - \dot{z}) + m\ddot{z}_d \end{array} \right] + \left[\begin{array}{c} 0 \\ 0 \\ mg \end{array} \right] \right) \cdot \left[R \left[\begin{array}{c} 0 \\ 0 \\ 1 \end{array} \right] \right]$$

$$F_{BZ} = C_{xyz} \cdot \left(R \left[\begin{array}{c} 0 \\ 0 \\ 1 \end{array} \right] \right)$$

$$B_{des} = \left[\begin{array}{ccc} \cos\psi_d & \sin\psi_d & 0 \end{array} \right]$$

$$b_{3d} = \frac{C_{xyz}}{|C_{xyz}|}$$
$$b_{1d} = b_{2d} \times b_{3d}$$
$$b_{2d} = \frac{b_{3d} \times B_{des}}{|b_{3d} \times B_{des}|}$$

$$R_d = \left[\begin{array}{ccc} b_{1d} & b_{2d} & b_{3d} \end{array} \right]$$

$$S(\omega_d) = R_d^T \dot{R}_d \qquad e_R = \frac{(R_d^T R - R^T R_d)}{2}$$
$$e_\omega = \omega - R^T R_d \omega_d$$

$$\tau = -K_R e_R - K_\omega e_\omega + \omega \times J\omega - \underline{J(S(\omega)R^T R_d \omega_d - R^T R_d \dot{\omega}_d)}$$

Optional, it could be
overwhelmed by PD terms

Note that the control is based on a guide vector regulated by three thrusters (the components of the desired rotation matrix), which are dependent on the same guide vector.

Graphically it looks as in Figure 3-20 (*note that the full operations are described in the previous equations and, as you have already seen, dynamic effects can be added to obtain a more accurate controller).

If you want to add remote controllers, they could modify the desired values of X, Y, Z, and yaw, or the torques and force, as in the case of the previous designs.

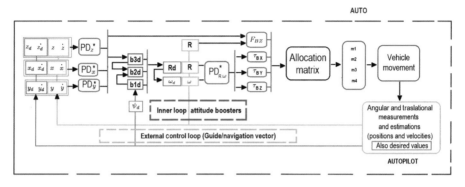

Figure 3-20. *Graphic sequence of the geometric control*

The following section provides an introduction to the Lyapunov method to demonstrate stability of systems. This, together with the previously deduced equations, will allow you to immerse yourself with less difficulty into the previous references.

Introduction to Lyapunov Stability

This section is for those who want to know more about the extended and formal proofs available in the aforementioned articles which are based on the Lyapunov stability theory and that complete the previous section. There are two Lyapunov methods, one for linear systems, and the other for nonlinear systems. Given the scope of the second method and the fact that the linear is a particular case of it, we will briefly explain its use through examples and also its graphic interpretation.

Step 1

Given a system, for example the first order system and the damped harmonic oscillator without a control input, remember the fact that we arrive at these systems once we apply closed loop controllers to our dynamic systems, as you can see in the previous sections.

$$\dot{e} = -e$$
$$\ddot{e} + \dot{e} + e = 0$$

A virtual energy can be proposed. This is a scalar function of several variables that is always positive except in its minimum value, where it is zero, or a total immobility condition, or a stable condition. In general, this function depends on the variables that we are analyzing.

$$V(e, e, ..e^n) > 0$$
$$V(0) = 0$$

For the first system, a function that satisfies the previous conditions is the following (notice that its graphical representation is a concave parabola):

$$V = \frac{e^2}{2}$$

For the second system, another example of function that satisfies both conditions is this one (its graphical representation is an elliptic paraboloid that is also concave):

$$V = \frac{e^2}{2} + \frac{\dot{e}^2}{2}$$

From now on, note that a Lyapunov function is usually denoted by the letter V (it is possible that this is because V seems to be the graphical representation of a concave function). Also, note that they are frequently divided by 2 in order not to drag the factor of 2 when deriving the Lyapunov squared functions.

Observe that a Lyapunov function usually has the shape displayed in Figure 3-21 (at least as it can be represented as such when it depends on only one or two variables). It looks like concave vessels, not necessarily curved. Some of them look like inverted pyramids (the idea can be extended for more than two variables).

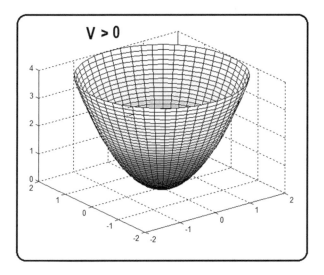

Figure 3-21. *A 3D example of a Lyapunov function*

Step 2

The derivative of the Lyapunov function with respect to the time must be negative, or at least negative semidefinite, and must depend on one or more of our variables of interest. This has a lot to do with the graphical analogy. Remember that Lyapunov functions are concave and closed containers, and their slope seen from any point on their surfaces is negative. See Figure 3-22. This implies that the states of a system "placed" on said energy surface "will slide" towards the minimum point of the surface, or condition of stability, or null energy, or simply that the system will stop at the minimum value of energy.

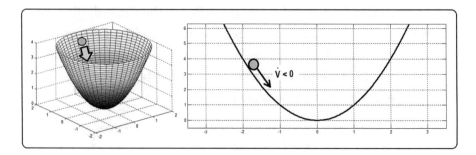

Figure 3-22. *The derivative of a Lyapunov function (3D and 2D examples)*

$$\dot{V}(e, e, ..e^n) = \frac{dV(e,e,..e^n)}{dt} = \frac{dV(e,e,..e^n)}{d(e,e,..e^n)} \frac{d(e,e,..e^n)}{dt} = \leq 0$$

For the first order system:

$$V = \frac{e^2}{2}$$
$$\dot{V} = e\dot{e}$$

And replacing the system for which said Lyapunov function was designed:

$$\dot{e} = -e$$
$$\dot{V} = e\dot{e} = -e^2 \leq 0$$

This derivative is negative semidefined and depends totally or partially on the states of our interest.

For the damped harmonic oscillator system, we have

$$V = \frac{e^2}{2} + \frac{\dot{e}^2}{2}$$
$$\dot{V} = e\dot{e} + \dot{e}\ddot{e}$$

And replacing the system for which said Lyapunov function was designed:

$$\ddot{e} + \dot{e} + e = 0$$
$$\ddot{e} = -\dot{e} - e$$

$$\dot{V} = e\dot{e} + \dot{e}\ddot{e} = e\dot{e} - \dot{e}^2 - \dot{e}e = -\dot{e}^2 \leq 0$$

This derivative is negative semidefined and depends totally or partially on the states of our interest. (In this case, it does not depend on the error but on its derivative. Soon we will see how to deal with this problem.)

If for the first order system we had proposed

$$V = \frac{K_p e^2}{2}$$
$$\dot{V} = K_p e\dot{e} = -K_p e^2$$
$$K_p > 0$$

the derivative of the Lyapunov function would not alter its negativity, nor the Lyapunov function its positivity while the constant Kp was positive. You will remember this fact soon.

Note that we can only say that the states with respect to which the Lyapunov derivative depends tend to the behavior of the minimum energy of the Lyapunov function; that is, they tend to 0. If the rest of the states do not appear, we cannot ensure anything about them, and we must design and try a new Lyapunov function.

Step 3

By using auxiliary postulates, known as Barbalat's lemma or Lasalle's principle (they are used according to the type of system you have, so you must investigate them), it must be evaluated when V and its derivatives are zero if the states of the system also tend to zero. This is because local valleys may occur, as in Figure 3-23. In these valleys, the energy value is zero, but the system will not reach the minimum value of the Lyapunov function, but a local trap.

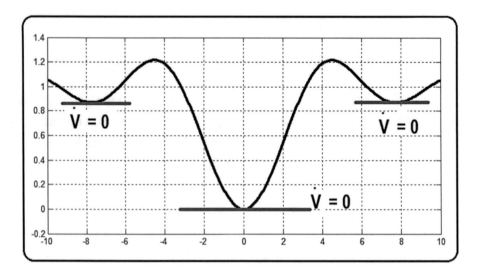

Figure 3-23. *Local and global minimal values at a Lyapunov function*

For the first example, let's see what happens when the derivative of V is equal to zero:

$$\dot{V} = e\dot{e} = -e^2 = 0$$

$$-e^2 = 0$$
$$e = 0$$

and also

$$e\dot{e} = 0$$
$$\dot{e} = 0$$

This result could also be reached with the system equation:

$$\dot{e} = -e$$

Thus,

$$e \to 0$$
$$\dot{e} \to 0$$

For the second system, we proceed in the same way:

$$\dot{V} = e\dot{e} + \dot{e}\ddot{e} = e\dot{e} - \dot{e}^2 - \dot{e}e = -\dot{e}^2 = 0$$
$$-\dot{e}^2 = 0$$
$$\dot{e} = 0$$

and also

$$V = \tfrac{e^2}{2} + \tfrac{\dot{e}^2}{2} = 0$$
$$e = -\dot{e} = 0$$

Solving for the double derivative of e by replacing the found values of e and its first derivative:

$$\dot{V} = e\dot{e} + \dot{e}\ddot{e} = 0$$
$$\ddot{e} = 0$$

This result could also be reached with the system equation:

$$\ddot{e} = -\dot{e} - e$$

Thus,

$$\ddot{e} \to 0$$
$$\dot{e} \to 0$$
$$e \to 0$$

Additionally, a very common way to work with Lyapunov functions is based on quadratic equations.

For example, the Lyapunov function of the damped harmonic system can be rewritten like this:

$$V = \frac{e^2}{2} + \frac{\dot{e}^2}{2}$$

$$V = \begin{bmatrix} e & \dot{e} \end{bmatrix} \begin{bmatrix} \frac{1}{2} & 0 \\ 0 & \frac{1}{2} \end{bmatrix} \begin{bmatrix} e \\ \dot{e} \end{bmatrix}$$

$$\dot{V} = \begin{bmatrix} \dot{e} & \ddot{e} \end{bmatrix} \begin{bmatrix} \frac{1}{2} & 0 \\ 0 & \frac{1}{2} \end{bmatrix} \begin{bmatrix} e \\ \dot{e} \end{bmatrix} + \begin{bmatrix} e & \dot{e} \end{bmatrix} \begin{bmatrix} \frac{1}{2} & 0 \\ 0 & \frac{1}{2} \end{bmatrix} \begin{bmatrix} \dot{e} \\ \ddot{e} \end{bmatrix}$$

$$= \begin{bmatrix} e & \dot{e} \end{bmatrix} \begin{bmatrix} 0 & -1 \\ 1 & -1 \end{bmatrix} \begin{bmatrix} e \\ \dot{e} \end{bmatrix}$$

If you look at

$$\begin{bmatrix} \frac{1}{2} & 0 \\ 0 & \frac{1}{2} \end{bmatrix}$$

$$\begin{bmatrix} 0 & -1 \\ 1 & -1 \end{bmatrix}$$

The direct concern is to demonstrate that these matrices are respectively the equivalent of positive and negative or what in linear algebra is known as a positive definite matrix, a negative definite matrix, or semidefinite matrices. By using the linear algebra theory, it is obtained through the eigenvalues criterion that the first matrix is positive definite while the second is negative semidefinite, which matches with the original results. This matrix representation is found in many texts on control systems, including Taeyoung Lee's demonstrations in the previously indicated articles.

Proposing Lyapunov functions and also demonstrating that their derivatives (where the systems and their controllers usually appear) are defined negative is an extensive branch of a science called nonlinear control theory. Each dynamic system represents a challenge in finding its stability through Lyapunov functions; even each individual result represents a book or a new science.

What helps a lot in this research is the capacity to do algebraic operations with the controller. As an example, in Chapter 4, there is a section dedicated to the state-space representation, where it is indicated that a non-linear system of differential equations (including a multicopter) can be represented as follows:

$$\dot{x} = f(x, u)$$

where x are the states of the system and u their control signals.

In this way, following the Lyapunov method

$$V(x) > 0$$
$$V(0) = 0$$
$$\dot{V}(x) = \nabla V(x)\dot{x} = \nabla V(x)f(x, u)$$

and as the following is expected:

$$\dot{V}(x) = \nabla V(x)f(x, u) \leq 0$$

The way to achieve this is by modifying the control u as appropriate.

For example, let's analyze the case of the second order system (damped harmonic oscillator) with non-free input (with the presence of a force u instead of a simple 0).

The goal is that the variable Y tends to a desired value known as Yd.

We will have two equations: the real system equation and the control equation.

So here we have two options:

1. A controller is tested and if it works correctly, we directly try to demonstrate the stability of the closed loop system. This is not entirely recommended, but most people do it this way, especially because almost everything works with a PD or PID and people only want to answer the reasons.

As said, we have a system and a control that is already useful:

$$\ddot{Y} + \dot{Y} + Y = u$$
$$u = \ddot{Y}_d + K_d(\dot{Y}_d - \dot{Y}) + K_p(Y_d - Y)$$

The closed loop is analyzed:

$$\ddot{Y} + \dot{Y} + Y = \ddot{Y}_d + K_d(\dot{Y}_d - \dot{Y}) + K_p(Y_d - Y)$$
$$\ddot{Y} = \ddot{Y}_d + K_d(\dot{Y}_d - \dot{Y}) + K_p(Y_d - Y) - \dot{Y} - Y$$

Some dominant assumptions are made. The following is valid for positive Kp and Kd values and also greater than 1:

$$-K_d\dot{Y} \gg -\dot{Y}$$
$$-K_pY \gg -Y$$

$$\ddot{Y} = \ddot{Y}_d + K_d(\dot{Y}_d - \dot{Y}) + K_p(Y_d - Y)$$
$$0 = (\ddot{Y}_d - \ddot{Y}) + K_d(\dot{Y}_d - \dot{Y}) + K_p(Y_d - Y)$$

Renaming:

$$Y_d - Y = e$$

And also renaming its derivatives, we have this system:

$$0 = \ddot{e} + K_d\dot{e} + K_pe$$

And finally, its closed loop stability is demonstrated in a similar way to the second order system previously analyzed:

$$V(e) = \frac{K_p e^2}{2} + \frac{\dot{e}^2}{2}$$
$$\dot{V}(e) = K_p e \dot{e} + \dot{e}\ddot{e} = K_p e \dot{e} + \dot{e}(-K_d \dot{e} - K_p e) = -K_d \dot{e}^2 \leq 0$$

2. The stability of the original system is demonstrated and the control is designed on the process.

For example, this Lyapunov function is proposed and then its derivative:

$$V(Y_d - Y, \dot{Y}_d - \dot{Y}) = \frac{(K_p[Y_d - Y])^2}{2} + \frac{(\dot{Y}_d - \dot{Y})^2}{2}$$
$$\dot{V} = (K_p[Y_d - Y])(\dot{Y}_d - \dot{Y}) + (\dot{Y}_d - \dot{Y})(\ddot{Y}_d - \ddot{Y})$$

We introduce the dynamics of the system into the Lyapunov derivative:

$$\ddot{Y} + \dot{Y} + Y = u$$
$$\ddot{Y} = u - \dot{Y} - Y$$
$$\dot{V} = (K_p[Y_d - Y])(\dot{Y}_d - \dot{Y}) + (\dot{Y}_d - \dot{Y})\left(\ddot{Y}_d - \left[u - \dot{Y} - Y\right]\right)$$

In this moment, it is not possible to say that

$$\dot{V} \leq 0$$

But it is possible to design u, for example:

$$u = \ddot{Y}_d + K_d(\dot{Y}_d - \dot{Y}) + K_p(Y_d - Y)$$

Then the term

$$\ddot{Y}_d - \left[u - \dot{Y} - Y\right] = \ddot{Y}_d + \dot{Y} + Y - \ddot{Y}_d - K_d(\dot{Y}_d - \dot{Y}) - K_p(Y_d - Y)$$
$$= \dot{Y} + Y - K_d(\dot{Y}_d - \dot{Y}) - K_p(Y_d - Y)$$

Again, we can make these assumptions

$$K_d\dot{Y} \gg \dot{Y}$$
$$K_p Y \gg Y$$
$$\ddot{Y}_d - \left[u - \dot{Y} - Y\right] = \dot{Y} + Y - K_d(\dot{Y}_d - \dot{Y}) - K_p(Y_d - Y)$$
$$\approx -K_d(\dot{Y}_d - \dot{Y}) - K_p(Y_d - Y)$$

under these considerations

$$\dot{V} = (K_p[Y_d - Y])(\dot{Y}_d - \dot{Y}) + (\dot{Y}_d - \dot{Y})(\ddot{Y}_d - \left[u - \dot{Y} - Y\right])$$
$$\approx (K_p[Y_d - Y])(\dot{Y}_d - \dot{Y}) + (\dot{Y}_d - \dot{Y})\left[-K_d(\dot{Y}_d - \dot{Y}) - K_p(Y_d - Y)\right]$$
$$\dot{V} = -K_d(\dot{Y}_d - \dot{Y})^2 + K_p\left[(Y_d - Y)(\dot{Y}_d - \dot{Y}) - (Y_d - Y)(\dot{Y}_d - \dot{Y})\right]$$
$$= -K_d(\dot{Y}_d - \dot{Y})^2 \leq 0$$

Note that, as in the case of the Taeyoung Lee's aforementioned articles, sometimes it is not specifically proven that the Lyapunov functions and their derivatives are strictly defined positive and negative, but simply that some of their equation terms are bounded (this means that their maximum and minimum values cannot exceed a certain value), and due to the fact that they are bounded, they can be dominated in their effects by other negative definite or positive defined terms. Also, these limits allow finding the physical restrictions of the vehicle and its operating ranges.

Finally, it must be mentioned that the stability analysis by using Lyapunov methods is optional in linear systems, since they have many other tools. But in non-linear systems, as was the geometric control case, Lyapunov's method is the most popular option, and not because of the simplicity (which does not exist), but because it has a specific method. Said method is represented in Figure 3-24.

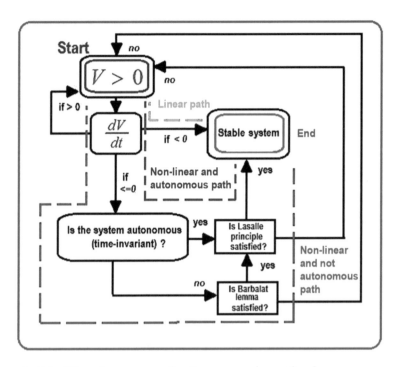

Figure 3-24. *Usual sequence for Lyapunov's method*

You have learned about robot and vehicle mode controllers and also the basis of the Lyapunov theory. Let's close this chapter with a section on the desired values (remember that they are a component of the error which defines our controllers).

Definition of Desired Values: Regulation, Trajectory, or Point-to-Point

In Chapter 4, we will verify most of the controllers explained here and we will note (especially in the geometric case) that the kind of path alters the way the control is tuned (and not only in the selection of gains, but also in the inclusion or omission of specific terms).

In this way, we can ask ourselves if there is a way to follow trajectories without depending directly on the execution time, but directly on the mobility of the vehicle, for example its speed, acceleration, jerk (first derivative of acceleration), or even its snap (second derivative of acceleration).

Let's start by defining some concepts related to the desired value. Other concepts can be found in the article by Kelly in the Appendix (for example, in order to define a haptic error).

Regulation: A regulation task is when a system is placed in a constant value. In this case, a good example is the hovering task of a multicopter, which implies that the vehicle reaches a point in the space and once there it keeps a "static" position.

Trajectory tracking: This is when the vehicle is commanded to follow a time-dependent reference (a circle, a cosine, etc.). The basic task is to follow a reference in critical times, and it will be achieved as long as the motors and the system by itself are able to move at the speed, acceleration, etc. Here it is relevant to replicate the reference and its motion characteristics, for example a vehicle chase.

Point-to-point tracking: This is a special case of the previous one, where the maximum characteristics of the drone (speed, acceleration, etc.) are considered. The objective here is that our drone follows a route without exceeding its own limit values, avoiding forcing the motors and damaging the aircraft due to sudden inertial changes.

It consists of splitting a given trajectory into specific segments and carrying out said trajectory as a motion between points; see Figure 3-25. This way the designer is able to control the speed and acceleration (or more derivatives) profiles between the target points, in order that these profiles are under the maximum values of the vehicle. There are many ways to do it, such as splines, Hermite, Catmull-Rom polynomial interpolation of n degree, interpolation by using trigonometric, or exponential Fourier series. The main concern for defining point-to-point values is to achieve a smooth execution for the motors. It is not relevant to replicate the execution time of a reference but the reference only, and it is useful, for example, in object-search tasks or the execution of predefined movements for body rehabilitation.

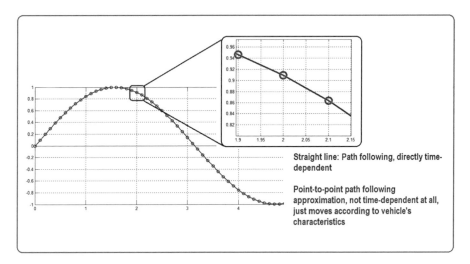

Straight line: Path following, directly time-dependent

Point-to-point path following approximation, not time-dependent at all, just moves according to vehicle's characteristics

Figure 3-25. *Point-to-point path approximation when a soft function is tracked*

Note that the closer the points are, the point-to-point tracking is also closer to the trajectory tracking behavior. In other words, the larger the order of the interpolation, the vehicle will behave in a less "robotic motion" way, all at the cost of damaging the vehicle's actuators. This represents a tradeoff between the mobility performance and the safety of the motors. Remember also that the closer the points are, the easier that oversampling errors may occur and consequently you could damage your vehicle. Conversely, while the distance between points is larger, undersampling tracking may occur. You will see with the given examples that the intermediate values between the points do not necessarily follow the original profile of the trajectory.

Note also that if the path to be followed has by itself a slow and smooth performance with respect to the limits of the vehicle (for example, following a low-frequency cosine signal), point-to-point tracking can be replaced by the trajectory tracking (in order to experiment, go to the simulation section in the geometric control part and modify the code to follow trigonometric functions from lower to higher frequencies).

Of course, point-to-point tracking is useful when a trajectory cannot be defined by using standard functions or when the functions to be followed are not smooth (for example, squares, triangles, etc.). The planning of trajectories can by itself generate a complete book, if we contemplate trajectories with minimum time, acceleration, or other motion profile derivatives, also trajectories with multiple points, or point-to-point trajectories, trajectories with a single variable or with multiple variables, translational, orientational, or combined trajectories, trajectories based on polynomials or trigonometric functions, and so on.

Let's continue. Suppose that we want to follow the square path displayed in Figure 3-26 (as you will see, tracking figures or paths with vertices represents a challenge for any controller).

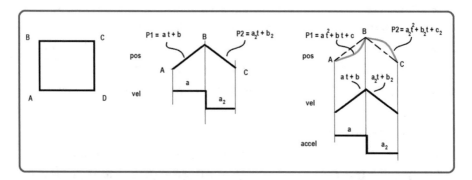

Figure 3-26. *Position, velocity, and acceleration profiles of a non-smooth function tracked by polynomials*

Part of this path implies that we must go through the ABC points. The intuition based on the shortest distance tells us that we can do it in a straight line (by using two first-degree polynomials).

The problem is that the derivative of the straight line trajectories takes an abrupt shape when inflection points occur (the derivative is a step function). To avoid this, a second order polynomial could be used (but now the square trajectory becomes an approximation, where only ABCD points are achieved).

Following the same reasoning, the second order polynomial no longer presents sudden changes at the speed level but at the acceleration level (again, where the inflection or transition point between the two polynomials occurs) and this also damages the motors. Then, the solution is simply to use polynomial trajectories of third order. A deeper demonstration, which is also based on the previous physical reasonings and the minimization of cost functions of Euler Lagrange equations, can be found in the MOOC, articles, and thesis of Kumar and his team, indicated in the Appendix.

Note that even with this, the derivative of the acceleration will continue presenting abrupt changes and thus indefinitely with each level of derivative when incorporating new polynomial degrees. However, this is not entirely relevant because we are interested in soft velocity values for which the accelerations are small (tending to zero) and even with these abrupt changes, their effects will not be important.

However, if we are interested in aggressive motion, then we must consider higher-order polynomials as shown by Kumar (see the Appendix) that perform point-to-point planning at the snap level (second derivative of the acceleration).

From this moment on, we can introduce speed values that are compatible with those that the vehicle can by itself generate in the following way (always considering a starting point and an ending point, although there are multipoint algorithms).

First, we observe that we have a desired polynomial of order three and that we will have a polynomial of this type for each desired value. This means that if we are interested in defining the desired values for the variables X, Y, and Z, we must repeat the procedure for each of these variables:

$$x_d, y_d, z_d = val_d = P_d = C_0 + C_1 t + C_2 t^2 + C_3 t^3$$

This implies that we require four equations to calculate the four coefficients. To avoid problems and confusion with the letters, we will continue the example with the X variable, but you should repeat it for all other variables.

We have two equations, one that depends on the final position and the other that depends on the initial position. Note that it is necessary to evaluate at the initial time and at the final time, so the maximum speed of the vehicle is considered here.

$$x_0 = x(t_0) = P_d(t_0)$$
$$x_f = x(t_f) = P_d(t_f)$$
$$x_0 = C_0 + C_1 t_0 + C_2 t_0^2 + C_3 t_0^3$$
$$x_f = C_0 + C_1 t_f + C_2 t_f^2 + C_3 t_f^3.$$

The other two equations are generated with the initial and final velocities. For this, we see that the derivative or the speed profile of our polynomial is

$$\dot{P}_d = 3C_3 t^2 + 2C_2 t + C_1$$

And therefore the equations with the initial and final velocities are

$$\dot{x}_0 = \dot{x}(t_0) = \dot{P}_d(t_0)$$
$$\dot{x}_f = \dot{x}(t_f) = \dot{P}_d(t_f)$$
$$\dot{x}_0 = C_1 + 2C_2 t_0 + 3C_3 t_0^2$$
$$\dot{x}_f = C_1 + 2C_2 t_f + 3C_3 t_f^2$$

Note that the coefficients of these polynomials must be recalculated as the initial and final points change. It is convenient to rewrite our four equations with four unknowns in matrix mode:

$$x_0 = C_0 + C_1 t_0 + C_2 t_0^2 + C_3 t_0^3$$
$$x_f = C_0 + C_1 t_f + C_2 t_f^2 + C_3 t_f^3$$
$$\dot{x}_0 = C_1 + 2C_2 t_0 + 3C_3 t_0^2$$
$$\dot{x}_f = C_1 + 2C_2 t_f + 3C_3 t_f^2$$

$$
\begin{bmatrix} x_0 \\ x_f \\ \dot{x}_0 \\ \dot{x}_f \end{bmatrix} =
\begin{bmatrix} 1 & t_0 & t_0^2 & t_0^3 \\ 1 & t_f & t_f^2 & t_f^3 \\ 0 & 1 & 2t_0 & 3t_0^2 \\ 0 & 1 & 2t_f & 3t_f^2 \end{bmatrix}
\begin{bmatrix} C_0 \\ C_1 \\ C_2 \\ C_3 \end{bmatrix}
$$

And the calculation of the polynomial will be updated in this way:

$$
\begin{bmatrix} C_0 \\ C_1 \\ C_2 \\ C_3 \end{bmatrix} =
\begin{bmatrix} 1 & t_0 & t_0^2 & t_0^3 \\ 1 & t_f & t_f^2 & t_f^3 \\ 0 & 1 & 2t_0 & 3t_0^2 \\ 0 & 1 & 2t_f & 3t_f^2 \end{bmatrix}^{-1}
\begin{bmatrix} x_0 \\ x_f \\ \dot{x}_0 \\ \dot{x}_f \end{bmatrix}
$$

$$P_d = C_0 + C_1 t + C_2 t^2 + C_3 t^3$$

In each new calculation, the starting position value, the starting speed, and the starting time must be taken from the previous final values. If we also want to include initial and final accelerations, the polynomial must be the fifth order.

Where is the maximum speed of the vehicle included?

Observe that the maximum speed value on the X axis can be approximated by

$$V_x \max = \frac{x_f - x_0}{t_f - t_0}$$

Position values are unalterable as they define our starting and final points. Another thing that we cannot alter is the initial time, so we can only modify the final time according to our maximum speed:

$$t_f = \frac{x_f - x_0}{V_x \max} + t_0$$

In this way, our design can do the following:

$$t_f \geq \frac{x_f - x_0}{V_x \max} + t_0$$
$$\dot{x}_0 \leq V_x \max$$
$$\dot{x}_f \leq V_x \max$$

As the vehicle does not generate more speed than that produced by its motors, the final time could be affected and this distorts the desired polynomial trajectory. To counteract this effect, a higher order polynomial can be used to introduce acceleration profiles, or these calculations can be avoided by working with exceeded values in this way:

$$t_f \gg \frac{x_f - x_0}{V_x \max} + t_0$$
$$\dot{x}_0 \ll V_x \max$$
$$\dot{x}_f \ll V_x \max$$

For defining attitude paths, depending on whether the used tools are directly Euler angles, quaternions, rotation matrices, etc., there are more considerations. Some of them can be found in the book of Peter Corke indicated in the Appendix, also at `https://robotacademy.net.au/masterclass/paths-and-trajectories/`, and finally in the book of modern robotics by Lynch and Park.

Finally, we will mention that the PD represents by itself a smooth polynomial of infinite order at the error level (a point-to-point tracking, where the starting point is the measured value and the final point the desired value), so a PD control could be performed without defining polynomial paths.

This is because the PD equation has an associated exponential behavior

$$PD(Error) \rightarrow Error \approx e^{-t}$$

and an exponential function, which according to the Taylor series is a nth order polynomial (much larger than a third, fifth, or higher order approximation)

$$e^{-t} = 1 - t + \tfrac{1}{2}t^2 - \tfrac{1}{6}t^3 + \tfrac{1}{24}t^4 + ...(-1)^n \tfrac{t^n}{n!}$$

$$Error \approx 1 - t + \tfrac{1}{2}t^2 - \tfrac{1}{6}t^3 + \tfrac{1}{24}t^4 + ...(-1)^n \tfrac{t^n}{n!}$$

However, there is no way to regulate the final time (this can be done with polynomial trajectories) unless there is something additional controlling the proportional and derivative gains of the PD based on the final time. This could be achieved with intelligent algorithms or with the TBG (time base generator) controller. See the concept of TBG in Parra's article in the Appendix. Additionally, as already said, the PD is based on an error that depends on two values. For this reason, it can only be applied at point-to-point tracking, while trajectory planning, according to the algorithm, also allows generating a trajectory that covers more than two points. In summary, see Table 3-1.

Table 3-1. *Type of Desired Values and Their Characteristics*

Type of desired value	Use
Constant	Regulation tasks where it is desired to stay indefinitely at a constant value (hovering drone tasks, for example)
Time-dependent trajectory	Tasks where the trajectory has a slow and smooth evolution with respect to the maximum speeds or accelerations of the vehicle
Point-to-point or multi-point trajectory by using n-th order polynomials (or other methods based on trigonometric functions)	Tasks where the trajectory cannot be defined by known functions, or where there is an abrupt evolution of the path causing sudden performances on the speed or the acceleration of the vehicle, or where the designer wants to restrict the speed, acceleration, or their derivatives with respect to the maximum values that the vehicle can reach

Summary

In this chapter, you learned useful concepts on control theory related to drones. In this case, the concepts were also applied to quadcopters but they are widely used in other types of aircraft. You explored two families of controllers, those of the vehicle kind and those of the robot type. In both cases, we presented four of the most used controllers in articles and books: the linear control, the variable yaw control, the spherical dynamic compensation controller, and the geometric control. With all of them you will be able to design from smooth operations to acrobatic flight modes. The chapter concluded with notions about trajectory planning. In the next chapter, you will learn details about drone simulation.

CHAPTER 4

Simulation

This chapter has both maker and scientific impacts. It will show you a topic discarded in practically all the books and available references, and which consists of the generic simulation of drones. In this particular case, we will use the MATLAB/Simulink tools due to their popularity and simplified use among the scientific community, but the knowledge is extendable to any other programming environment, including open source simulators. The approach is based on the use of state-space variables and a graphic representation through processing blocks. As a result, you will be able to design your own vehicles by using software tools and also to extend this type of knowledge to other robots.

Types of Simulators

We have four kinds of simulators:

- **Numeric with symbols**: They only require equations, specifically the system's mathematical model and its controller. This kind of simulator is any program capable of solving these equations. Depending on the complexity of the model, the program will be able or not to solve it. In the case of a drone, this can be done with a standard programming language where you can code an algorithm for the numerical resolution of

© Julio Alberto Mendoza-Mendoza, Victor Javier Gonzalez-Villela,
Carlos Fernando Aguilar-Ibañez, Leonardo Fonseca-Ruiz 2021
J. A. Mendoza-Mendoza et al., *Drones to Go*, https://doi.org/10.1007/978-1-4842-6788-2_4

ordinary differential equations such as Euler, RK4, etc. This simulator requires at least two sections of code: the solver and the system to solve.

- **Numeric with blocks**: Similar to the previous case, but instead of a symbolic representation of the equations and the controller, they have a graphical representation based on blocks. This is a much more visual form of programming than the symbolic one, and it facilitates the interconnection of components (except when they are many components). Known examples are LabView, Simulink, or Scilab/Scicos. In the case of using blocks, the solver is the command interface by itself, and the system to be solved is a file with diagrams.

- **Animated**: In this case, they are interfaces with three-dimensional graphics that allow simulating a system. Examples are V-rep, Gazebo, or the Mission Planner GUI and its virtual SITL (software in the loop) simulator. In general, they consist of two parts: the animated object and its world, and the modeling file. Many of these simulators have a physics engine, which includes effects of the environment like wind or pressure.

- **Interactive**: Here we find the ability to interact among simulators of any of the previous types, or the interaction with hardware. Examples are X-Plane or the Mission planner with its HITL (hardware in the loop) mode.

In the case of this text, we will focus on the two simplest to use (from the point of view of the installation): the numerical ones. Of course, they require mathematics but users can make them as simple or complicated as they want. Additionally, many simulators can be used assembled and interactively with the methodology described below.

Having decided which kind of simulators we will use, let's continue with the state space representation, which is a tool that allows us to work with simulators.

State Space Representation

If you have a differential equation of order n, it can be transformed into *n* differential equations of order one. This is useful for using a single collective integrator block in the simulator, or handling vector and matrix operations instead of scalar ones.

$$(1x1)$$
$$y^{(n)} + a_1 y^{(n-1)} + \ldots a_{n-1}\dot{y} + a_n y = u$$
$\Rightarrow$
$$(nx1)$$
$$\dot{x} = f(x, u)$$

For example, remember that the mass spring damper system is a second order system:

$$\boxed{m\ddot{x}} + b\dot{x} + kx = u$$
$$n = 2$$

This way, it will require two state space variables. In these cases, the most convenient selection is to take as state space variables those that have lower orders with respect to the system's order. In this equation, the position and velocity are chosen as state space variables:

$$\begin{bmatrix} x_1 \\ x_2 \end{bmatrix} = \begin{bmatrix} x \\ \dot{x} \end{bmatrix}$$

Obtaining the derivative, we arrive at the required expression:

$$\dot{x} = f(x, u) = \begin{bmatrix} \dot{x}_1 \\ \dot{x}_2 \end{bmatrix} = \begin{bmatrix} \dot{x} \\ \ddot{x} \end{bmatrix}$$

The last equation is solvable from the original equation of the system:

$$\begin{bmatrix} \dot{x}_1 \\ \dot{x}_2 \end{bmatrix} = \begin{bmatrix} \dot{x} \\ \ddot{x} \end{bmatrix} = \begin{bmatrix} \dot{x} \\ \dfrac{u - kx - b\dot{x}}{m} \end{bmatrix}$$

Replacing the state space variables, this results in

$$\begin{bmatrix} \dot{x}_1 \\ \dot{x}_2 \end{bmatrix} = \begin{bmatrix} \dot{x} \\ \ddot{x} \end{bmatrix} = \begin{bmatrix} \dot{x} \\ \dfrac{u - kx - b\dot{x}}{m} \end{bmatrix} = \begin{bmatrix} x_2 \\ \dfrac{u - kx_1 - bx_2}{m} \end{bmatrix}$$

remaining only two first order equations as expected.

A quadcopter can have, according to its dynamic model, twelve state space variables (six equations of the second order; remember that three of these equations are related to the translational dynamics and the rest with the rotational dynamics):

$$F_{BZ} \begin{bmatrix} \theta \cos \psi_d + \phi \sin \psi_d \\ \theta \sin \psi_d - \phi \cos \psi_d \\ 1 \end{bmatrix} + m \begin{bmatrix} 0 \\ 0 \\ -g \end{bmatrix} = m \begin{bmatrix} \ddot{x} \\ \ddot{y} \\ \ddot{z} \end{bmatrix}$$

$$\begin{bmatrix} \tau_\phi \\ \tau_\theta \\ \tau_\psi \end{bmatrix} \approx \begin{bmatrix} J_x \ddot{\phi} \\ J_y \ddot{\theta} \\ J_z \ddot{\psi} \end{bmatrix}$$

If we select the state space variables in the following way (this is a possible choice alternating positions and speeds), we have

$$
\begin{bmatrix}
x_1 \\ x_2 \\ x_3 \\ x_4 \\ x_5 \\ x_6 \\ x_7 \\ x_8 \\ x_9 \\ x_{10} \\ x_{11} \\ x_{12}
\end{bmatrix}
=
\begin{bmatrix}
x \\ \dot{x} \\ y \\ \dot{y} \\ z \\ \dot{z} \\ \theta \\ \dot{\theta} \\ \phi \\ \dot{\phi} \\ \psi \\ \dot{\psi}
\end{bmatrix}
\qquad
\begin{bmatrix}
\dot{x}_1 \\ \dot{x}_2 \\ \dot{x}_3 \\ \dot{x}_4 \\ \dot{x}_5 \\ \dot{x}_6 \\ \dot{x}_7 \\ \dot{x}_8 \\ \dot{x}_9 \\ \dot{x}_{10} \\ \dot{x}_{11} \\ \dot{x}_{12}
\end{bmatrix}
=
\begin{bmatrix}
\dot{x} \\ \ddot{x} \\ \dot{y} \\ \ddot{y} \\ \dot{z} \\ \ddot{z} \\ \dot{\theta} \\ \ddot{\theta} \\ \dot{\phi} \\ \ddot{\phi} \\ \dot{\psi} \\ \ddot{\psi}
\end{bmatrix}
=
\begin{bmatrix}
x_2 \\ \frac{F_{BZ}}{m}\left(x_7 \cos x_{11d} + x_9 \sin x_{11d}\right) \\ x_4 \\ \frac{F_{BZ}}{m}\left(x_7 \sin x_{11d} - x_9 \cos x_{11d}\right) \\ x_6 \\ \frac{F_{BZ}}{m} - g \\ x_8 \\ \tau_\theta/J_y \\ x_{10} \\ \tau_\phi/J_x \\ x_{12} \\ \tau_\psi/J_z
\end{bmatrix}
$$

Note also that the control input u has four values. They are the thrust force and the three torques:

$$
\dot{x} = f(x, u) = f(x, [F_{BZ}, \tau_\theta, \tau_\phi, \tau_\psi])
$$

Another possible choice could be done by first selecting all the positions and then all the speeds, or simply another sequence different from the one presented here. Whichever you choose, it must be respected for its later use.

The second tool that is useful for our simulations is the block representation. Let's talk about it.

Block Representation

In this case, the blocks are a graphical representation of the state space variables. They are useful for making diagrams or for simulating with visual languages such as Simulink or Labview, which are designed to use blocks.

Returning to the mass spring damper example and specifically its representation in state space variables, we can do the following to obtain its block representation.

First, note that there are two state space equations, so two main blocks are required. These blocks represent integrators; see Figure 4-1. In this example, we added labels to the states, which is a good practice for programming and understanding, but such labeling is not frequently done.

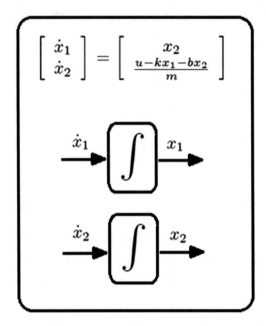

Figure 4-1. *Block representation of an ODE, first step*

The standard implies that what is placed on the right of the block is the output, and what is on the left is the input. We will start with the definition of the derivative of x1.

We make the connection shown in Figure 4-2, which defines the x1 derivative.

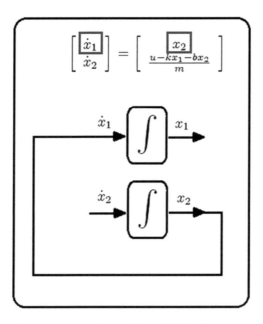

Figure 4-2. *Block representation of an ODE, first equation connection*

In the same way, you can notice that the derivative of x2 is a sum. For this reason, we will need another block. You should also note that at the output of said block there must be a gain; see Figure 4-3.

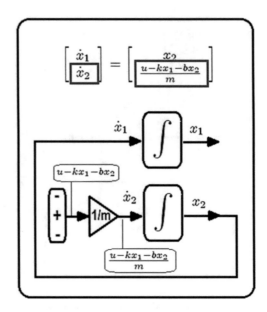

Figure 4-3. *Block representation of an ODE, second equation connection*

And finally, following the previous logic, we arrive at Figure 4-4.

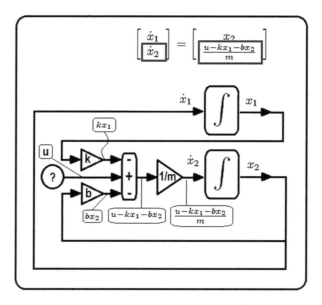

Figure 4-4. *Block representation of an ODE, full connection (without control)*

Even though this system only has a few equations and terms, its block representation required many icons and connectors (also note that the value of u has not been defined and this can increase the number of blocks).

One way to simplify this is by working with matrices and vectors, relegating the equations to just one block, as indicated in Figure 4-5.

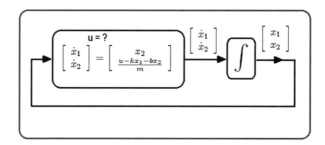

Figure 4-5. *A reduced block representation with the system in a "text file" (without control)*

In this way, an aggregate such as u can be reduced to some lines of code instead of a large number of blocks. Also, the variable u, for example, can be a PD controller that depends on a trajectory, which also depends on the time. See Figure 4-6. Observe that you need a clock block.

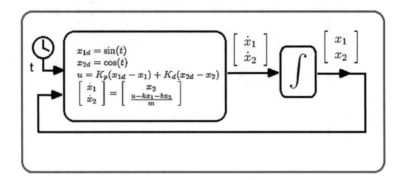

Figure 4-6. *A reduced block representation with the system in a "text file" (with control)*

Note that if the system has many equations and each of them have several terms, as in the case of the quadcopter, this simplified model of blocks is very convenient. This is exactly what we will do in the next section by using the Simulink-MATLAB combination.

Simulation with Simulink and Interpreted MATLAB Functions

If you want to use free software such as Scilab or Python, it is advisable to read this section. Based on what you learn here and the references of this chapter (which you can find in the Appendix), you could search for the equivalent commands or blocks in the mentioned programs and programming languages.

Keep in mind that through the multiple libraries that this combination has (MATLAB/Simulink), you can interact with animated or interactive simulation software such as Gazebo, X-plane, the Ardupilot libraries, the Pixhawk autopilot, or CAD software with physics engines.

Let's continue. This is a special mode among the many that Simulink has to perform simulations. It offers the practicality of the blocks in one of their most simplified forms, where a text file is used exclusively for writing the equations of the system and its controller. In this manner, a set of equations with many terms are relegated to the text file, and a general template is placed in a block file. The block file contains preprogrammed equation solvers such as Euler or RK4 and is developed for an easy interconnection and processing. This method is valid for MATLAB 2012b versions or higher. The best thing about this type of representation and simulation is that multiple modifications and uses can be made with the input and output signals (filtering, plot edition, introducing delays, etc.). This is not possible in simulators that do not use blocks.

Required Blocks

The Simulink blocks here described have at least one of the following three properties: an input signal, an output signal, and a way for setting up their own parameters. See Figure 4-7.

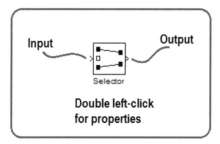

Figure 4-7. *Properties of a Simulink block*

These are the seven most usable blocks for our purposes.

Interpreted MATLAB function: This block is used to link the text file containing the dynamic model of the system and its controller with the block file. See Figure 4-8.

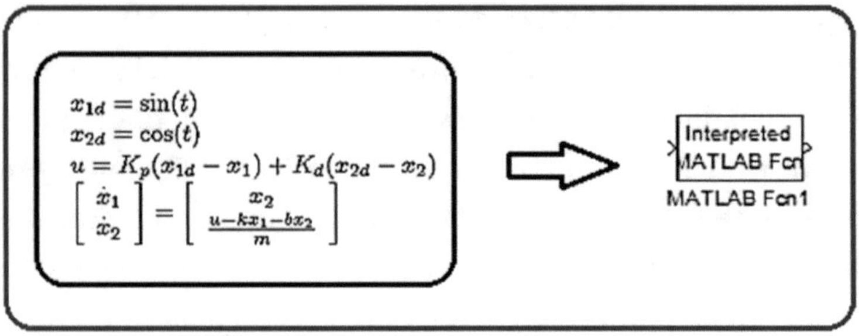

Figure 4-8. *Interpreted MATLAB function block*

The input of this block is a bus or data channel with n signals (states, time, auxiliary values, etc.). The output of this block is also a bus or data channel with m signals (states, auxiliary values, signals to be plotted, etc.).

The important properties of this block in which we are interested are (do not modify the other properties):

1. The name of the file that contains the dynamic model of the system and its controller. This name must be identical to the text file that contains said model and without the file extension.

2. The size of the output bus (measured in the number of variables).

Once these parameters have been modified, just click OK and close the block's dialog box. See Figure 4-9.

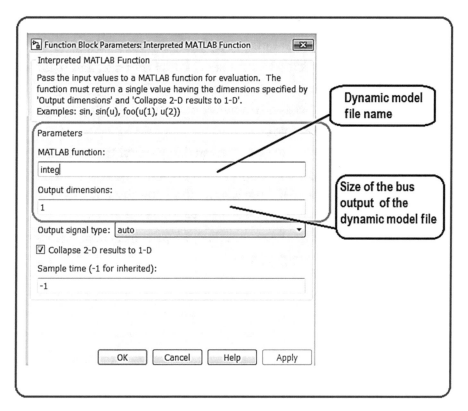

Figure 4-9. *Interpreted MATLAB function block parameters*

Note that we use the previous block for practicality, but you should also investigate the MATLAB Function and the S-function blocks.

Integrator: It allows integrating a bus of signals. See Figure 4-10.

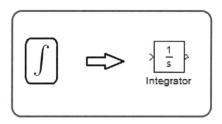

Figure 4-10. *Integrator block*

This block is used to integrate signals. In Simulink, there are different types of integrators, but for our purposes, this is the one that we use.

The input of this block is a bus or data channel with n signals (the derivatives of the system states, for example).

The output of this block is also a bus or data channel with n signals (the system states, for example).

The only parameter that we are interested in modifying is the initial conditions or the starting point of our system to simulate. If this is a single equation, just write a scalar. If there is more than one equation, the initial values must be introduced as follows: [val1 val2 val3 valN].

Once this parameter has been modified, we just click OK and close the properties dialog box. See Figure 4-11.

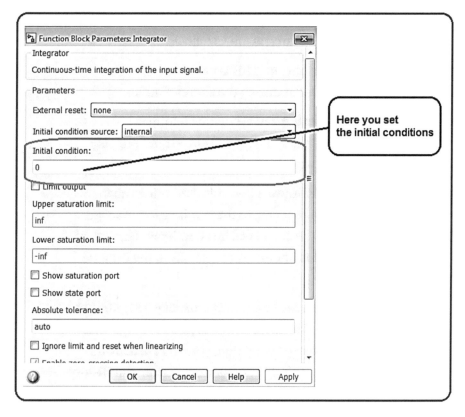

Figure 4-11. *Integrator block parameters*

Scope: This block allows seeing the graphs of our simulation directly in the block-diagram file, either during the simulation or at the end of it. See Figure 4-12.

Figure 4-12. *Scope block*

This block does not have outputs. Its inputs are buses with n signals to be plotted. Its relevant parameters are as follows:

1. **The autoscale button**: This is useful to adjust the graph at the end or during the simulation.

2. **The properties button**: When this button is pressed, an auxiliary menu will appear. We are only interested in two options:

- **The number of input axes**: This determines how many independent graphs there will be in the scope. Each input to the scope will be an independent bus of n variables. This option is accessed from the General menu.

- **The limit data checkbox**: This is usually activated, and it only displays the last 5,000 data points. If you want to see an extensive simulation, you must deactivate this checkbox. This option is accessed from the History menu. See Figure 4-13.

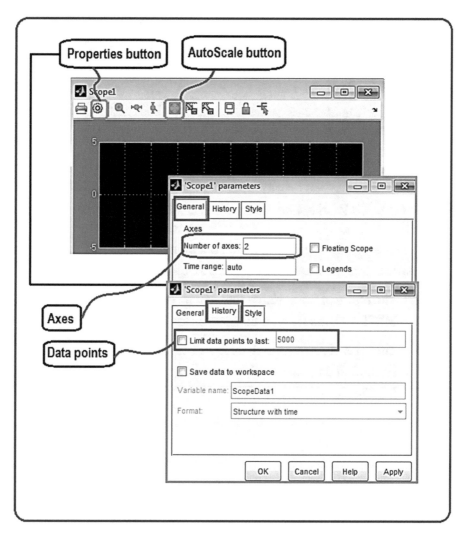

Figure 4-13. *Scope block parameters*

As in the previous cases, you must click OK and close the auxiliary menus in order to save the modifications.

You can also experiment with the Style menu of the Scope parameters if you want to modify the presentation and the colors of the plot.

To Workspace block: This block allows using specific data outside the Simulink interface in order to carry out further processing or editing (for example, exporting the plots for editing their graphs to be used in a publication). See Figure 4-14.

Figure 4-14. *To Workspace block*

This block only has an input, which is a data bus.
Its parameters of interest for our purposes are only two:

1. The name of the variable that will be used from the MATLAB console for editing the information

2. The type of the output data. In our case and for a simplified data access, this must always be an array. See Figure 4-15.

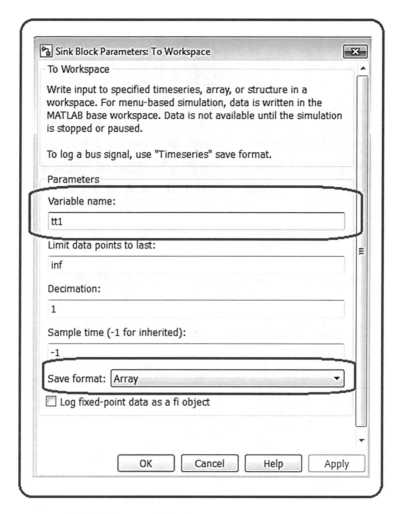

Figure 4-15. *To Workspace block parameters*

Selector: This block is used for selecting one or more signals from a bus. See Figure 4-16.

Figure 4-16. *Selector block*

The input to the block is a data bus with n variables. Its output is another bus with p variables, where p goes from just one signal to the n signals. The size of p will simply depend on which signals you want to extract.

Its parameters of interest are

1. The output signal index in scalar format if only one signal is chosen, or in the vector format [val1 val2 val3 valN] if more than one signal is required.

2. The size of the input bus. See Figure 4-17.

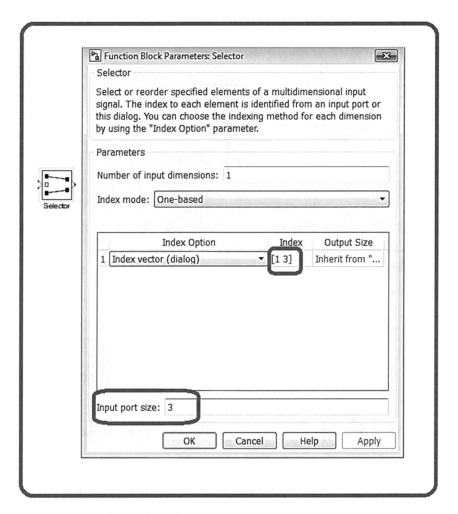

Figure 4-17. *Selector block parameters*

Let's analyze the given example. Note that it is graphically intuitive. The block in the figure receives a data bus with three variables, and its output is another bus with two variables, specifically the first and third values of the input bus.

Mux: It is a multiplexer and its function is to generate a single bus from the input of two or more data buses. The opposite block is called Demux. This block is useful for plotting in a single channel of a scope. We simply select all the variables of interest from different blocks in order to send them to the scope by using a Mux. See Figure 4-18.

Figure 4-18. *Mux block*

Its inputs are several buses of *n* variables each, and its output is a single bus with all the collected variables from all the input buses.

Its only parameter of interest for our applications is the number of input buses, as indicated in Figure 4-19.

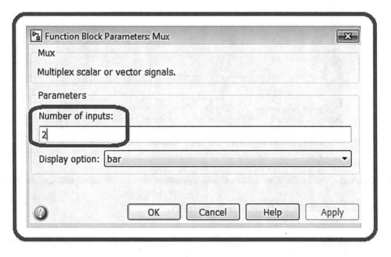

Figure 4-19. *Mux block parameters*

Clock: This is very useful for defining trajectories (time-variant functions). This block does not have inputs, and its only output is the simulation time (this time is not real-time). See Figure 4-20.

Figure 4-20. *Clock block*

For the purposes of this book, this block does not have parameters that must be modified.

Other blocks that may be useful: For more information, refer to the gain block, the derivative block, the sum block, the constant block, the math function block, the goto labels, and the saturation block, among many others.

Now that you know how to work with blocks, state space variables, and the basic blocks that we will use with MATLAB, we can start with our simulations.

Quadcopter Example, Text File

Note that this file would be enough if we wanted to simulate our drone and we only had a basic programming language such as C++ or Python, of course by incorporating an ODE solver.

Remember that the model will be as precise as you want by adding more dynamic effects. In this case, we will use the previous models that have no aerodynamic effects, but they serve to test some details in the control design, such as the fact that planar PDs cannot exceed the value of 2Pi (remember that these PDs represent desired angles and they cannot reach values greater than 2Pi). One way to improve the model is by adding more effects or by inducing noise in the states by means of random functions, or even by creating a delay in the signals to simulate the behavior of the sensors. The text file called quadmodel.m is displayed in Listing 4-1.

Listing 4-1. Quadmodel Code, a Controller with a Desired Yaw
Value Equal to Zero

```
function outp=quadmodel(inpt)

% system inputs: states and time
% x1-x, x2-xdot, x3-y, x4-ydot, x5-z, x6-zdot
% x7-theta, x8-thetadot, x9-phi, x10-phidot, x11-psi, x12-
psidot
x1=inpt(1);
x2=inpt(2);
x3=inpt(3);
x4=inpt(4);
x5=inpt(5);
x6=inpt(6);
x7=inpt(7);
x8=inpt(8);
x9=inpt(9);
x10=inpt(10);
x11=inpt(11);
x12=inpt(12);
t=inpt(13);

% constant parameters: mass, inertial values, gravity
m=1;
g=9.8;
Jx=0.2;
Jy=0.2;
Jz=0.2;

% control gains: notice the small values at x and y gains
because they
% define an angle
kpx=0.1;
```

```
kdx=0.09;
kpy=0.1;
kdy=0.09;
kpz=1;
kdz=0.7;
kptet=3;
kdtet=1;
kpfi=3;
kdfi=1;
kppsi=3;
kdpsi=1;

% planar desired values
x1d=5;
x2d=0;
x3d=-6;
x4d=0;

% planar PD: remember that these PD define desired angular
values
PDx=(kpx*(x1d-x1))+(kdx*(x2d-x2));
PDy=(kpy*(x3d-x3))+(kdy*(x4d-x4));

% altitude and attitude desired values
x5d=8+sin(t);
x6d=cos(t);
x7d=PDx;
x8d=0;
x9d=-PDy;
x10d=0;
x11d=0;
x12d=0;
```

```
% altitude and attitude PDs
PDz=(kpz*(x5d-x5))+(kdz*(x6d-x6));
PDteta=(kptet*(x7d-x7))+(kdtet*(x8d-x8));
PDfi=(kpfi*(x9d-x9))+(kdfi*(x10d-x10));
PDpsi=(kppsi*(x11d-x11))+(kdpsi*(x12d-x12));

% vehicle's forces and torques
Fbz=PDz+(m*g);
taoteta=PDteta;
taofi=PDfi;
taopsi=PDpsi;

% vehicle's dynamic model xp notation implies xdot or xpoint or x
% derivative
x1p=x2;
x2p=(Fbz/m)*((x7*cos(x11d))+(x9*sin(x11d)));
x3p=x4;
x4p=(Fbz/m)*((x7*sin(x11d))-(x9*cos(x11d)));
x5p=x6;
x6p=(Fbz/m)-g;
x7p=x8;
x8p=taoteta/Jy;
x9p=x10;
x10p=taofi/Jx;
x11p=x12;
x12p=taopsi/Jz;

% output: derivatives of the system states and vehicle's force
and
% torques
outp=[x1p;x2p;x3p;x4p;x5p;x6p;x7p;x8p;x9p;x10p;x11p;x12p;Fbz;ta
oteta;taofi;taopsi];

end
```

Attention: The name of the textfile that contains the dynamic model of the system (the one with the .m extension) must be identical to the word that we wrote in the function line, as indicated in Figure 4-21.

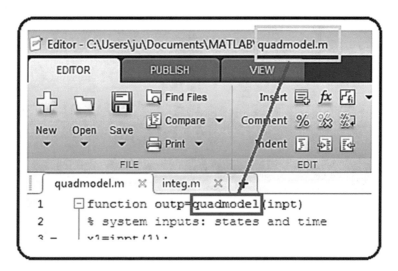

Figure 4-21. *Text file for the interpreted MATLAB function block quadmodel.m*

Remember that as an alternative to MATLAB and Simulink, you can use Scilab, which has a block simulator called Scicos or Xcos depending on the version. Scilab is a free software tool and you must search for the equivalent of the seven blocks shown here (for example, the Scicos user defined functions).

Quadcopter Example, Block File

In the following block file called blockquad.slx (see Figure 4-22; in Simulink versions prior to the 2013a, the extension is .mdl), we have used all of the seven basic blocks previously mentioned. Note that the complexity of the model remains in the text file. For this reason, the number of blocks is reduced. This block file can be used as a template for any other model. It only changes the size of the buses and the text file that contains the system.

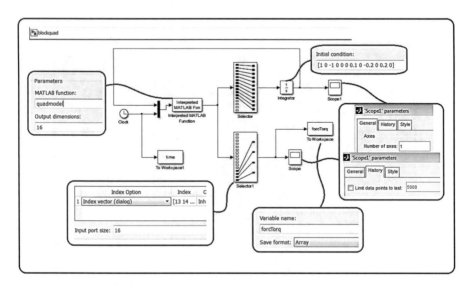

Figure 4-22. *Block file for using the interpreted MATLAB function block, blockquad.slx*

Into Figure 4-22 a zoom to the parameters to be modified is displayed.

Use of the Simulators

As indicated, to solve a differential equation, it is required to have a solver or method to solve it, along with the file that contains the model or differential equations associated with that model.

When using the proposed Simulink method, both files must be in the same folder, as indicated in Figure 4-23.

If the blockquad.slx file does not exist, click the Simulink library icon and create this file, as also indicated in Figure 4-23.

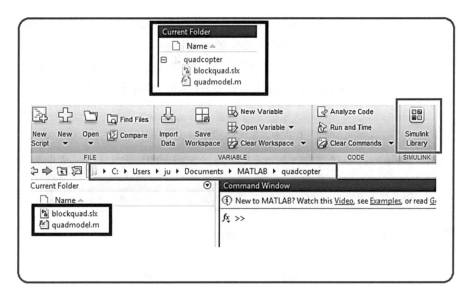

Figure 4-23. *Files location for their execution*

If the quadmodel.m file does not exist, you must generate it by using
the NewScript button, as shown in Figure 4-24. Never try to start the
simulation from the file with the .m extension. This must be done from the
block diagram file.

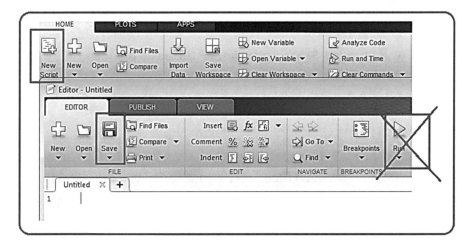

Figure 4-24. *Text file additional instructions*

Once in the block file, and with the text file filled with the code provided, in the Simulink window you will notice some drop-down menus. If you go to the Simulation menu and then to the Model Configuration Parameters option, you can choose from a variety of solvers. See Figure 4-25.

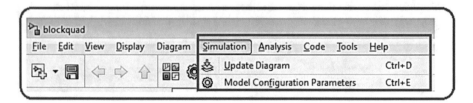

Figure 4-25. *Simulink model configuration parameters*

The features that we want to modify are the following:

- **Type of step**: Here you choose if the step is fixed or variable. This means that the simulation time is executed unalterably in a fixed unit of time, or that it is adapted as the simulation evolves.

- **Step duration**: In the case of choosing fixed steps, the duration of the step will determine how accurate and consequently how slow the simulation will be. A smaller step will imply a more detailed simulation (this will be reflected in the graphs and the result qualities), but it will take longer to run.

- **Method**: Here you choose the type of solver to be used. The most common are Euler and RK4.

The combination of the method and the duration of the step influences the result and the execution time. It is recommended to use a simple method with a relatively reduced step. For example, the Euler method with fixed steps of 0.001 seconds is an acceptable option for a quadcopter; see

Figure 4-26. In general, this combination will be used with the rest of our simulations.

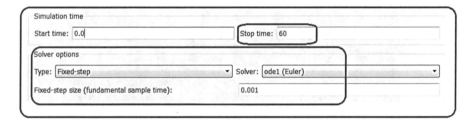

Figure 4-26. *Simulink solver, time, and step size selection*

Once you have selected the solver and you have set the aforementioned characteristics, you must define the total time to be simulated. Click OK, close the auxiliary window, and save the changes. See Figure 4-27 to the left side.

Press the play button and wait for the result; see Figure 4-27. Note that the simulation time and the real time are not the same. The simulation time will depend on the machine processor, and it is desirable that the simulation be executed as fast as possible. If this was not the case, a simulation time of 10,000 seconds would imply waiting almost 3 hours.

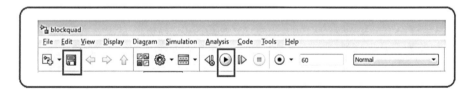

Figure 4-27. *Simulink final instructions for the simulation*

When pressing any scope in the block file, the simulation graphs will appear; see Figure 4-28. In this example, the states converge to the desired values with the given controller and references set up in the quadmodel.m file. It is convenient to press the autoscale button in the scope menu.

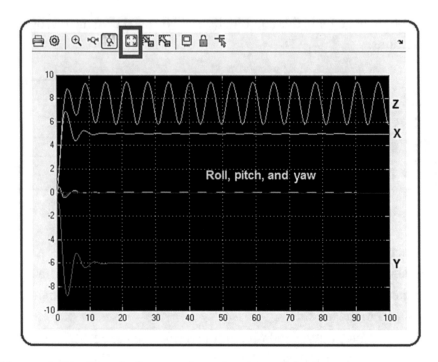

Figure 4-28. *Simulation result and autoscale button*

If we want to use the graphs beyond the simulator scopes, we use the To Workspace blocks and the MATLAB command window; see Figure 4-29.

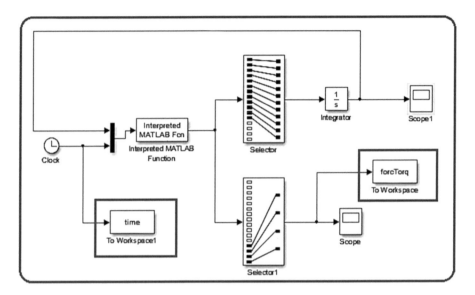

Figure 4-29. *Using To Workspace blocks*

In the given example, two data buses were sent to the workspace: the simulation time called time, and the forces and torques called forcTorq.

Once the simulation has been run, just go to the MATLAB command window and type this to use the aforementioned data: plot (time, forcTorq). The graph displayed in Figure 4-30 will appear.

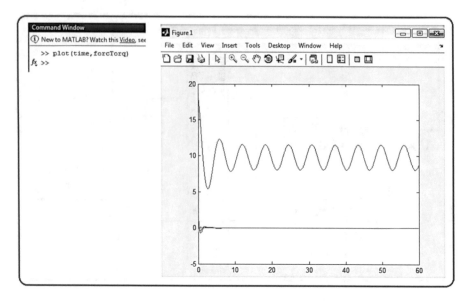

Figure 4-30. *Plotting from the command window*

Note that simulations here developed will omit the motors' effect because they focus on controlling the vehicle's center of gravity. It is assumed that the allocation matrix only has a linear effect on the control transmission towards the motors due to the previously indicated facts of symmetry, balance, and point-mass distribution. If you want to analyze the effect of the motors, it would be enough to take the thrust force and torque signals from the simulation and multiply these values by the corresponding allocation matrix (obviously it would be necessary to include scaling factors to make it compatible with real motors). This is done as indicated in Listing 4-2.

Listing 4-2. Allocquadmodel Code, Controller with a Desired Yaw Equal to Zero and Modified for Displaying the Value of Each Motor

```
function outp=allocquadmodel(inpt)

% system inputs: states and time
% x1-x, x2-xdot, x3-y, x4-ydot, x5-z, x6-zdot
```

```
% x7-theta, x8-thetadot, x9-phi, x10-phidot, x11-psi, x12-
psidot

x1=inpt(1);
x2=inpt(2);
x3=inpt(3);
x4=inpt(4);
x5=inpt(5);
x6=inpt(6);
x7=inpt(7);
x8=inpt(8);
x9=inpt(9);
x10=inpt(10);
x11=inpt(11);
x12=inpt(12);
t=inpt(13);

% constant parameters: mass, inertial values, gravity
m=1;
g=9.8;
Jx=0.2;
Jy=0.2;
Jz=0.2;

% control gains notice that in order to make visible the motor
effects
% we reduce the original differential gains
kpx=0.1;
kdx=0.03;
kpy=0.1;
kdy=0.03;
kpz=1;
kdz=0.7;
```

```
kptet=3;
kdtet=0.5;
kpfi=3;
kdfi=0.5;
kppsi=3;
kdpsi=1;

% planar desired values
x1d=5;
x2d=0;
x3d=-6;
x4d=0;

% planar PD: remember that these PD define desired angular values
PDx=(kpx*(x1d-x1))+(kdx*(x2d-x2));
PDy=(kpy*(x3d-x3))+(kdy*(x4d-x4));

% altitude and attitude desired values
x5d=8+sin(t);
x6d=cos(t);
x7d=PDx;
x8d=0;
x9d=-PDy;
x10d=0;
x11d=0;
x12d=0;

% altitude and attitude PDs
PDz=(kpz*(x5d-x5))+(kdz*(x6d-x6));
PDteta=(kptet*(x7d-x7))+(kdtet*(x8d-x8));
PDfi=(kpfi*(x9d-x9))+(kdfi*(x10d-x10));
PDpsi=(kppsi*(x11d-x11))+(kdpsi*(x12d-x12));
```

```
% vehicle's forces and torques
Fbz=PDz+(m*g);
%Fbz=20;
taoteta=PDteta;
taofi=PDfi;
taopsi=PDpsi;

% vehicle's dynamic model
x1p=x2;
x2p=(Fbz/m)*((x7*cos(x11d))+(x9*sin(x11d)));
x3p=x4;
x4p=(Fbz/m)*((x7*sin(x11d))-(x9*cos(x11d)));
x5p=x6;
x6p=(Fbz/m)-g;
x7p=x8;
x8p=taoteta/Jy;
x9p=x10;
x10p=taofi/Jx;
x11p=x12;
x12p=taopsi/Jz;

% Here goes the motor effects throught the allocation matrix
W=[1,-1,1,1;1,1,-1,1;1,1,1,-1;1,-1,-1,-
1]*[Fbz;taoteta;taofi;taopsi];
w1=W(1);
w2=W(2);
w3=W(3);
w4=W(4);

% output: derivatives of system states and vehicle force and
torques
%outp=[x1p;x2p;x3p;x4p;x5p;x6p;x7p;x8p;x9p;x10p;x11p;x12p;Fbz;
taoteta
```

```
%taofi;taopsi];
% here we change the end of the line above by replacing forces and
% torques by the motor velocities, the Simulink® file does not need
% modifications
outp=[x1p;x2p;x3p;x4p;x5p;x6p;x7p;x8p;x9p;x10p;x11p;x12p;w1;w2;
w3;w4];
end
```

If we analyze the new plots, the stabilization effect is now achieved around 30 seconds in the angular variables, and with high presence of oscillations in X and Y; see Figure 4-31. This will affect the behavior of each motor at least around 30 seconds, and then they will work identically; see Figure 4-32 (the drone will remain fixed and without change its attitude, just its altitude; this way the motors will have an identical behavior).

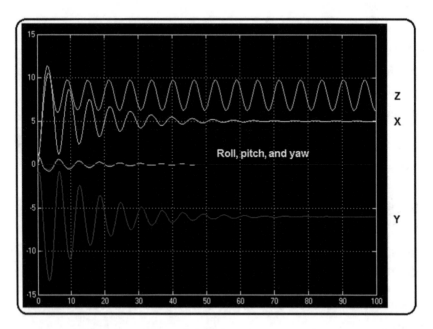

Figure 4-31. *Simulation modified for observing the action of the motors (notice the designed oscillations)*

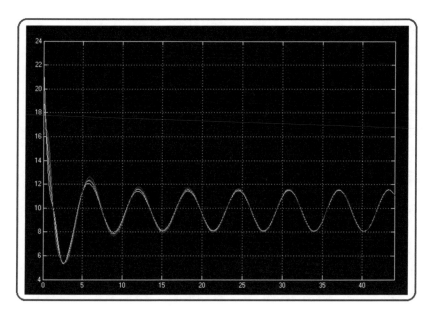

Figure 4-32. *The action of each motor*

Now, the file quadmodel.m gets modified as indicated in Listing 4-3 to perform a variable yaw control, see Figure 4-33. The blockquad file remains intact.

Listing 4-3. Quadmodel2 Code, Controller with a Variable Value of Yaw

```
function outp=quadmodel2(inpt)
% system inputs: states and time
% x1-x, x2-xdot, x3-y, x4-ydot, x5-z, x6-zdot
% x7-theta, x8-thetadot, x9-phi, x10-phidot, x11-psi, x12-psidot

x1=inpt(1);
x2=inpt(2);
x3=inpt(3);
x4=inpt(4);
x5=inpt(5);
```

```
x6=inpt(6);
x7=inpt(7);
x8=inpt(8);
x9=inpt(9);
x10=inpt(10);
x11=inpt(11);
x12=inpt(12);
t=inpt(13);

% constant parameters: mass, inertial values, gravity
m=1;
g=9.8;
Jx=0.2;
Jy=0.2;
Jz=0.2;

% control gains
kpx=0.2;
% sometimes because of the noise or just the control
interaction
% differential gains could be greater than proportional ones
% try the opposite and see the resulting behavior
kdx=0.35;
kpy=0.2;
kdy=0.35;
kpz=1;
kdz=0.7;
kptet=5;
kdtet=2;
kpfi=5;
kdfi=2;
kppsi=3;
kdpsi=1;
```

```
% planar desired values
x1d=5;
x2d=0;
x3d=-6;
x4d=0;

% planar PDs: remember that these PDs define desired angular
values
PDx=(kpx*(x1d-x1))+(kdx*(x2d-x2));
PDy=(kpy*(x3d-x3))+(kdy*(x4d-x4));

% altitude desired values
x5d=8+sin(t);
x6d=cos(t);

% yaw desired values
x11d=0.3*sin(t)+0.9;
x12d= 0.3*cos(t);

% roll and pitch desired values, instead of x11d, try changing
to x11
x7d=(1/g)*((PDx*cos(x11d))+(PDy*sin(x11d)));
% instead of cero try to change x8d to the x7d derivative
x8d=0;
x9d=(1/g)*((PDx*sin(x11d))-(PDy*cos(x11d)));
% instead of cero try to change x10d to the x9d derivative
x10d=0;

% altitude and attitude PDs
PDz=(kpz*(x5d-x5))+(kdz*(x6d-x6));
PDteta=(kptet*(x7d-x7))+(kdtet*(x8d-x8));
PDfi=(kpfi*(x9d-x9))+(kdfi*(x10d-x10));
PDpsi=(kppsi*(x11d-x11))+(kdpsi*(x12d-x12));
```

```
% vehicle's force and torques
Fbz=PDz+(m*g);
taoteta=PDteta;
taofi=PDfi;
taopsi=PDpsi;

% vehicle's dynamic model
x1p=x2;
x2p=(Fbz/m)*((x7*cos(x11d))+(x9*sin(x11d)));
x3p=x4;
x4p=(Fbz/m)*((x7*sin(x11d))-(x9*cos(x11d)));
x5p=x6;
x6p=(Fbz/m)-g;
x7p=x8;
x8p=taoteta/Jy;
x9p=x10;
x10p=taofi/Jx;
x11p=x12;
x12p=taopsi/Jz;

%output: derivatives of the system states and vehicle's force and
%torques
outp=[x1p;x2p;x3p;x4p;x5p;x6p;x7p;x8p;x9p;x10p;x11p;x12p;Fbz;
taoteta;taofi;taopsi];

end
```

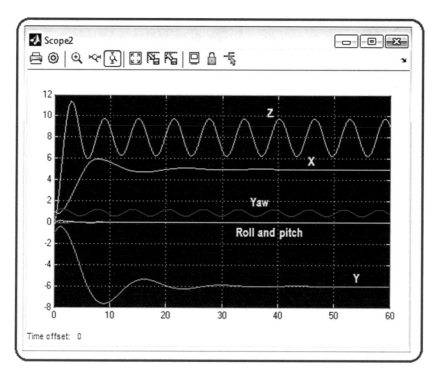

Figure 4-33. *Simulation of the variable yaw control*

Finally, the simulation of the geometric control is shown. We use a set of trajectories similar to that found in the publications of Taeyoung Lee previously indicated, but with a slower motion profile in order to use a simple PD controller. If you want to go further, you can modify the following code by adding the required terms until you achieve a high-speed performance as in said articles.

Listing 4-4 shows the geoquad.m file.

Listing 4-4. Geoquad Code, Geometric Controller

```
function outp=geoquad(inpt)
% system inputs: states
% x xderivative y yder z zder
x1=inpt(1);
```

```
x2=inpt(2);
x3=inpt(3);
x4=inpt(4);
x5=inpt(5);
x6=inpt(6);

% w and R (angular velocity and orientation)
w1=inpt(7);
w2=inpt(8);
w3=inpt(9);
r11=inpt(10);
r12=inpt(11);
r13=inpt(12);
r21=inpt(13);
r22=inpt(14);
r23=inpt(15);
r31=inpt(16);
r32=inpt(17);
r33=inpt(18);
% we need also Rdesired derivative
r11dp=inpt(19);
r12dp=inpt(20);
r13dp=inpt(21);
r21dp=inpt(22);
r22dp=inpt(23);
r23dp=inpt(24);
r31dp=inpt(25);
r32dp=inpt(26);
r33dp=inpt(27);

% time
t=inpt(28);
```

```
% constant parameters: mass, inertial values, gravity
m=1;
g=9.8;
Jx=0.2;
Jy=0.2;
Jz=0.2;

% building the desired Rotation matrix from its components

Rdp=[r11dp,r12dp,r13dp;r21dp,r22dp,r23dp;r31dp,r32dp,r33dp];

% building also the rotation matriz and the skew angular
velocity
% matrix
R=[r11,r12,r13;r21,r22,r23;r31,r32,r33];
S=[0,-w3,w2;w3,0,-w1;-w2,w1,0];

% control gains
kpx=0.3;
% sometimes because of the noise or due to control interaction
% differential gains could be greater tham propotional ones
% try the opposite and see the resulting behavior
kdx=0.5;
kpy=0.3;
kdy=0.5;
kpz=0.7;
kdz=0.5;
KR=50;
Kw=30;

% cartesian translational desired values
% this is an helical trajectory
x1d=0.4*t;
x2d=0.4;
```

```
x3d=0.4*sin(t/2);
x4d=0.2*cos(t/2);
x5d=0.6*cos(t/2);
x6d=-0.3*sin(t/2);

% planar PD
PDx=(kpx*(x1d-x1))+(kdx*(x2d-x2));
PDy=(kpy*(x3d-x3))+(kdy*(x4d-x4));
PDz=(kpz*(x5d-x5))+(kdz*(x6d-x6));

% Main thrust
Fbz=dot((([PDx;PDy;PDz]+[0;0;m*g]),(R*[0;0;1]));

% try to increase the angular frequency of these motion profile in
% order to disrupt the control loop by increasing velocities and
% accelerations as a consequence, in this case add the full
controller
% above described, or an improvement, because here we are
simulating
% just a simple PD

% Rd definition notice the indirect regulation of the yaw by means
% of the Bdes vector (a circular motion)
psid=t/3;
Bdes=[cos(psid);sin(psid);0];
b3d=[PDx;PDy;PDz]+[0;0;m*g]/norm([PDx;PDy;PDz]+[0;0;m*g]);
b2d=cross(b3d,Bdes)/norm(cross(b3d,Bdes));
b1d=cross(b2d,b3d);
Rd=[b1d,b2d,b3d];
```

```
% here the desired rotation matrix is decomposed into its
% components in order to be sent as a vector in the output of
% this model,we need to send them in this order to calculate
% their derivatives
r11d=Rd(1,1);
r12d=Rd(1,2);
r13d=Rd(1,3);
r21d=Rd(2,1);
r22d=Rd(2,2);
r23d=Rd(2,3);
r31d=Rd(3,1);
r32d=Rd(3,2);
r33d=Rd(3,3);

% definition of the rotation and angular velocities errors
Rmul=transpose(Rd)*Rdp;
eRM=(transpose(Rd)*R)-(transpose(R)*Rd);
w=[w1;w2;w3];
wd=[Rmul(3,2);Rmul(1,3);Rmul(2,1)];

ew=w-(transpose(R)*Rd*wd);
eR=[eRM(3,2);eRM(1,3);eRM(2,1)]/2;

% simple rotational PD
PDrw=-KR*eR-Kw*ew;

% here PDrw is decomposed in order to be injected into the 3 body
% torques
Tbx=PDrw(1);
Tby=PDrw(2);
Tbz=PDrw(3);
```

```
% vehicle's dynamic model traslational
% velocities
xp=[x2;x4;x6];
% accelerations
xpp=(R*[0;0;Fbz])-[0;0;m*g];

% we do this in order to send state variables for integration
% xdot xdoubledot ydot ydoubledot zdot zdoubledot
x1p=xp(1);
x2p=xpp(1);
x3p=xp(2);
x4p=xpp(2);
x5p=xp(3);
x6p=xpp(3);

% vehicle's rotational dynamics
w1p=(Tbx-(w2*w3*Jz)+(w2*w3*Jy))/Jx;
w2p=(Tby-(w1*w3*Jx)+(w1*w3*Jz))/Jy;
w3p=(Tbz-(w1*w2*Jy)+(w1*w2*Jx))/Jz;

% auxiliar kinematics of rotation
Rp=R*(S);

% we decompose Rderivative into its components for sending to the
% output the integrating and obteining R elements, notice that
we need
% R initial values at the Simulink® solver
r11p=Rp(1,1);
r12p=Rp(1,2);
r13p=Rp(1,3);
r21p=Rp(2,1);
r22p=Rp(2,2);
r23p=Rp(2,3);
```

```
r31p=Rp(3,1);
r32p=Rp(3,2);
r33p=Rp(3,3);

% output:
% translational system states, elements 1-6
% angular velocities, elements 7-9
% derivative of rotation matrix, elements 10-18
% desired rotation matrix for obtaining its derivative,
elements 19-27
% desired translational values just for plotting, elements 28-30

outp=[x1p;x2p;x3p;x4p;x5p;x6p;w1p;w2p;w3p;r11p;r12p;r13p;r21p;
r22p;r23p;r31p;r32p;r33p;r11d;r12d;r13d;r21d;r22d;r23d;r31d;
r32d;r33d;x1d;x3d;x5d];
end
```

Figure 4-34 shows the Simulink block file called geocopt.slx with the required modifications. For data management, the rotation matrix was handled as a vector (deconstructed element by element). Figures 4-35 and 4-36 show the translational values, and Figure 4-37 shows the rotational ones displayed as components of rotation matrices.

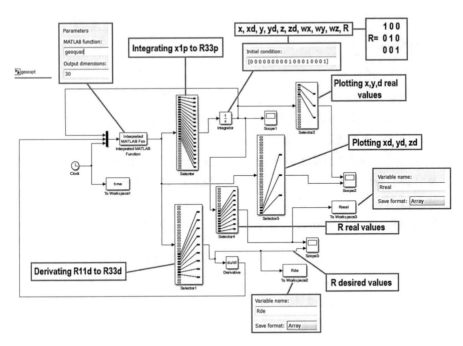

Figure 4-34. *Block file for the geometric control simulation*

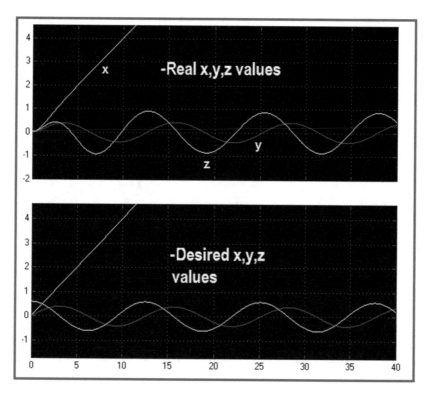

Figure 4-35. *Real vs. desired position values (individually)*

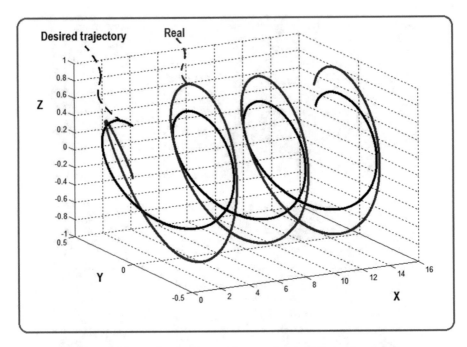

Figure 4-36. *Real vs. desired position values (3D trajectory)*

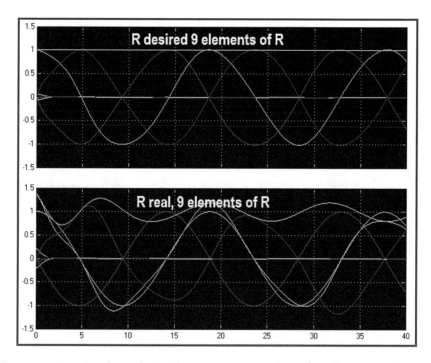

Figure 4-37. *Real vs. desired orientation values (as elements of rotation matrices)*

In addition to the translational trajectories, the desired and measured rotation matrices are shown. For better visualization of these attitude results, you can remember that

$$R = R_{z_\psi} R_{x_\phi} R_{y_\theta}$$

$$R = \begin{bmatrix} c\psi c\theta - s\phi s\psi s\theta & -c\phi s\psi & c\psi s\theta + s\phi s\psi c\theta \\ s\psi c\theta + s\phi c\psi s\theta & c\phi c\psi & s\psi s\theta - s\phi c\psi c\theta \\ -c\phi s\theta & s\phi & c\phi c\theta \end{bmatrix}$$

215

So, doing the following operations (if you choose another rotation matrix, you must determine its corresponding analysis):

$$\psi = \arctan 2(-R_{1,2}/R_{2,2})$$
$$\theta = \arctan 2(-R_{3,1}/R_{3,3})$$
$$\phi = \arctan 2(R_{3,2}/(\tfrac{R_{3,3}}{\cos\theta})) = \arctan 2\left(\sqrt{\frac{R_{3,2}^2}{R_{1,2}^2+R_{2,2}^2}}\right)$$

For wide-range rotations such as the yaw angle, the function that should be used is atan2, in order to avoid redundancies or inconsistencies, but for small angular motions, something more direct can be used as in the case of

$$\phi \approx \arcsin(R_{3,2})$$

In this way, the following code that uses the information obtained from the To Workspace blocks (which must be used at the end of the simulation), serves as a guide to determine what happens with the respective Euler angles; see Figure 4-38 (this can be executed directly in the command window or by using a m-file as indicated in Listing 4-5).

Listing 4-5. Plotting the Euler Angles from the Rotation Matrices, plotR.m File

```
subplot(3,1,1)
% phi
plot(time,asin(Rde(:,8)))
hold on
plot(time,asin(Rreal(:,8)),'m')

subplot(3,1,2)
% psi
```

```
plot(time,atan2(-Rde(:,2),Rde(:,5)))
hold on
plot(time,atan2(-Rreal(:,2),Rreal(:,5)),'m')

subplot(3,1,3)
% teta
plot(time,atan2(-Rde(:,7),Rde(:,9)))
hold on
plot(time,atan2(-Rreal(:,7),Rreal(:,9)),'m')
```

Note that the indexes have the following format that we use for working with the To Workspace block:

$$
\begin{bmatrix}
R_{11} & R_{12} & R_{13} \\
R_{21} & R_{22} & R_{23} \\
R_{31} & R_{32} & R_{33}
\end{bmatrix}
\rightarrow
\begin{bmatrix}
R_{11} & R_{12} & R_{13} & R_{21} & R_{22} & R_{23} & R_{31} & R_{32} & R_{33}
\end{bmatrix}
$$

Observe that this example is valid because the angles (with the exception of psi) had small values during the simulation. See Figure 4-38.

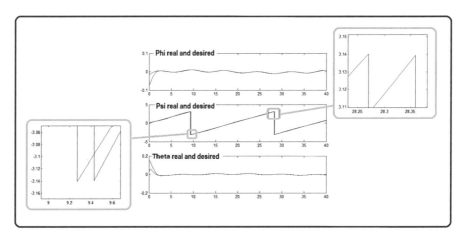

Figure 4-38. *Real vs. desired orientation values (as Euler angles)*

Note the small delay between the desired signal and the control signal. This is evident because the desired signal requires processing. This consists of generating the error, defining the control, and injecting this controller to the motors. For slow computers, the delay is even more notorious. In this case, we could say that it is not relevant.

As desired, in addition to following a helical trajectory, the drone makes it while continuously rotating around its Zb axis. In Figure 4-38, it looks like a motion from -180 degrees or -pi radians to 180 degrees or pi radians, but is identical to a 0-360 degrees rotation; see Figure 4-39.

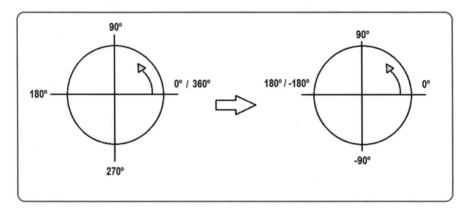

Figure 4-39. *Two equivalent angular ranges*

The interpretation is as follows.

The vector that controls the rotation in the body axis of the vehicle is defined as

$$B_{des} = \begin{bmatrix} \cos \psi_d & \sin \psi_d & 0 \end{bmatrix}$$

In this case, Psi desired depends on the time:

$$\psi_d = \tfrac{t}{3}$$

$$B_{desX} = \cos(t/3)$$
$$B_{desY} = \sin(t/3)$$

$$\psi_d = \arctan 2\left(\tfrac{\sin(t/3)}{\cos(t/3)}\right)$$

This can be presented graphically as in Figure 4-40.

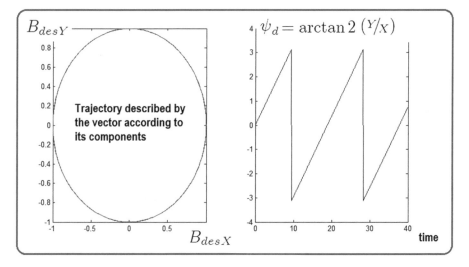

Figure 4-40. *Bdes vector behavior as a dependency on the desired yaw motion*

Figure 4-40 was plotted with the code available in Listing 4-6.

Listing 4-6. Code for Plotting Bdes and the Desired Yaw as a Time Function

```
t=[0:0.1:40];

x=cos(t/3);
y=sin(t/3);

% trayectory around body axes
subplot(1,2,1)
plot(x,y,'m')

% angle between this axes (psi/yaw)
subplot(1,2,2)
plot(t,atan2(y,x),'k')
```

Before closing this chapter, let's talk about some alternatives to simulation, also available within the Simulink and MATLAB environment.

Simulation Alternatives with the Simulink and MATLAB environment

In this section, alternative simulation methods for using MATLAB/ Simulink are presented. For this purpose and in order to make the procedures understandable and compact, the general solution of a mass spring damper system will be simulated (with an input force equal to zero and with non-zero initial conditions, this system should return to zero). Note that this is the closed-loop behavior of a PD controller with acceleration compensation as previously seen or a PID. Based on these examples, you can modify them as you wish in order to simulate a quadcopter or any other system or aircraft.

The concrete system to be exemplified in this section is the following:

$$0.7\ddot{x} + 0.5\dot{x} + 0.5x = 0$$

with the initial conditions given by

$$x_1 = x = 5$$
$$x_2 = \dot{x} = 0$$

There are more ways to simulate a system with MATLAB and Simulink, but these are the five that we consider the most useful.

Blocks and Interpreted MATLAB Functions

This is the case already seen in all the previous simulations but this time with the aforementioned reduced system so you can compare it with other available techniques. This is the one that we recommend given its practicality and the ease of use. In general, this method is the most compatible with other Simulink blocks and MATLAB functions in an intuitive and not so laborious way compared with the others that will be presented later.

Figure 4-41 illustrates the block file called `msdmatBlockSim.slx`. Observe that we include two blocks that facilitate the interconnection in terms of spacing and aesthetics (the Goto and From tags). Without them, the user would simply make direct and entangled connections.

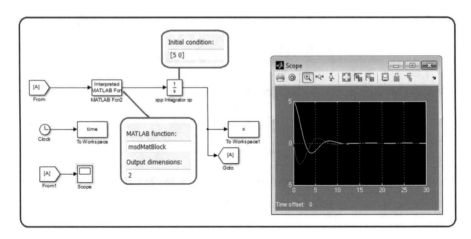

Figure 4-41. *Mass spring damper simulation by using blocks and interpreted MATLAB functions*

The dynamics and control code (in this case, the control is zero) is in a file called msdMatBlock.m, which is displayed in Listing 4-7.

Listing 4-7. Code for Using the Blocks and Interpreted MATLAB Functions Method

```
function outp=msdMatBlock(X)

% as you know you can modify the following dynamics with the
dynamics
% and control that you want, for example a quadcopter
x1=X(1);
x2=X(2);

B=0.5;
K=0.5;
M=0.7;

x1d=x2;
x2d=(1/M)*((-B*x2)-(K*x1));
```

```
outp=[x1d;x2d];
end
```

Only Blocks

Figure 4-42 also illustrates the previous case but by only using a file of blocks. In this example, it is called msdBlock.slx.

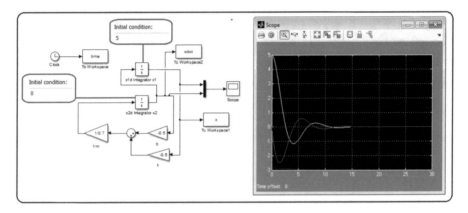

Figure 4-42. *Mass spring damper simulation by using only blocks*

This type of simulation is still useful because there are some hardware devices that are linked with Simulink and for some reason they do not allow interaction with user-defined functions. The biggest disadvantage of this technique, as already indicated, is that in a larger system, the blocks also become numerous in quantity. Remember that each equation requires blocks for all its symbols and operators (sums, products, exponents, matrices, etc.). When you have more equations, it is convenient that you read about the use of subsystems, and especially on how to create a subsystem from Selection. You can find this information in the following link:

www.mathworks.com/help/simulink/ug/creating-subsystems.html

Blocks and S-Functions

An S-Function can be considered an evolution of the interpreted MATLAB function, which contains the differential dynamics in the text file (it does not require the use of an integrator; it only needs feedback). It has several advantages, such as the possibility of being used with hardware and software external to MATLAB and Simulink. The biggest problem that exists with these functions is related to the time management. In the example presented below, the Simulation is useful with variable-step ODE solvers but not with fixed-step ODE solvers (the most demanding task when working with S-Functions is that you must be careful with the compatibility of the simulation times).

Figure 4-43 shows the block file called `msdSfuncBlock.slx`.

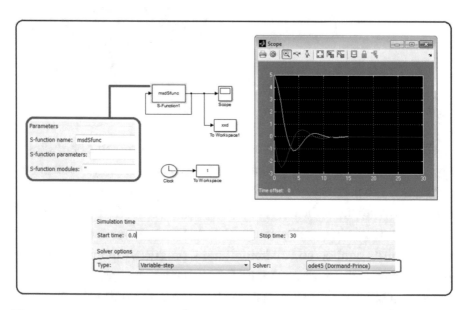

Figure 4-43. *Mass spring damper simulation by using blocks and S-Functions*

Listing 4-8 is the corresponding text file called msdSfunc.m. Its
description is reserved for you to investigate, since as indicated, they are
not so intuitive and they have a variety of configurations. You can start your
research on this topic with the book about sliding mode control by Jinkun
Liu indicated in the Appendix. In this book, there are a lot of examples that
use the S-Function approach.

Listing 4-8. Code for Using the Blocks and S- Functions Method

```
function [sys,x0,str,ts]=msdSfunc(t,x,u,flag)
switch flag,
case 0,
    [sys,x0,str,ts]=mdlInitializeSizes;
case 1,
    sys=mdlDerivatives(t,x,u);
case 3,
    sys=mdlOutputs(t,x,u);
case {2, 4, 9 }
    sys = [];
otherwise
    error(['Unhandled flag = ',num2str(flag)]);
end
function [sys,x0,str,ts]=mdlInitializeSizes
sizes = simsizes;
sizes.NumContStates   = 2;
sizes.NumDiscStates   = 0;
sizes.NumOutputs      = 2;
sizes.NumInputs       = 2;
sizes.DirFeedthrough = 0;
sizes.NumSampleTimes = 0;
sys=simsizes(sizes);
x0=[5 0];
```

```
str=[];
ts=[];

function sys=mdlDerivatives(t,x,u)

B=0.5;
K=0.5;
M=0.7;

sys(1)=x(2);
sys(2)=(1/M)*((-B*x(2))-(K*x(1)));
function sys=mdlOutputs(t,x,u)
sys(1)=x(1);
sys(2)=x(2);
```

Text Mode with Predefined Commands

In this case, only a text file and an auxiliary file for plotting (optional) are required (the auxiliary file can be replaced by typing directly into the command window). As the name implies, predefined functions are used (in the following example, the command ode45).

The disadvantage of this method is that its interaction with Simulink is extremely difficult and any additional signal processing implies that you must write auxiliary code (this becomes very difficult when feedback is required). On the other hand, note that for converting this code into an interpreted MATLAB function, you must make some simple adjustments (the dynamics file already has a structure similar to an interpreted MATLAB function).

Listing 4-9 shows the code of the msdPredefinedFuncSys.m file and the way to convert this file into an interpreted MATLAB function code.

Listing 4-9. Code for Using the Text Mode with Predefined
Commands

```
function out=msdPredefinedFuncSys(t,inpt)
% for converting this file into an Interpreted MATLAB® function
% just delete the letter t from the function arguments and add the
% word end after the output line

x1=inpt(1);
x2=inpt(2);

B=0.5;
K=0.5;
M=0.7;

x1d=x2;
x2d=(1/M)*((-B*x2)-(K*x1));

out=[x1d;x2d];
```

The use of this file is described in the lines of Listing 4-10 (observe the part where the time and initial conditions are set):

Listing 4-10. Complementary Code for Running the Simulation and
Plotting While Using the Text Mode with Predefined Commands

```
[t,X]=ode45(@msdPredefinedFuncSys,[0 30],[5;0]);
plot(t,X)
```

The previous commands can be introduced directly into the command window or by using an auxiliary file. In the case of this book, it's the file msdPredefinedFuncPlot.m. The result of this kind of simulation is displayed in Figure 4-44.

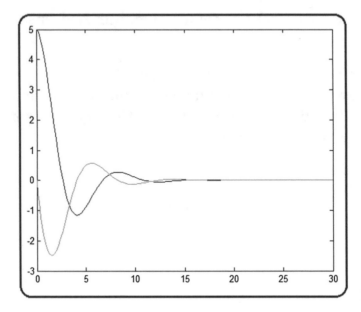

Figure 4-44. *Mass spring damper simulation by using only text files (with predefined or customized commands)*

Text Mode with Customized Commands

This is identical to the previous case, but the user is free to generate their own ODE solvers (non-predesigned functions). This implies a direct way to migrate to other programming languages. Just remember that the syntax will change but not the algorithms or the equations.

Listing 4-11 shows the system code (msdCustomSys.m). Remember that in this case the controller is zero. At this point, you should have already noticed the simulation pattern (a file with the dynamics of the system, another file with the ODE solver, and a line, code segment, or execution interface for running the simulation).

Listing 4-11. Code for Using the Text Mode with Customized
Commands

```
function h=msdCustomSys(t,X)

x1=X(1);
x2=X(2);

B=0.5;
K=0.5;
M=0.7;

x1p=x2;
x2p=(-(B*x2)-(K*x1))/M;

h=[x1p;x2p];
```

The execution lines are as indicated in Listing 4-12, and they are
contained in the msdCustomPlot.m file (which is optional since they can be
executed from the command window).

Listing 4-12. Complementary Code for Running the Simulation and
Plotting While Using the Text Mode with Customized Commands

```
X0=[5;0];
t = linspace(0,30,5000);

X=ode3('msdCustomSys',t,X0);
plot(t,X)
```

The plot is practically identical to Figure 4-44. The solver file called
ode3 is available for download at www.mathworks.com/matlabcentral/
answers/98293-is-there-a-fixed-step-ordinary-differential-
equation-ode-solver-in-matlab-8-0-r2012b in the folder called
ODE_Solvers.zip, which appears throughout that post.

Observe that the code provides in an extensive way its own numerical method. For other solvers, you can consult the Appendix.

Summary

In this chapter, you learned about different methods to simulate the behavior and control of drones by using MATLAB and Simulink tools. However, it is presented to you in such a way that you can use the knowledge learned with other tools and programming languages. The chapter conclusion is that, in order to simulate an aircraft and in general any system, you will require at least three programs: the dynamic model with its control code, the numerical solver for your system of equations, and an execution environment. If you want to include graphics or user interaction, some options were mentioned but finally and in any case you will need to know the basic notions of the three aforementioned programs. This knowledge is complemented in the Appendix. In the next chapter, you will see implementation details focused on signal processing, high-level UART communication, and SDKs programming.

CHAPTER 5

Implementation

This chapter has a scientific and maker impact and you will learn about topics that are also discarded in many publications, related to core implementation details such as signal processing for sensors and actuators, data transmission, the ways to program a drone, and a glossary with the main commands used with the most popular software development interfaces. As a result, you will be able to understand concisely how to program a drone or any other robotic vehicle. You will also be able to advance your knowledge with the selected references in the Appendix.

Tasks of a Drone

There are six basic tasks of a drone:

- **Motor**: This is the most basic and important task. In general, it consists of an automatic open loop control that is a function of other closed loop controllers of the vehicle. The speed of each motor is modified, having an effect on the behavior of the drone. This task is the one that presents the fastest variation and consequently needs a high frequency update. Motors must receive the propulsion or allocation matrix in an automatic way.

© Julio Alberto Mendoza-Mendoza, Victor Javier Gonzalez-Villela,
Carlos Fernando Aguilar-Ibañez, Leonardo Fonseca-Ruiz 2021
J. A. Mendoza-Mendoza et al., *Drones to Go*, https://doi.org/10.1007/978-1-4842-6788-2_5

- **Attitude or orientation**: This is the second most relevant task (also in the frequency of execution). It is more important than the altitude task because it implies that the aircraft is adequately balanced. If this was not the case, the drone could move randomly around the plane and in the worst case fall down. Due to the relevance in the flight of the vehicle, it is usually a fully automatic closed loop.

- **Altitude or elevation**: This is the third in importance because any aircraft implies being able to float. For this reason, people with an introductory knowledge believe that this task is the most important, but as we already indicated, lack of balance tends to destabilize the drone. It is usually an automatic closed loop, but you can give it a semi-automatic behavior through the remote control.

- **Planar**: This is the fourth in relevance. It involves controlling the drone position, which is perpendicular to the elevation axis (the position that the aircraft keeps along the ground). This task can also be automatic or semi-automatic.

- **Trajectory planning**: In this case, this is the simultaneous variation of the attitude, altitude, and planar tasks. This variation is carried out as a function of the time or a specific point-to-point path. It can be automatic or semi-automatic. Basically it is the navigation through a collection of points.

- **Remote control**: This is the manual component of the flight tasks. It is a human closed loop control because the pilot is the one who regulates the error according to the measurement provided by their sight and the action of the control buttons. Since the action is human-dependent, this task is as slow and imprecise as the pilot's abilities. Its use with the other tasks gives them a semi-automatic mode. In some cases, the pilot only alters the desired values and in others modifies directly the effect of the control. It is not recommended that the remote control directly modifies the orientation tasks (buttons and sticks move slower and more abrupt than the required automatic attitude action).

Now that you now about the tasks of a drone, let's talk about the kind of controllers that they use.

Loops and Kinds of Controllers for a Drone

A quadcopter is a system that serves as a good example to describe various types of controllers and control loops. They are covered in the following sections.

Control Loops

Open and Closed Loops

In general, the altitude, planar position, and orientation of a drone are closed loops, which means that their error correction is based on feedback. However, there is a task that depends on an open loop. It is the speed control of the motors. An open loop is the one where the task is executed more as an effect of proportionality than by error correction. In the case of the motors, a voltage is sent and we observe a proportional motor speed without having a closed loop to verify and correct this speed.

Inner and Outer Loops

A quadcopter has four motors, and due to their geometric configuration, it can directly control four variables, which are the altitude and the attitude (its three orientations). This is called an inner loop. However, as it is required that the vehicle can also move in the XY plane, this is done in a dependent way with respect to the roll and pitch orientations in an outer control loop.

Dependent and Independent Loops

The independent loops occur in all the variables whose control does not require the monitoring of an additional variable; examples are the altitude control and the yaw control. On the other hand, the dependent loops require the information of one or more additional variables; examples are the controls of X and Y that depend on the vehicle's orientation.

Pose and Speed Loops

A quadcopter is a vehicle whose pose loops (orientation and position) depend on the speed open loop of each one of its motors. Servomotors are pose actuators, and brushless DC motors are usually speed actuators.

Kinds of Controllers

Model-Free and Non–Model-Free Controllers

Certain variables such as the roll, pitch, and yaw orientations could be regulated with a "simple" PD controller. This means that compensation for their partial or full dynamics is not required. On the other hand, when controlling the altitude, it is necessary to introduce a compensation element for the vehicle's weight (a partial non–model-free controller).

Robust and Adaptive Controllers

In the case of the regulated variables by using PDs without any type of compensation, it is assumed that the PDs are large enough with respect to the vehicle dynamics. In this case, the control is called dominant or robust (as long as the motors allow this robustness). Another example of robust controllers are the sliding mode family. Basically they don't require the model of the system, just the error loop. In the case of the altitude, as the weight is compensated, this is a very rudimentary example of adaptive control. However, if the PD gains are large enough and the motors can counteract this effect by themselves, the compensatory term can be omitted. Generally, adaptive controllers are designed to compensate partial or full dynamics or unmodeled perturbations.

Unrestricted and Bounded Controls

An unrestricted control is the one that can use an unlimited range of values, such as all the positive and negative values. This kind of control does not exist but you can think that is a viable option because of the simulators. On the other hand, bounded controllers introduce operating limits. The first bounded control found in a quadcopter is given by the motors since they have maximum and minimum values of speed and torque. The second bounded control is very noticeable when using brushless motors (assuming they are not bidirectional). This is the presence of exclusively positive operating values. And the last bounded control, not so evident in drones, is determined by physical effects such as the response time.

In the first restriction, saturations are used. In the second, scaling factors are required. In the third, delay control techniques are used. The last effect is not so evident on regular drones due to the fast response of autopilots and computers, and is usually omitted, but in aircraft that use bidirectional propellers, it is relevant to consider these delays since the propellers do not change their sense of rotation instantaneously.

Linear and Nonlinear Control

This kind of control is determined by the operating conditions. You saw some flight modes where the motion is smooth and the angles are restricted to a small vicinity around zero, so it was a right decision to linearize both the model and the controller. However, we also described some flight-modes where the angles are not bounded and the vehicle can perform aggressive motions; therefore the control and the model have non-linearities.

Continuous Operation and Based on Events

In this case, a control that is always continuous and that must be present throughout the full operation of the aircraft is the attitude controller. The one that depends on events, like time-based signals or the interaction with the remote controller, is the trajectory control.

Continuous and Discrete Controllers

Here comes a second definition of continuity and it is related to how small the sampling time is. This depends on two factors: the first is the computer and the second the actuators and sensors.

In the case of computers, today almost all of them are fast enough to consider their operation as continuous models or systems based on differential equations. However, by varying the technology of the actuators from electric brushless motors to internal combustion motors, you will notice that the latter kind of engines have slower response times with respect to the electric ones (they have a lot of components, friction, and operating cycles) and they require difference equations for their analysis (their modeling with differential equations is no longer possible).

Electrical and Mechanical Control

We abuse some of the technology because the electrical and electronic components are guaranteed by the manufacturer to operate properly so, for example, we do not worry about the operation of the ESCs. Also, we rely on the fact that electrical devices are faster with respect to the mechanical components. For these reasons, our design ignores electrical and electronic components and we just consider the drone as a system with purely mechanical modeling and control. However, modern designs that introduce a closed loop control in the speed of the motors can be seen as an intermediate or electromechanical control, where the mechanical speed of the motors depends on electrical variables such as the electrical phases of the ESCs. See the Appendix for references on closed loop motor control.

You have learned about the drone tasks and most of the controllers that this vehicle/robot can use. Let's continue with the basic signal processing that a drone requires and an example of application.

Drone Signal Processing

Maybe you are tempted to implement the previous controllers. However, some steps are required before this implementation. The most common are the following:

- Signal filtering, which is used in the sensors

- Signal mapping, which is used in the sensors, the remote control sticks, during data transmission, etc.

- Signal casting or data conversion, which is used to inject the control value into the motors or during serial data transmission

- Signal saturation, which is used to limit the values to send to the motors, or to limit the values that are read from a remote control stick

- Signal normalization, which is used to impose an operating range in the sensors

Signal Filtering

As you can see in the previous chapters, the main component of the closed loop controllers is the error, which also depends on the measured variables, and this is achieved with the sensors. However, these sensors usually have electrical noise due to their own behavior or because of their interaction with the environment.

Therefore, a filtering stage is required in order to reduce or suppress the electrical noise. As a computational or electronic processing is implied, noise suppression is an agreement between smoothing the noise signal and delaying the smoothed signal. There are several ways to achieve this. Some examples are the following:

- **Passive**: Here, additional devices are used, which by their own nature absorbs some of the environmental noise. Examples are dissipative sponges or fluids for mechanical motion, lenses that absorb a frequency of light, or passive electronic devices that can be used as filters.

- **Active by electronic filtering**: Low-pass, high-pass, band-pass, and band-reject circuits are well known examples.

- **Active by mathematical filtering**: The signal is sent to a mathematical filter. Among the best known filters are the Kalman Filter and the Luenbenger observer.

- **Active by space transformation**: The signal is converted into a different space in order to perform a simple filtering in the new space, such as filtering at a frequency level instead of at a time-based level. This method can also be considered as a mathematical filter, but it has its own line of research. Examples are Fourier and Wavelets transformations.

- **Active by intelligent filtering**: This is done by using any algorithm that employs an artificial intelligence.

The trade-off between the noise reduction and the signal delay can be seen in Figure 5-1 (the code of a generic low pass filter was used). In Listing 5-1, you can see a high-level generic code for using this type of filters (in this case, MATLAB).

Listing 5-1. Generic Code for Filtering a Signal as Available in Many Programs (Syntax May Change)

```
filteredSignal=lowpassFilter(noisySignal)
```

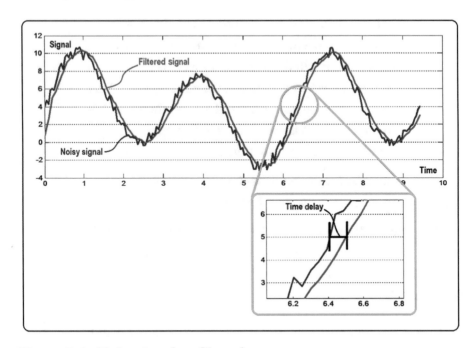

Figure 5-1. *Noisy signal vs. filtered one*

Saturation

In this case, it is necessary to impose limit values on the controllers, in order that the maximum and minimum values to be injected do not exceed the motor limits. Another application is to limit the values that a user can reach in the stick of the remote control.

This saturation can be done abruptly (for example, by using a sign function which is equivalent to the action of turning on and off) or continuously (by using a function called saturation). Even a continuous function can be smooth or sharp (you could use a lot of functions among a family of saturators called sigmoidal functions).

Typically, the non-restricted part of the saturator copies the original signal as a standard linear function, as illustrated in the code of Listing 5-2. However, in order to counteract an undesired performance (for example, the abrupt behavior of a remote control stick), sometimes other types of sigmoids are used.

Figure 5-2 illustrates two things. The upper part is a family of saturators, in this case the sign function, the saturation function, and the hyperbolic tangent function. Obviously the designer must modify them so that they reach minimum and maximum values according to their applications and not only -1 and 1. The lower part is the application of the saturation function with a given signal, in this case the minimum and maximum allowed values go from 0 to 7.

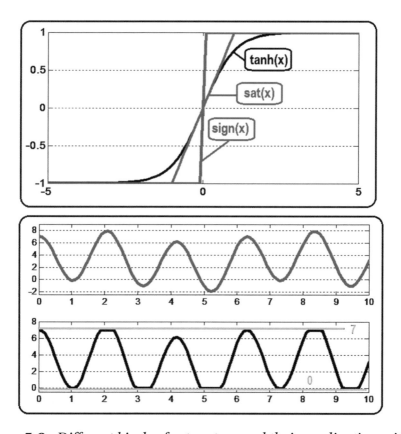

Figure 5-2. *Different kinds of saturators and their application with a signal*

The code used in Figure 5-2 is really simple and is displayed in Listing 5-2.

Listing 5-2. Generic Code for a Saturation Function (the Linear One)

```
Mini=0
Maxi=7
if(signal<=Mini)
    satsignal=Mini;
elseif(signal>=Maxi)
    satsignal=Maxi;
else
    satsignal=signal;
end
```

Biasing and Mapping

Another important task is to transform the control signal (a signal with positive and negative values) into one signal compatible with the motors (for example, within a range of values between 1000 and 2000 in brushless RC motors). Another example is the range of the sensors, which can be arbitrary and must be converted into a standard working range (0 to 360 degrees, -180 to 180 degrees, -1 to 1 meter etc.). See Figure 5-3. In this case, scaling and translation functions are used.

One of the most used biasing and mapping techniques is the equation of the line between two points known as linear mapping, which adjusts an input value to the equation of a straight line (the output value). For this, the input signal must previously be constrained in a way that it does not exceed maximum and minimum input limits.

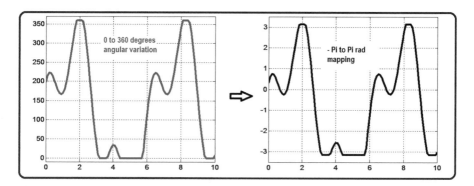

Figure 5-3. *Mapping a signal from a range of input values to a range of output values*

The code is also simple and is shown in Listing 5-3 (note that this mapping code describes a line between two points).

Listing 5-3. Generic Code for a Mapping (the Linear One)

```
mininput=0;
minoutput=-pi;
maxinput=360;
maxoutput=pi;
mapsignal=(signal - mininput) * (maxoutput - minoutput) /
(maxinput - mininput) + minoutput;
```

Data Casting

This is another important signal adaptation, and it is the one to be carried out when a command only admits one type of data and is provided with data of another type. For example, the commands for writing to a PWM-type RC motor usually require data of integer type and the provided values are floating numbers or fractions. In this case, we use what in programming is called as casting, which is the transformation from one data type to another. This can involve two things:

- The casting does not exist and the user must design this program.

- The casting generates aliasing, which affects the quality of the measurements or the executions (for example, a controller can go from a smooth and natural motion to an abrupt and robotic one, or from a high definition image to one with poor quality).

Figure 5-4 shows a common example. The red signal represents a calculated control value (with a large number of decimal places) and at the moment of injecting this signal into the motors, as the writing command admits other type of data (uint8 for example), the precision of the original value is reduced. In appearance they look similar, but if we see in detail, a stepped effect called aliasing is presented. This effect could imply a less smooth behavior in the motion of a drone.

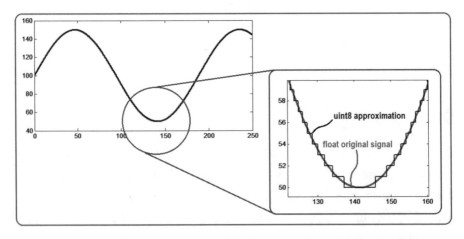

Figure 5-4. *Aliasing of a signal when data casting is performed*

Depending on the programming language, the casting commands may or may not exist (the user must create them), but in general they adopt the form displayed in Listing 5-4.

Listing 5-4. A Generic Example of Data Casting

```
signal=100+50*sin(t/30);
castSignal = uint8(signal);
```

Observe that if the casting exists, it means that there are functions that force a signal or input data to change its data type (uint8, in this example).

Redundancies and Singularities Normalization

This is a common problem found in angular sensors and it lies in the fact that they have a jump from their maximum value to their minimum value, for example from 359 degrees to 0 degrees, or redundant values known as singularities such as 0 degrees and 360 degrees (this also happens with -180 degrees and 180 degrees if the sensor works in this way). See Figure 5-5.

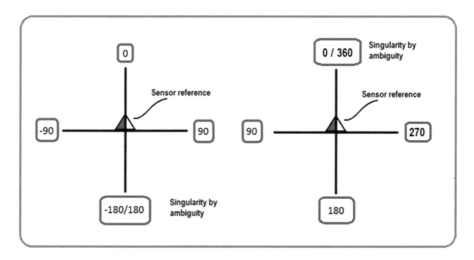

Figure 5-5. *Angular redundancies and singularities*

To handle these conditions of singularity, ambiguity, or redundancy, there are many normalization methods. One of them (which considers the case on the left side of Figure 5-5) is based on the symmetric definition of the angular error with respect to the measured value. See my book *Advanced Robotic Vehicles Programming* for more details.

$$e_\psi = \psi_d - \psi$$

$$e_{\psi\,Norm} = \begin{cases} e_\psi - 360 \text{ if } e_\psi > 180 \\ e_\psi + 360 \text{ if } e_\psi < -180 \\ e_\psi \text{ in another case} \end{cases}$$

This is a dynamic normalization, whose additional objective is to reduce the rotation to be made by the vehicle in a way that implies a shorter distance. To achieve a desired orientation, a vehicle can do it by rotating to the left or to the right. This algorithm, in addition to preventing singularities, chooses whether it is better to move in clockwise or in counterclockwise sense.

You should also develop or investigate alternative normalization methods that are based on the desired value rather than the measured one, or based on an absolute reference instead of the vehicle reference, or methods based on multiple rotations and methods for angular measurements from 0 to 360 degrees, etc.

Example of Use

Figure 5-6 presents a modification of the semi-automatic controller without yaw motion (or very small) as previously described. This variation incorporates the five basic signal processing methods in this way: mapping and saturation of the remote control is applied to adapt its values in order to have acceptable angular commands. Filtering is applied to the pose sensors to reduce their levels of noise. The angular error is normalized. Before injecting the allocation matrix into the motors, a scaling is applied to make their signals positive. In general, drone motors have a fixed sense of rotation, and their speed can be varied from zero or starting value, up to their maximum speed, so a saturation is applied in the motor signals in order not to exceed their starting and maximum values. Finally, a casting is done because in general the commands for writing to the motors request a type of integer and the control signals are floating values.

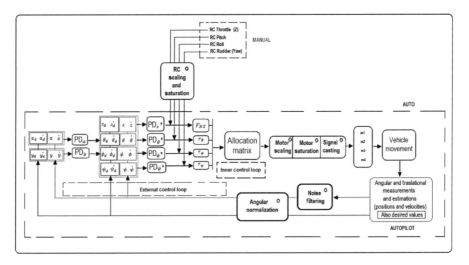

Figure 5-6. *Signal processing applied to the controller of a drone*

You learned the basis of signal processing for drones. Let's continue with the basis of data transmission theory, which is used for most of the drone programming environments that are usually based on the UART type serial transmission.

Data Transmission Theory

Data transmission theory is considered a topic of high relevance given that it allows the communication between a team of drones or between a single drone and a remote base. Among the available presentations, here we describe the UART type (Universal Asynchronous Receiver-Transmitter), because is one of the most basic and employed protocols with decades of use and is really common to find in drone SDKs.

Data Types and Subtypes

Before talking about this standard, it is convenient to talk about data types and subtypes. This topic is related to the data conversion previously introduced. We will use C/C ++ concepts in the following paragraphs because this is the most common programming language found in different SDKs for developing drone applications. However, this is a really common topic among other programming languages and each one of them has the following basic types (or very similar). See Table 5-1.

Table 5-1. *Basic Data Types*

Type	Description
int	Used for integer numbers
float	Used for numbers with decimal values
double	Increases the accuracy of the floats and is useful for scientific or engineering calculations
char	Allows the use of characters
bool	Allows the use of logical values

However, according to the operations being carried out, such as time management, memory management, and communication protocols, it is common to find variants of these fundamental types of data. These variants are identified by the incorporation of prefixes and suffixes. In drone programming, it is very common to use variants of the integer type. For example, uint8 has a prefix u and a suffix 8.

In general, the prefix indicates a sign restriction and the suffix a range restriction based on bits. There are 8, 16, 32, and 64 bit integers, and they can store up to 255 (255 = 2 raised to eighth power minus 1, in order to start from the element 0), 65535, 4294967295, and 18446744073709551615, respectively. The prefix u indicates that the possible values to use have only a positive sign and 0. So in the case of uint8, its useful range is from 0 to 255. Instead, if we use the option int8, we will also have 255 values but between a range from -128 to 127.

The usefulness of the prefixes and suffixes is described with examples.

Let's imagine a process that must be executed in microseconds. If we use an uint8 data subtype, we will only have 255 microseconds, which is not even a millisecond of time. If we use an uint16, we will only have 65 milliseconds. Finally, by selecting an uint32 subtype, the equivalent in seconds is 4294 or around 71 minutes.

Let's advance a little further on the use of the UART to indicate that this is a communication that only supports unsigned 8-bit blocks. In this way, the use of subtypes 16 and 32 is not possible, much less the subtype with negative values. For this reason, here is where the utility of the uint8 subtypes is found.

Finally, you will find in many programming environments the aggregate t in the numerical suffix (uint16t, for example). This only has the property of being a compatible data between different hardware platforms. When the data types 8, 16, and 32 were developed, they diverged in memory consumption between different computing platforms. Thus the manufacturers came to an agreement on the portability of the code by creating a standard that is identified with the letter t.

UART Introduction

Notice that it is assumed a SDK with high-level UART commands such as `read ()`, `write ()`, `begin ()`, or `available ()`, like the one presented in Arduino or Ardupilot. The use of a low-level UART is reserved for books about machine language, assembly language, or microcontrollers.

UART transmission is described because it is one of the most widely used with the current autopilots and their respective SDKs. It is bilateral but asynchronous (without a timer involved and consequently without ensuring transmission and reception times). We have also indicated that this standard is based on the management of 8-bit positive and integer data packets.

To continue, we ask the following questions.

Given the limitations indicated,

- How do you work with negative data?

- How do you work with decimal data (a number with decimal places)?

- How are the reading and writing actions guaranteed, if there's no timer to read or write?

- And, how do you work with data greater than the value 255?

To answer these questions, we start with the concept of a cyclic counter. This is simple to understand if we refer to the rotary motion.

In a rotary motion, a body can be oriented from 0 to 360 degrees or from 0 to 2pi radians, depending on the standard that you employ. Values higher than this range imply making multiple rotations or placing in the modulo operation of the indicated value with 360 or 2pi.

Thus, 800 degrees is equivalent to two rotations of 360 degrees and a surplus of 80 degrees. Note that any angle is a function of the modulo or remainder of base 360 or 2pi, and the quotient of said angle with the same base (observe that we are interested only in the integer parts of the modulo and the quotient).

$$N = N \bmod(360) + 360(quotient(N/360))$$

For the previous example,

$$800 = 800 \bmod(360) + 360(quotient(800/360))$$
$$800 = 80 + 360(2)$$

Using this logic, the serial transmission implies that our base is the number 256 (from 0 to 255 there are 256 values), and any number to be sent can be decomposed into the modulo with that base and the quotient with the same base:

$$N = N \bmod(256) + 256(quotient(N/256))$$

For example,

$$7515 = 7515 \bmod(256) + 256(quotient(7515/256))$$
$$7515 = 91 + 256(29)$$

In short, to work with values greater than 255, a number must be decomposed into two sections, one related to the modulo of said number and the other to its quotient:

$$7515 = \boxed{7515 \bmod(256)} + 256(\;\boxed{quotient(7515/256)}\;)$$

The next question to solve is the way to send negative numbers.

The answer is that there are two options and each one will depend on the data range to be used (the range of a sensor, for example).

The first of them is basically to waste one of the 8 bits to be sent for indicating that said bit has a value of 0 if the number to send is positive or 0, and that has a value of 1 if the number is negative. However, our communication base will no longer be 256 but 128 (with the remaining 7 bits, we can only form 128 different numbers).

The second is to carry out a saturation and mapping (translation and scaling) of the values (the operations seen in the previous section). When performing the saturation, we establish limits for our signal and these limits are required to define the minimum and maximum input values in our mapping function. The translation allows us to move towards a positive reference, for example to move from a range of values from [-100 100] to one of [0 200]. The scaling is optional if the input has large values with respect to the output, for example going from [-1000 1000] to [0 200]. Notice that the mapping function already has both effects.

The effect of the excessive scaling (with large numbers it becomes more noticeable) is the presence of numbers with a fractional part. Now we will answer how to work with them.

The first thing to do is to establish the degree of precision that we want. We must evaluate if we are interested in one, two, or more decimal places. For example, if in our range [0 200] we are interested in working with numbers like 199.3 or in numbers like 199.15.

To communicate with these numbers, we also have two basic options.

The first is to separate the integer part from the fractional part and send them as two different numbers. In the example of the number 199.15, a 199 will be sent separately and then a 15. The problem with this approach is that one of the two numbers could get lost on the way.

The other option is to apply a scaling. In this way, if we are only interested in one decimal place, it would be enough that we multiply our initial range by 10, so using the given examples, 199.3 would become 1993 and 199.15 would become 1991. Instead, if we want two decimal places, the factor would be 100, sending 19930 and 19915, respectively. In this way, a scaled number is sent. For this purpose, it is required that both the receiver and the emitter know the scale factor. Obtaining a high level of precision with this approach is a problem because quite possibly the number to send must be divided into two parts or more. The application is simple. For example, if we want two decimal places, instead of mapping from [-1000 1000] to [0 200], we should do it from [-1000 1000] to [0 20000].

Note that almost any operation can be done in the sender and the receiver, including floating or double operations. But the data transmission is exclusively for positive integer values. For this reason we must make the aforementioned adjustments (there are development interfaces like Arduino that include functions that automatically make these conversions; for this reason, it seems that they support not only positive integers).

Finally, to answer the remaining question about how the communication is guaranteed, we will indicate how the components of the UART communication are implemented.

The basis for this procedure is to understand the binary operations that are equivalent to those previously presented (modulo and quotient) and some other binary check operations. This is because it is convenient to simplify the data processing tasks at the computer in a language that the processor knows. These operations are sending, receiving, checking, and communication agreement.

UART Sending

The starting point is this equation:

$$N = N \bmod (256) + 256(quotient(N/256))$$

In decimal format, the operations to get the modulo and the quotient are obtained from the division, as indicated in Figure 5-7.

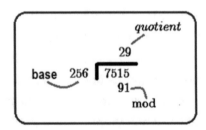

Figure 5-7. *Quotient and modulo of a decimal base number*

In binary format, the quotient can be obtained from the non-cyclic right shift operation (replacing the shifted numbers with zeros). This is applied to the last 8 bits of the binary equivalent of the number to be partitioned. This operation is represented as >> 8 in C ++ as a reference for other programming languages. On the other hand, the module is obtained with the AND operation applied with 255 or 1111 1111 in binary base. This is represented as & in C ++ as a reference for other programming languages.

Using the same example:

7515=1110101011011(bin)

11101 0101 1011(bin) >>8 = 0000 0000 11101(bin) = 29(dec)

On the other hand:

11101 0101 1011 (bin)

& 00000 1111 1111 (bin)

= 00000 0101 1011 (bin) = 91 (dec)

In this way, the number (7515 in this case) is sent as two groups of 8 bits:

0101 1011 (bin) = 91 (dec)

0001 1101(bin) = 29(dec)

Of course, before sending these numbers, they were obtained with the operations described previously (>>8 and & 1111 1111).

UART Receiving

Receiving consists of applying the following equation:

$$N = N \bmod(256) + 256(quotient(N/256))$$

Directly in some programming languages or by using the following binary equivalent: 8-bit non-cyclic left shift, and the OR operations (<< 8 and | in C ++):

Binary value = Binary Quotient part << 8 | Binary Module part

Using the previous example:

0001 1101(bin) = 29 (dec) << 8 = 0000 11101 0000 0000 = 7424 (dec)

Having this result, we continue with the OR operation. Note that there are more than 8 bits, but remember that this is processed by the receiving computer once the data is received. This is not the case for the communication channel that requires 8-bit messages.

11101 0000 0000

| 00000 0101 1011 (bin) = 91 (dec)

= 11101 0101 1011(bin) = 7515(dec)

The reading and writing processes are summarized in Figure 5-8.

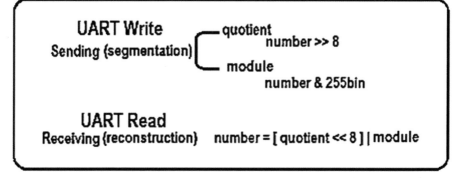

Figure 5-8. *UART reading and writing processes sumarized*

Now you know how to send and receive information. However, how do you verify the data? And how do you know if you are able to communicate? This is answered with the following operations.

UART Checking

In this case, the incorrect information is discarded, the simplest algorithm is the checksum, and its improvement is the XOR checksum.

An easy explanation is done from the decimal base.

Suppose the following data are sent:

val1Send=50

val2Send=30

A third value to send can be the sum of the previous quantities (the sum part of the checksum algorithm):

valsumSend=val1+val2=80

The same data should arrive to the receiver:

Val1Rec=50

Val2Rec=30

valSumRec=80

And then the check part of the algorithm is built:

Check=Val1Rec+Val2Rec=80

In this way, Check and valSumRec are the same and this is a valid collection of data.

Now let's suppose that the receiver reads an incorrect value:

Val1Rec=20

Val2Rec=30

valSumRec=80

We build the check part again:

Check=Val1Rec+Val2Rec=50

In this way, Check is different from valSumRec and the data collection is discarded, or the information is requested again.

As can be seen, the checksum algorithm has some important problems:

1. The sum may exceed the value of 255 and it will be required to send the number as two or more groups of data.

2. The sum of the incorrect data can result in a correct check.

For example, the sender writes

val1Send=50

val2Send=30

valsumSend=val1+val2=80

The receiver reads

Val1Rec=60

Val2Rec=20

valSumRec=80

And, as the check remains equal to 80, this incorrect data packet will not be discarded.

3. The data arrive correctly but the sum is corrupted.

The sender writes

val1Send=50

val2Send=30

valsumSend=val1+val2=80

And the receiver reads

Val1Rec=50

Val2Rec=30

valSumRec=10

Since the value of the check=80 is different from valSumRec, the information is discarded despite having arrived correctly.

In order to reduce these problems (at least the overflow problem), binary checksums are used. One of them is the XOR checksum (^ operator in C ++). Note that the rest of the problems are still present.

If you want to send a sum value that exceeds 255, for example 520, the first thing to do is a binary transformation:

1000001000(bin)=520(dec)

After that, the XOR addition is made element by element:

(1)xor(0)xor(0)xor(0)xor(0)xor(0)xor(1)xor(0)xor(0)xor(0)=0

So, the additional data to send is simply 0.

For example:

Val1Send=250

Val2Send=250

Val3Send=20

ValSum=520

Valsum cannot be sent, but instead the XOR sum of its binary components is sent:

XORSend=(1)xor(0)xor(0)xor(0)xor(0)xor(0)xor(1)xor(0)xor(0)xor(0)=0

The receiver reads

Val1Rec=250

Val2Rec=10

Val3Rec=20

XORRec=0

Then, the check is built:

Check=Val1Rec+Val2Rec+Val3Rec=280

The XOR sum is done with the binary components of the Check:

100011000(bin)=280(dec)

XORCheck=(1)xor(0)xor(0)xor(0)xor(1)xor(1)xor(0)xor(0)xor(0)=1

Since the result is different from XORRec, the data are discarded or requested again.

Turn Agreement

In this case, additional information is sent to indicate which devices are the receivers and which are the transmitters during the communication process. The algorithm consists of sending and evaluating a logical value. This is having two or more drones that contain communication devices; all of them have a variable that works as a traffic light or flag. One of them has this variable in the ON state and the others in the OFF state. Only the one that starts with the ON state can write while the others read. As soon as the one that started with the ON state finishes, it changes its flag or semaphore to OFF. When the other members of the team read that the flag of the initial emitter changes to OFF, they initiate a sequence to determine which of them is the next to change their flag to ON. This is repeated cyclically, alternately, or just once. Basically, it is like a polite conversation where each participant asks or rotates their turn to communicate while waiting for the one who is talking to finish.

Generic UART Algorithm

The generic algorithm for the UART communication using the aforementioned operations is as follows. (The specific appearance of each operation is underlined; note that the checksum is a shared operation. To improve this sequence, each process may depend on a timer to accelerate or ensure its execution or just to avoid delays.)

1. The flag or <u>turn</u> of the communication device is checked.

2. If the current turn involves <u>writing,</u>

    - The information to send is divided into 8-bit segments. This information is segmented into two parts: the modulo and the quotient.

- The sum of all the information to send is performed, and from the result is obtained the XOR sum of its binary components.

- Channel availability is verified.

- The information is sent.

- The variables employed for writing are cleaned for their later use.

- The state of the flag is changed to reading.

3. If the turn implies reading,

- The received data is read.

- The XOR check is performed and then it is verified with the received sum.

- If they do not coincide, the designer will prescribe the procedure to follow, which can be from discarding the information to requesting the information again.

- If they coincide, the information is reconstructed with the indicated bit shifting and the OR operation.

- The variables employed for reading are cleaned for their later use.

- The state of the flag is changed to writing.

4. The process continues indefinitely until the user, the code, or the power supply interrupts the communication.

Now that you know about control, signal processing, and UART communications, the next sections will guide you on the ways to code your drone. First, we will show you the available environments for programming your aircraft.

Available Ways to Program a Drone

Currently, there are two ways to code your drones, the GUI and the SDK.

The GUI

A GUI is a simplified and highly visual interface designed for the user with limited or null programming skills.

In this case, this is a graphical user interface. Many of the closed architectures for programming drones have one of them. These closed architectures are characterized by allowing the user to modify basic parameters such as the path to follow, the gains of preloaded controllers, and the rudimentary calibration of sensors and actuators. More specialized tasks are closed to the user. Some of the most common GUIs are Mission Planner and LibrePilot.

The SDK

An SDK is a software development kit. The user is required to know a programming language in all cases.

SDK Level 1

For SDK Level 1, non-specialized users in drone control or robotics can program a drone for purposes other than recreational. The architecture is not completely open, and only allows the user to design some high-level controllers in a way as if the vehicle were a particle able to move in X, Y, Z, and rotate around its Z axis. See Figure 5-9.

One of the best known examples is the Dronekit SDK based on Python. In this type of SDK, the user can only modify the desired references of X, Y, Z, and yaw, or their speeds. Nothing can be done about the thrust force and drone torques, and of course, about the allocation matrix.

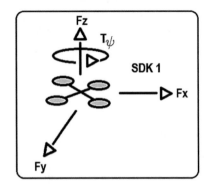

Figure 5-9. *SDK level 1*

SDK Level 2

The architecture in SDK Level 2 is a little more open and allows control of the vehicle at the force-torque level. That is, it allows users who are familiar with drone control and robotics to incorporate their own algorithms and controllers into predesigned vehicles that are compatible with the SDK. One of the best known examples is the Parrot Bebop-autonomy SDK based on C ++, and also a flight mode of the PX4 libraries.

In this type of SDK, the user can only modify the thrust force and the torques of a drone. Nothing can be done about the allocation matrix. See Figure 5-10. As the thrust force and the drone torques are a function of a spatial reference (X, Y, Z, and yaw), this SDK has a higher level than the type 1 SDKs.

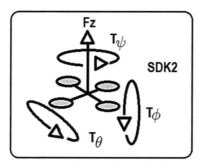

Figure 5-10. *SDK level 2*

SDK Level 3

SDK Level 3 is totally open and allows the user to control the vehicle at motor level; see Figure 5-11. It also allows programming their own communication protocols, incorporating their own sensors, monitoring their parameters of interest, and more. In short, it allows the user to design their own vehicles, even if these vehicles have no precedent. The best known examples are the Ardupilot libraries and the PX4 libraries based on C++.

In this type of SDK, the user must provide the allocation matrix, which is a function of the thrust torques and the forces of the drone, which in turn are a function of the desired position and orientation values. Therefore this kind of SDK has a higher level than type 2 and 1 SDKs.

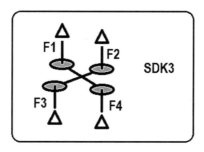

Figure 5-11. *SDK level 3*

You learned where to code, but what about how to code? This is introduced in the next section.

Some Useful Commands Available in Most SDKs

The following are the most employed commands to program aerial drones, and any other type of vehicle in general. They are found in three of the most used SDKs: Ardupilot, PX4, and Dronekit. These commands are presented in a thematic way and are compatible with C ++, C ++ for ROS, and Python, respectively (although these SDKs have variants for other programming languages, operating systems, and computational architectures). A detailed description and examples can be found in the official webpages or in my book *Advanced Robotic Vehicles Programming* described in the reference section in the Appendix. With regard to the aforementioned libraries, it must be indicated that the only one that allows the user to incorporate real-time tasks is Ardupilot, the simplest to use is Dronekit, and the one that has multiple compatibilities because is based on ROS is PX4, which as a disadvantage has limited and not very understandable documentation (at least up to now).

Official Webpages

Ardupilot

```
http://ardupilot.org/dev/docs/apmcopter-programming-libraries.
html
```

Dronekit

```
https://dronekit-python.readthedocs.io/en/latest/
```

Px4

```
https://dev.px4.io/master/en/index.html
```

Input Commands

Ardupilot keyboard input (serial monitor):

```
hal.console->read()
```

Ardupilot remote control input:

```
hal.rcin->read()
```

Dronekit keyboard input:

```
input() or raw_input()
```

Dronekit remote control input:

```
vehicle.channels[channel]
```

PX4 message for keyboard input:

```
PX4_INFO
```

PX4 message for remote control input:

```
manual_control_setpoint.msg
```

Output Commands

Ardupilot user output (serial monitor):

```
hal.console->printf()
```

Dronekit user output:

```
Print
```

PX4 message for user output:

```
PX4_INFO
```

Sensor Commands

Ardupilot analog reading:

```
ch =hal.analogin->channel(channel)
read=ch->voltage_average()
```

Ardupilot digital reading:

```
hal.gpio->read(pin)
```

Ardupilot GPS reading (XYZ positions and velocities):

```
inertial_nav.get_position()
inertial_nav.get_velocity();
```

Ardupilot attitude reading (orientations and angular velocities):

```
ahrs
ins.get_gyro()
```

Ardupilot barometer's altitude:

```
barometer.get_altitude()
```

Dronekit analog reading:
Indirect, for example, analog ports on Raspberry Pi
Dronekit digital reading:
Indirect, for example, digital ports on Raspberry Pi
Dronekit GPS reading (XYZ positions and velocities):

```
vehicle.gps_0
vehicle.velocity
vehicle.location
```

Dronekit attitude reading:

```
vehicle.attitude
```

PX4 message for analog reading:

```
adc_report.msg
```

PX4 message for digital reading:

```
gpio_led start
```

PX4 messages for GPS reading (XYZ positions and velocities):

```
vehicle_gps_position.msg
vehicle_odometry.msg
```

PX4 messages for angular positions and velocities:

```
vehicle_odometry.msg
sensor_combined.msg
```

Actuator Commands

Ardupilot digital writing:

```
hal.gpio->write(pin,value)
```

Ardupilot writing to motors and servos (PWM RC for brushless or brushed motors):

```
hal.rcout->write()
```

Dronekit digital writing:
Indirect, for example digital ports on Raspberry Pi
Dronekit vehicle writing (not to the motors because of the SDK type):

```
send_ned_velocity(vx,vy,vz,time)
```

PX4 message for writing to motors or to the vehicle (PX4 is a SDK type 1, and a type 3):

```
actuator_controls.msg
for writing to a vehicle
```

```
actuator_direct.msg
test_motor.msg
for writing to the motors
```

Signal Processing Commands

Ardupilot noisy signals filtering:

```
LowPassFilter2pfloat filtername(parameters)
filtername.apply(signal);
```

> Dronekit noisy signal filtering:
> Indirect through specialized Python libraries
> PX4 procedure

```
https://dev.px4.io/v1.9.0/en/middleware/modules_estimator.html
```

Communication Commands (Wired and Wireless)

Ardupilot serial communication:

```
hal.uart#->write()
hal.uart#->read()
with #=A,B,C,D
```

> Dronekit serial communication:
> Indirect by using Python libraries and Raspberry ports
> PX4 procedure

```
https://mavlink.io/en/
```

Time Commands

Ardupilot current time, delays, and real-time:

```
hal.scheduler->millis(),micros()
hal.scheduler->delay()
scheduler.run(time)
```

Dronekit current time, delays, and real-time:
Python time commands, for example time.sleep(time)
Real time is not possible by using these libraries
PX4 (there is no way to generate a real time scheduler)

```
hrt_absolute_time();
```

Miscellaneous Commands

Ardupilot onboard memory storage:

```
DataFlash.WriteBlock(package,size)
```

Ardupilot battery monitor:

```
battery.read( )
```

Dronekit memory storage:
Based on Python, for example file.write or MAVLINK commands
Dronekit battery monitor:

```
vehicle.battery
```

PX4 procedure for using the onboard memory:

```
https://dev.px4.io/v1.9.0/en/log/ulog_file_format.html
```

PX4 message for using the battery monitor:

```
battery_status.msg
```

Summary

In this chapter, you learned about the tasks of a drone as well as the basic types of signal processing that are required to use it. The explained signal processing were signal filtering, signal saturation, signal mapping, data casting, and the normalization of redundancies and singularities. All of them can be used with sensors, actuators, and with the communication or control stages. For the communication task, you learned about the usual parts of a high-level UART. Finally, you learned about the four ways to program a drone, including a thematic list of drone commands with an approach based on three of the most used SDKs.

With this chapter, we finished the topics of the book, but we recommend that you continue with the Appendix. It contains topics related to drones such as the estimation of their maximum power and speed limits, sliding modes, differential flatness, a brief on linear control, some alternative ways for representing the orientation of a vehicle, and how you can extend the topics described in this book to other types of aerial vehicles instead of just quadcopters.

APPENDIX

Additional Resources

In this appendix, you will find selected topics such as differential flatness, sliding modes, alternative rotational representations, a brief on linear control, and the way to use these topics with other kinds of aircraft. Furthermore, we've included a section on drone power consumption and consequently motor selection through analytical calculation or through simulation. Each section has its own set of selected references.

Differential Flatness and Multicopters

This is a recurring topic in the study and design of multicopters so for this reason it is briefly explained below.

The differential flatness technique is usually employed in the analysis of non-linear systems. Basically it is a linearization method in which a dynamic or kinematic feedback compensation is applied to transform a non-linear system to a linear one in order to simplify the control design. Designing controllers for linear or linearized systems is generally much simpler than doing it for non-linear systems, starting with the fact that there are many books and tools for linear systems, while for non-linear systems, each case or family of cases is usually a publication or a book by itself.

The most extended works on this topic belong to M. Flies and Sira-Ramirez (see the references).

© Julio Alberto Mendoza-Mendoza, Victor Javier Gonzalez-Villela,
Carlos Fernando Aguilar-Ibañez, Leonardo Fonseca-Ruiz 2021
J. A. Mendoza-Mendoza et al., *Drones to Go*, https://doi.org/10.1007/978-1-4842-6788-2

There are three complicated parts while working with differential flatness:

- The first is to find the linearizing transformation associated with a system (which is not unique and could be partial or non-existent).

- The second is that the linear transformation is valid only for the analyzed model, so if the system has other not-specified phenomena, they will be outside the linearization.

- The third is that the domain of the linearizing transformation may be lower in the operating range than the original system.

For example, for the case of the quadcopter without yaw variation and smooth flight, a linearizing transformation is deduced as follows (observe the imposed restrictions, and the fact that if another flight mode is desired, then another linearizing transformation is required).

The equations for this system in the XYZ space and the roll, pitch, and yaw angles are

$$
\begin{bmatrix} F_{BZ}\left(\sin\theta\cos\psi + \sin\phi\cos\theta\sin\psi\right) \\ F_{BZ}\left(\sin\theta\sin\psi - \sin\phi\cos\theta\cos\psi\right) \\ F_{BZ}\cos\phi\cos\theta \end{bmatrix} + m \begin{bmatrix} 0 \\ 0 \\ -g \end{bmatrix} = m \begin{bmatrix} \ddot{x} \\ \ddot{y} \\ \ddot{z} \end{bmatrix}
$$

$$
\begin{bmatrix} \tau_\phi \\ \tau_\theta \\ \tau_\psi \end{bmatrix} \approx \begin{bmatrix} J_x \ddot{\phi} \\ J_y \ddot{\theta} \\ J_z \ddot{\psi} \end{bmatrix}
$$

With the flight restriction concerning the yaw angle equal to zero, and assuming that inertial values are directly compensated (by control domination), these equations become

$$\begin{bmatrix} F_{BZ} \sin \theta \\ -F_{BZ} \sin \phi \cos \theta \\ F_{BZ} \cos \phi \cos \theta \end{bmatrix} + m \begin{bmatrix} 0 \\ 0 \\ -g \end{bmatrix} = m \begin{bmatrix} \ddot{x} \\ \ddot{y} \\ \ddot{z} \end{bmatrix}$$

$$\begin{bmatrix} \tau_\phi \\ \tau_\theta \\ \tau_\psi \end{bmatrix} \approx \begin{bmatrix} \ddot{\phi} \\ \ddot{\theta} \\ \ddot{\psi} \end{bmatrix}$$

Observe that this is still a nonlinear system.

The following variable changes produce a linear version of the previous system in the space XYZ and alpha, beta, and yaw. In some texts about differential flatness, the new variables usually appear with the names of z1 to zn (in this case, they should be from z1 to z6). We omit this nomenclature to avoid confusion with the vertical Z axis. Observe carefully the equations used to define this change of variables, and also note that in general there are no methods to obtain them (there are some methods based on Lie algebra, but they persist the fact of proposing or identifying a suitable linearizing function). In other words, this change of variables represents by itself an investigation and a research article.

$$F_{BZ} = \frac{m(r_Z + g)}{\cos \phi \cos \theta}$$

$$\alpha = \frac{-\ddot{y}}{\ddot{z}+g} = \frac{F_{BZ} \sin \phi \cos \theta}{F_{BZ} \cos \phi \cos \theta} = \tan \phi$$

$$\beta = \frac{\ddot{x}}{\ddot{z}+g} = \frac{F_{BZ} \sin \theta}{F_{BZ} \cos \phi \cos \theta} = \frac{\tan \theta}{\cos \phi}$$

If we interact with these equations

$$\frac{F_{BZ} \cos \phi \cos \theta}{m} = (r_Z + g)$$

$$(r_Z + g) \beta = \frac{F_{BZ} \cos \phi \cos \theta}{m} \frac{F_{BZ} \sin \theta}{F_{BZ} \cos \phi \cos \theta}$$

$$= \frac{F_{BZ} \sin \theta}{m} = \ddot{x}$$

$$(r_Z + g) \alpha = \frac{F_{BZ} \cos \phi \cos \theta}{m} \frac{\sin \phi}{\cos \phi}$$

$$= \frac{F_{BZ} \sin \phi \cos \theta}{m} = -\ddot{y}$$

by obtaining the time derivatives of alpha and beta as many times as required (in this case, only two times in order to obtain their dynamics or acceleration behavior). Note that the original control terms emerge in the second derivatives, which is a distinctive behavior of the differential flatness linearization (at least with this system).

$$\dot{\alpha} = \left(\tan^2 \phi + 1 \right) \dot{\phi}$$

$$\ddot{\alpha} = \left(\tan^2 \phi + 1 \right) \ddot{\phi} + 2 \left(\tan \phi \right) \left(\tan^2 \phi + 1 \right) \dot{\phi}^2$$

$$= \frac{\ddot{\phi}}{\cos^2 \phi} + \frac{2 (\tan \phi) \dot{\phi}^2}{\cos^2 \phi} = \frac{1}{\cos^2 \phi} \left[\tau_\phi + 2 (\tan \phi) \dot{\phi}^2 \right] = r_\alpha$$

$$\dot{\beta} = \frac{1}{\cos \phi \cos^2 \theta} \dot{\theta} + \frac{\tan \theta \tan \phi}{\cos \phi} \dot{\phi}$$

$$\ddot{\beta} = \ddot{\theta} \frac{1}{\cos \phi \cos^2 \theta} + \ddot{\phi} \frac{\tan \theta \tan \phi}{\cos \phi} + \frac{2 \tan \theta}{\cos^2 \theta \cos \phi} \dot{\theta}^2 + \frac{2 \tan \phi}{\cos^2 \theta \cos \phi} \dot{\phi} \dot{\theta} + \left(\frac{\tan \theta}{\cos^3 \phi} + \frac{\tan \theta \tan^2 \phi}{\cos \phi} \right) \dot{\phi}^2$$

$$\ddot{\beta} = \tau_\theta \frac{1}{\cos \phi \cos^2 \theta} + \tau_\phi \frac{\tan \theta \tan \phi}{\cos \phi} + \frac{2 \tan \theta}{\cos^2 \theta \cos \phi} \dot{\theta}^2 + \frac{2 \tan \phi}{\cos^2 \theta \cos \phi} \dot{\phi} \dot{\theta} + \left(\frac{\tan \theta}{\cos^3 \phi} + \frac{\tan \theta \tan^2 \phi}{\cos \phi} \right) \dot{\phi}^2$$

$$= r_\beta$$

In this way, the linearized equations are obtained:

$$\ddot{z} = r_z$$
$$\ddot{x} = (r_z + g)\beta$$
$$\ddot{y} = -(r_z + g)\alpha$$
$$\ddot{\beta} = r_\beta$$
$$\ddot{\alpha} = r_\alpha$$
$$\ddot{\psi} = \tau_\psi$$

Note also that a new control space is used, thus, while the original equations were controlled with

$$F_{BZ}, \tau_\phi, \tau_\theta, \tau_\psi$$

the new controllers are

$$r_Z, r_\alpha, r_\beta, \tau_\psi$$

This transformation is linearizing with respect to the new space of variables, and all the non-linearities were retransmitted to the new control elements. Therefore, they must be compensated at the moment of being injected into the original forces and torques. The easy part will be to design the control for the equivalent linear system; the difficult part will be to compensate the original torques and forces with respect to the new control variables (finally, these are the forces and torques that must be injected into the real system).

The other problem here is that this linear transformation, due to the properties of the arctangent function (even atan2 variants), is only valid while the angles are inside this range of values (although the flight conditions by themselves already indicate that they should not happen).

$\theta, \phi \in (-\pi/2, \pi/2)$. And as said before, the biggest problem is that if the model changes (for example, in conditions where the yaw is no longer intended to be zero), this linear transformation is no longer valid for the new model.

This linear transformation and the rest of the design can be found in Aguilar's article in the reference section. The signs differ because in that article they use a sense of rotation opposite to the one we use in this book, but for illustrative purposes this does not affect the objective of this section. Even more, it encourages you to be careful with your angular conventions.

Another possible linearizing transformation (which does not restrict the yaw operation to a value equal to zero) is given by the rudder-guide vector control equations of the drone as presented in the corresponding chapter of this book, and in Nguyen's article indicated in the reference section and also the geometric controller.

Sliding Modes and Multicopters

The sliding modes are not a linearizing transformation, but a robust control method. See Fridman's article in the reference section about the fifth generation of the sliding mode controllers for a historic context. In sliding modes, a kind of double control loop is established. That is, a high-frequency control loop regulates a sliding surface, and a slower control loop regulates the behavior associated when this surface is reached (for example, a spring damper system or PD).

The sliding modes in terms of the loop that regulate the sliding surface work with signum functions, and this is where their advantages and disadvantages lie.

Concerning the amplitude effect, the loop that regulates the sliding surface behaves like a high-gain bounded control (a straight line with a high slope, or ideally infinite). Therefore, the control is robust against amplitude variations or perturbations. In Figure A-1, the sign function behaves in a bounded way as an infinite slope. Also, the fact of being bounded makes it compatible with the motors of a system that physically have maximum and minimum values (for example, minimum and maximum values of speed and torque).

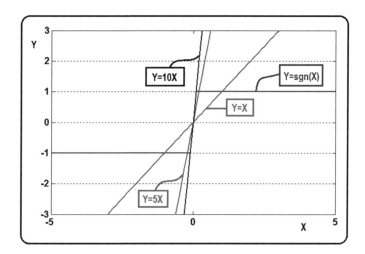

Figure A-1. *Comparison among a sign function and straight lines with high slope*

Regarding the effect in frequency, the shape like a step of the sign function, that implies to be in two places at the same time, also implies a very fast control. In Figure A-1, if the X axis were associated with the time, the change at the Y axis from -1 to 1 would be practically instantaneous, or equivalent to say that the function is in two places simultaneously. This is really good against fast disturbances until the control must interact with the motors that generally have slower response times (this interaction tends to produce destructive high frequency effects called chattering).

Therefore, the sliding modes are ideal for use with fast actuators, or if they are used with mechanical systems (which have a very slow action compared to the electrical and electronic systems), it is appropriate to use higher order sliding modes, or techniques based on them, such as the supertwisting method, or alternatives to the sliding modes called bounded input controllers, where the sign function effect is approximated by sigmoids or sigmoidal functions (these functions have these names because they look like a letter s, which is derived from the Greek letter sigma).

A simple example to understand this topic is the following. Suppose that we want to control the yaw angle of a multicopter. We chose this variable because in addition to being independent in most of the multicopters, it usually has one inertial element to be compensated (at least in the simplified model).

$$J_z \ddot{\psi} = \tau_\psi$$

The following sliding surface is proposed, the nomenclature of *s* is because of the word *sliding*. Observe that the sliding surface is a function of a quasiPD control dynamic (we could say that the derivative gain is equal to 1). Soon you will see why we selected this surface. Observe that in this case and in a lot of articles and books, the error definition is inverted with respect the rest of the error definitions previously defined. However, when the control is injected into the rest of the equations, it is made by introducing a negative sign. In short, you must not worry about your error definition but respect your Lyapunov conditions and other negativity and positivity criteria (eigenvalues or root locus, for example). In the end, these methods will introduce the required signs into your controller:

$$s = K_p e + \dot{e}$$
$$e = \psi - \psi_d$$
$$\dot{e} = \dot{\psi} - \dot{\psi}_d$$
$$\ddot{e} = \ddot{\psi} - \ddot{\psi}_d$$

And now we carry out a Lyapunov stability analysis, but unlike the examples seen in the corresponding section, the Lyapunov function is not directly dependent on the error but on the sliding surface:

$$V = \frac{s^2}{2} \geq 0$$
$$\dot{V} = s\dot{s} \leq 0$$
$$\dot{V} = s\dot{s} = (s)(K_p\dot{e} + \ddot{e})$$

Remember that the second derivative of the error is also a function of the yaw acceleration, and consequently we can introduce the original system in order to design the torque control:

$$\ddot{e} = \ddot{\psi} - \ddot{\psi}_d = \frac{\tau_\psi}{J_z} - \ddot{\psi}_d$$

$$\dot{V} = s\dot{s} = (s)\left(K_p\dot{e} + \frac{\tau_\psi}{J_z} - \ddot{\psi}_d\right)$$

in this way, if

$$\tau_\psi = J_z\left(-K_p\dot{e} + \ddot{\psi}_d - Gsgn(s)\right)$$
$$\dot{V} = -sGsgn(s) = -G\left|s\right| \leq 0$$

where G is a positive gain and sgn is the sign function. Again, observe how the combination of signs and the error definitions does not contradict our previous controllers. We decided to show you in this way because in a lot of papers you will find both approaches (the error definition inverted with an opposite sign in the controller), so it is required that you understand that they are the same.

Remember that when a value is multiplied by its corresponding sign, the result is an absolute value, and because this is always positive or zero, our Lyapunov derivative becomes negative semi-definite. Finally, using the Barbalat lemma, it is concluded that the minimum value of our Lyapunov candidate function is zero when the surface s is also equal to zero. This implies the following:

$$s = 0$$
$$s = K_p e + \dot{e} = 0$$

when s is equal to zero, the slowest dynamics, which is the error control dynamics, behaves in this case as an exponential system that tends to zero. Note that the dynamics of the surface s are faster due to the use of the sign function, whose effect is practically instantaneous with respect to the straight-line behavior of the error control dynamics.

$$e \rightarrow 0$$
$$\psi \rightarrow \psi_d$$

Finally, the control to be injected into the yaw torque is simply the following (compare this controller with those previously developed in the preceding sections):

$$\tau_\psi = J_z\left(-K_p\dot{e} + \ddot{\psi}_d - Gsgn(K_p e + \dot{e})\right)$$

One of the main complexities of the sliding modes, in addition to the reduction of the chattering effects and their stabilization times, is the design of their sliding surfaces.

They are called sliding surfaces because when they are equal to zero, if we draw the error plane we have what is shown in Figure A-2 (or hyperspace, depending on the number of variables that constitute the sliding surface, which in this case lies in a plane).

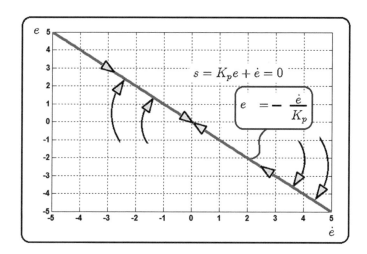

Figure A-2. *Sliding surface behavior*

In other words, if the error and its derivative start at a point outside of the sliding surface (in this case, the straight line), they are attracted to that surface (the sign function effect takes care of this). Once the sliding surface is reached, the error behaves like a first order system that tends to zero. Other sliding mode control applications to multicopters, in more than just one variable which in this case was the yaw angle, or in all of their variables, are available in the reference section.

Helicopters, Omnicopters, Airplanes, and More

In a similar way to the robotic arms, which have a generic equation that describes them (available through the Euler-Lagrange method) and that is used for designing their generic control laws, observe the similarity between this equation and a mass (in this case, an inertia matrix M), spring (in this case, the gravity vector G), and damper (in this case, a Coriolis matrix) system:

$$M(q)\ddot{q} + C(q,\dot{q})\dot{q} + G(q) = \tau$$

In this kind of robot, each particular case modifies the generic equation in a way that alters the mobility and transmissibility of the robots depending on their motors' position. It is worth mentioning that in some particular cases, other terms are added to improve their performance. Notice that this is really a vector equations system and not just a simple equation.

Considering the above, there is also a set of generic equations to model and design flight controllers for aircraft (especially if they are small-size units). Also, keep in mind that there exist conditions to transform the system of equations of an aircraft to the general equation of a robot previously indicated and vice versa.

These equations are at the translational level (kinematics and dynamics)

$$\dot{\xi} = v$$
$$m\dot{v} = mge_3 + Rf$$

and at the rotational level (kinematics and dynamics)

$$\dot{R} = RS(\omega)$$
$$J\dot{\omega} = \tau - \omega \times J\omega$$

with

$$e_3 = \begin{bmatrix} 0 \\ 0 \\ 1 \end{bmatrix}$$

So the question is, How do the implementation and simulation change for each type of aircraft? And the answer is as follows:

1. Each particular case changes the propulsion matrix that is influenced by the propellers, deflectors, or any other vectorization mechanism including drag surfaces such as wings. In some cases, the allocation matrix no longer has constant values and varies according to the action of a surface or servomotor. This makes it necessary to also control these surfaces or vectorization mechanisms, and not only the aircraft. That is why it becomes so complex to control a fixed-wing aircraft such as an airplane, since its deflection surfaces are many and they also have many restrictions in their operations.

2. Each particular case modifies the term RF (or the gravitational term if the analysis is carried out in the vehicle frame), which even in a simple quadcopter can imply the presence or exclusion of many terms depending on the type of flight to be performed (three-dimensionality, aggressiveness, smoothness, etc). Here, it is possible to perform certain omissions by linear approximations or keep the entire set of equations (for example, to perform stunts).

3. Each particular case may require the inclusion of additional terms, such as the wind drag in an aircraft with fixed wings and non-vertical take-off, or their omission for small vertical take-off drones and slow flight aircraft. Also, in this type of horizontal take-off aircraft, the thrust and lift forces (notice that in a quadcopter they are the same) are entities with other types of interdependence with respect to those

that exist in vertical take-off drones. In this way, it is frequent to see the addition of more aerodynamic effects in their basic models.

4. Each particular case may have a different frame for developing its equations. This way, it is necessary to choose if the analysis is carried out for convenience in the world frame, the fixed frame, or in a mixed frame (as in the case of multicopters), and this will depend on the flight convenience for each aircraft.

5. You must carry out an analysis of the equivalent forces and torques at your vehicle's center of interest, by means of which the forces and moments of each motor are transferred to said point (as previously explained, this is the way in which the propulsion or allocation matrix is built).

These five points are summarized in two concepts: omnidirectionality and thrust-vectoring. Both can be consulted in my other book and other texts available in the reference section.

The presence of common equations in such different aircraft should not surprise you. Basically it is due to the fact that the analysis, design, and control of an aerial vehicle is carried out in a point of interest. This point of design can be the center of gravity, masses, buoyancy, geometric, or even a variant point if the system, its symmetries, and its tasks allow it.

The conclusion is that the kinematics and the dynamics, both translational and rotational, are generic for almost any aerial drone. What you must verify is the allocation analysis, which relates the driving elements with the vehicle's design point as well as the vehicle's flight mode, which affects the degree of influence of the RF and gravitational terms, and the inclusion of additional terms that become perceptible during the flight (for example, the drag force and its effect on the wings of an airplane).

Other Rotational Representations for Drones

In this book, two types of rotational representations are used: one based on rotation matrices, and one based on Euler angles (the Tait-Bryan type). However, there are other useful representations (homogeneous matrices, screw theory, geometric algebra, exponential or logarithmic representations, quaternions, etc).

The use of quaternions is deduced as follows (it is explicitly included in this text because, along with the rotation matrices and the Euler angles, this is one of the three most common approaches for attitude representation with drones and aircraft). Given a vector p0, it can be rotated by using any of the following ways (its destination vector is called p1):

$$p_1 = Rp_0$$

$$p_1 = qp_0q^{-1}$$

where q is a unit quaternion and R is a rotation matrix. The quaternion is defined as

$$q = a + bi + cj + dk$$

and it is a unit quaternion because

$$a^2 + b^2 + c^2 + d^2 = 1$$

In the previous equations, it is said that a is the scalar or real part, and the elements b, c, and d are the vector or imaginary part.

A rotation matrix and a quaternion are related in this way:

$$R = \begin{bmatrix} a^2 + b^2 - c^2 - d^2 & 2bc - 2ad & 2bd + 2ac \\ 2bc + 2ad & a^2 - b^2 + c^2 - d^2 & 2cd - 2ab \\ 2bd - 2ac & 2cd + 2ab & a^2 - b^2 - c^2 + d^2 \end{bmatrix}$$

Just as we previously found a kinematic relationship between a rotation matrix and the angular velocity of a body, an equivalent way of finding the relationship between a unit quaternion and the angular velocity of a body can be deduced (and of course we will find some similarities with the procedure described for the rotation matrices). For the original procedure, see `www.euclideanspace.com/physics/kinematics/ angularvelocity/QuaternionDifferentiation2.pdf`.

Suppose an initial vector called R0 rotated by a quaternion q(t). We call the destination vector Rt:

$$R_t = q(t)R_0 q^{-1}(t)$$

Remember that in this case the R letters do not represent a rotation matrix but vectors. However, they are a convenient notation because certain terms will look similar to the kinematic reasoning used for rotation matrices. Additionally, the method described here is scalable for rotation matrices, remembering that they are a concatenation of three vectors (think of the example of the **noa** vectors we used in the geometric control section).

Deriving the above equation with respect to the time (note that R0 is a constant vector):

$$\frac{dR_t}{dt} = \frac{dq(t)}{dt}R_0 q^{-1}(t) + q(t)R_0 \frac{dq^{-1}(t)}{dt}$$

Solving in terms of Rt:

$$q(t)^{-1}R_t = R_0 q^{-1}(t)$$
$$R_t q(t) = q(t)R_0$$

$$\frac{dR_t}{dt} = \frac{dq(t)}{dt}R_0 q^{-1}(t) + q(t)R_0\frac{dq^{-1}(t)}{dt}$$
$$\frac{dR_t}{dt} = \frac{dq(t)}{dt}q(t)^{-1}R_t + R_t q(t)\frac{dq^{-1}(t)}{dt}$$

Since q (t) is a unit quaternion, it is also true that

$$q(t)q(t)^{-1} = 1$$

Therefore, deriving this equation with respect to the time, we have

$$\frac{dq(t)}{dt}q(t)^{-1} + q(t)\frac{dq(t)^{-1}}{dt} = 0$$
$$\frac{dq(t)}{dt}q(t)^{-1} = -q(t)\frac{dq(t)^{-1}}{dt}$$

Here the equations resemble the property of a rotation matrix multiplied by its transposed matrix previously used in this book. Solving the previous result in terms of the inverse of q (t), the following is obtained:

$$\frac{dR_t}{dt} = \frac{dq(t)}{dt}q(t)^{-1}R_t + R_t q(t)\frac{dq^{-1}(t)}{dt}$$
$$\frac{dR_t}{dt} = \frac{dq(t)}{dt}q(t)^{-1}R_t - R_t\frac{dq(t)}{dt}q(t)^{-1}$$

By doing the following change of variables, we have

$$\frac{dq(t)}{dt}q(t)^{-1} = p(t)$$
$$\frac{dR_t}{dt} = p(t)R_t - R_t p(t)$$

Next, we will use two facts.

1. As mentioned, if R0 is a vector, the result of its rotation called Rt will also be another vector. Consequently, the time derivative of Rt will be a vector or a quaternion of the vector type.

2. The terms pRt and Rtp produce a vector only if p is also a vector-type quaternion (with a scalar part equal to zero). There is an identity for vector-type quaternions that indicates the following (note its resemblance to the skew symmetric matrix used for rotation matrices):

$$p \times q = \tfrac{1}{2}(pq - qp)$$

In this case,

$$p = p(t)$$
$$q = R_t$$

so

$$\frac{dR_t}{dt} = 2\left[p(t) \times R_t\right]$$

On the other hand, we have the following equation that relates the linear velocity with the angular velocity at the vector level:

$$\frac{dR_t}{dt} = \omega \times R_t$$

Notice that in the case of the rotation matrix, a similar term appears, but instead of the cross product, it uses an antisymmetric matrix that contains the terms of the angular velocity. You must observe that a way to express a cross product as already indicated in the previous sections is by multiplying by a skew or antisymmetric matrix.

From the above,

$$2p(t) = \omega$$

$$2\frac{dq(t)}{dt}q(t)^{-1} = \omega$$

The kinematic relationship that we were looking for is finally

$$\frac{dq(t)}{dt} = \tfrac{1}{2}q(t)\omega$$

Note the similarity with the equations of a rotation matrix.
Developing the quaternion product as follows:

$$q_1 q_2 = (q_{1s}q_{2s} - q_{1v} \cdot q_{2v}) + (q_{1s}q_{2v} + q_{2s}q_{1v} + q_{1v} \times q_{2v})$$

where the letters s and v represent the scalar and vector parts of each quaternion.

If you remember that w is a vector-type quaternion (without scalar components), we have that

$$q(t)\omega = (q_s\omega_s - q_v \cdot \omega_v) + (q_s\omega_v + \omega_s q_v + q_v \times \omega_v)$$
$$= (-q_v \cdot \omega_v) + (q_s\omega_v + q_v \times \omega_v)$$

Developing these terms, the following expressions used in multicopters or other vehicles are obtained:

$$\frac{dq(t)}{dt}_{(4x1)} = \frac{1}{2}\begin{bmatrix} -q_v \cdot \omega_{(1x1)} \\ q_s\omega_{(3x1)} + q_v \times \omega_{(3x1)} \end{bmatrix}$$

$$= \frac{1}{2}\begin{bmatrix} -q_v \cdot \omega \\ [q_sI_3 + S(q_v)]\omega \end{bmatrix} = \frac{1}{2}\begin{bmatrix} \begin{pmatrix} -q_v^T \\ [q_sI_3 + S(q_v)] \end{pmatrix}\omega \end{bmatrix}$$

where

$$I_3 = \begin{bmatrix} 1 & 0 & 0 \\ 0 & 1 & 0 \\ 0 & 0 & 1 \end{bmatrix}$$

In summary, Figure A-3 shows the three generic equations of aerial vehicles. Notice that only the part related to the rotational kinematics changes and consequently the controller design. This can be seen when you compare the geometric control based on rotation matrices with the controllers based on Euler angles previously explained in this book.

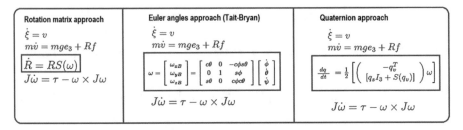

Figure A-3. *Usual orientation approaches for drones*

The preference for an attitude representation with respect to the others has advantages and disadvantages. Table A-1 shows a comparative description among the three approaches mentioned here.

Table A-1. *Usual Angular Representations for Drones and Their Characteristics*

Representation	Euler angles	Rotation matrix	Quaternions
Minimum number of elements to be used for a three-dimensional representation	3	9 (a 3x3 matrix has 9 elements)	4
Mathematical tool	Linear algebra	Linear algebra	Quaternion algebra (and of course complex numbers)
Interpolation and extrapolation (path planning)	Direct	With orthonormality restrictions	They are "simple" if you know the necessary mathematics, but they have their special methods (the slerp, for example).
Redundancies	They have due to the use of geometric functions, and they are partially avoidable with the use of atan2 functions. They also present the Gimbal lock effect.	They have due to the use of geometric functions. They also present the Gimbal lock effect.	By symmetry. A quaternion representation can have two associated values of orientation. To overcome this drawback, octonions are used.

(*continued*)

Table A-1. (*continued*)

Representation	Euler angles	Rotation matrix	Quaternions
Additional information	There are different conventions and uses. They have an ambiguity of value either from 360 to 0 degrees or from -180 to 180 degrees, and also their equivalent in radians.	There is also a considerable range of conventions, but if they are extended to the so-called homogeneous transformation matrix, they can also be used to indicate pose (position, rotation) and additionally scaling and perspective.	They are used as the basis for understanding a powerful computational tool called geometric algebra.
Drones applications	Smooth flights with small or moderate angular motion	Aggressive and acrobatic flights with severe angular variations	Aggressive and acrobatic flights with severe angular variations

Remember that there are ways to convert the attitude (orientation) values among these representations. An example was given in order to convert from rotation matrices to Euler angles in Chapter 4.

A Brief on Linear Control

The controllers studied in this book consist of two parts:

- A direct compensation of the non-linear elements of the system, which is a drawback if there are unmodeled dynamics. This could be optional if the next component has a dominant value.

- A desired dynamics injected through a "robust" linear controller.

You also saw that in some linear flight modes the compensation part is often omitted and dominated by the robust linear control.

For any of the previous cases, the objective of the control design is to deal with a linear or partially linearized version of the system (in a closed loop, which implies the system interacting with the controller).

A linear system satisfies two properties: inner or addition, and outer or scalar multiplication. In general, this is related to lines, planes, cubes, hypercubes, and so on. That is, this kind of scalar or vector equations:

$$y_{(1\times1)} = ax + b$$

In general,

$$y_{(1\times1)} = a_0 x_0 + a_1 x_1 + a_n x_n + b$$

Or in matrix form,

$$\dot{x}_{(n\times1)} = A_{(n\times n)} x_{(n\times1)} + B_{(n\times p)} u_{(p\times1)}$$

Observe that the y notation is used for the first two equations in order for you to quickly associate them with your geometry courses on the topics of straight lines and planes, but in the vector form, the usual notation found in control of linear systems is employed (read again the section on state space variables to remember the reason).

Also note that vector and matrix dimension suffixes are included as a reference for you to realize the type of entities that are used (scalars, vectors, and matrices).

Keep in mind that there are systems with the previous representations that are not necessarily linear (see the bilinear systems described in the papers of Sira-Ramirez).

Once we have a linearized system or a linear one in a closed loop with the injected control, a lot of tools are available to ensure that said system achieves a desired behavior. Since for each tool there are books or series of books, we will only mention these tools and indicate some useful references about them (see the reference section):

1. Analysis of differential equations, which implies solving directly the equations through different analytical methods for ODEs and then evaluating for a particular solution

2. Numerical analysis, where the equations are solved by using a numerical method (a simulation)

3. Poles and zeros analysis, which is an extension of the first method, which makes use of the Laplace transform

4. Graphical analysis of poles and zeros, which uses different techniques such as Bode, Nyquist, and Nichols plots

5. Modern control analysis by using linear algebra where, in this case, matrix equivalents of the poles and zeros are used through the properties of eigenvalues, determinants, and in general positivity and negativity of matrices

6. Modern control analysis by using the linear Lyapunov method, where in this case a simplified condition of the Lyapunov stability is verified (Lyapunov stability of linear systems)

7.   Intelligent analysis, which consists of using fuzzy logic, or neural networks, or genetic algorithms, or any other method used in artificial intelligence

As you can see, there is a huge variety for designing linear control techniques, and even within the ones described, there are a lot of variants. For this reason, it is relevant the attempt to convert the required system or its closed loop form into a total or a partial linear equivalent.

About the Power Consumption and Maximum Flight Features of a Drone

This section addresses topics on aerodynamics and very specifically the concept of drag. Unlike the rest of the book, given that we want to estimate the maximum speed and forces, and that they are modified by the vehicle's environment and design, it is necessary to consider some aerodynamic concepts whose effects on the control can be significative, but it is assumed that the control and specifically the motors are robust enough to deal with them.

This section will be explained with a quadcopter, but you should be able to modify this procedure for other types of aircraft.

Drag is the tendency of the environment to slow down the motion of a vehicle. In the case of aircraft, two models are handled: one quadratic (also called inertial) and one linear (also called viscous).

The complete drag model of an aircraft can be deduced with the Buckingham Pi theorem. Its deduction and description can be found on the Web, the French MOOC in the reference section, or the book *Fluid Mechanics* by F. White. These equations have two modes of operation and they are ruled by the Reynolds number.

- The first is when the speeds are low (basically when they are in magnitude less or equal to 1). In this case, the drag behavior is linear because the quadratic effect becomes negligible (the square of a number less or equal than 1 will be a smaller number or 1). This is also true for drones without exotic shapes and if the environment is non-turbulent air.

- The second is when the speeds are high (when in magnitude they exceed 1). In this case, the dominant behavior is the quadratic one (both the linear and the quadratic models are present, but the quadratic behavior dominates over the linear action).

In the case of the theoretical calculation of the maximum speed values, we must use a quadratic model because we want to know the maximum speed performance of an aircraft, and this will generally be a high value.

However, for simulating smooth flight operations where the drone will not be pushed to its limit, the linear approximation can be used. Note that if the quadratic approximation is used in the simulator, more restrictions will be required, including a difficult control tuning.

We will start with the theoretical calculation and then we will continue with the estimation through simulations.

Power is defined as the force multiplied by the speed. This is valid both at the translational and the rotational levels, evidently in the last case the linear speed is changed by the angular speed and the force by the torque. To get an idea of what power implies, a modern light bulb consumes around 25W, while a single motor of a small drone can easily consume 100W.

Now, it will be assumed that the angular velocities with respect to the horizontal axes are dependent on the effect of the horizontal linear velocities (at least this is valid for a quadcopter). This way just the linear velocities will be considered. This assumption is not made in the vertical axis because the motors, in addition to their combined thrust, also provide a combined torque. It is assumed that the aircraft has a symmetry such that it only presents inertial components in the main axes.

With these considerations, three types of power can be calculated according to the aircraft mobility. Observe that we only analyze the power consumed by the kinetic (K) and potential (U) energies.

1. Power consumed by dynamic flight or motion in four degrees of freedom (three translations and one rotation; remember that the planar translations are dependent on two rotations, but in this case we are interested in the power required to achieve the translational displacements):

$$P \approx \frac{dK}{dt} + \frac{dU}{dt} = \frac{d(mgz)}{dt} + \frac{d(\frac{1}{2}mv^2 + \frac{1}{2}J\omega^2)}{dt} = mg\frac{dz}{dt} + mv\frac{dv}{dt} + J\omega\frac{d\omega}{dt}$$

$$\approx \frac{mgz}{t} + \frac{mv^2}{t} + \frac{J\omega_z^2}{t} = mgv_z + ma \cdot v + J_{zz}\alpha_z\omega_z = F_{mg}v_z + F_a \cdot v + \tau_z\omega_z$$

$$v = \begin{bmatrix} v_x & v_y & v_z \end{bmatrix}$$
$$a = \begin{bmatrix} a_x & a_y & a_z \end{bmatrix}$$

2. Power consumed by hovering or floating flight, in which the vehicle floats static on the air (here the vehicle deals with the force of gravity, therefore an RMS effect of the vertical speed must be considered):

$$P \approx mgv_{zRMS} + \tau_z\omega_z$$

$$v \approx \begin{bmatrix} 0 & 0 & 0 \end{bmatrix}$$
$$a \approx \begin{bmatrix} 0 & 0 & 0 \end{bmatrix}$$

3. Power consumed by mixed flight, in which the vehicle remains stationary at a fixed altitude, but having X and Y planar displacements:

$$P \approx mgv_{zRMS} + ma_h \cdot v_h + \tau_z \omega_z$$
$$v_h = \begin{bmatrix} v_x & v_y & 0 \end{bmatrix}$$
$$a_h = \begin{bmatrix} a_x & a_y & 0 \end{bmatrix}$$

Observe that the speeds and accelerations are measured in the fixed frame, with the exception of the angular velocity that is already measured in the body frame. In the case of requiring the maximum values of speed and force, they will be determined with respect to the body frame, so these frames must be related by using the kinematic equations indicated in the previous chapters. Regarding the power, this is an invariant quantity no matter the frame used.

A simulation can be carried out for determining the speed values, then making the corresponding multiplications with the forces and torques, and finally calculating an approximation of the required power.

The task to be done will indicate which of the previous powers is higher. A lot of brushless electric motors that are widely used with drones usually have a worst-case efficiency of 80%, so it is convenient to select a set of motors such that the power of the motors exceed the calculated mechanical power in the following proportion (the calculated mechanical power must be less than the electrical power provided by the motors):

$$P_m = 1.25P$$

On the other hand, the electric power of the motors satisfies the following approximation:

$$P_m = V_m I_m$$

This is basically the voltage consumed by the current consumed. In most of the brushless motors, Vm has a constant value (the speed varies according to a PWM signal, but it is always taken from the same voltage value, for example 12V), so it is convenient to search in a motor catalog for ones whose current multiplied by said voltage provides the necessary power, and also check if these motors provide the necessary force and torque (this is usually available in their datasheets). In a drone, the required voltage is usually the same for all of the motors, so the current required must be multiplied by the number of motors to use.

As you can notice, the estimated power depends on the maximum values of forces, torques, linear speeds, and angular speeds of the vehicle. How are they calculated or approximated?

The procedure is as follows (remember that the selected motors must be able to achieve the required forces and torques as a group). The propellers are designed in such a way that their maximum thrust force is achieved with the vehicle in vertical motion (this is the case of the multicopters; you should be careful with this point for other types of aircraft). It is assumed that the dominant force is the vehicle's weight, so you must select a set of engines that can lift the drone. That is, Fbz must be at least greater than the weight of the aircraft. If the motors are the same and there are four of them, this implies that each motor must contribute a quarter of the value of Fbz. If you want other behavior in your vehicle, you must consider the effects that we have omitted (for example, non-perpendicular thrust components to the frame of the vehicle).

With respect to the maximum translational speeds (you can find the basis at `https://klsin.bpmsg.com/how-fast-can-a-quadcopter-fly/`), they are calculated as follows.

The simplest is the maximum vertical speed. We start with the translational equation in Z. Note that in this case we use the set of equations seen from the body frame (this is how it is required by this problem since we want to know the top speeds achieved by the vehicle at its own frame). The original equation presented previously in this book was developed in the world frame. To transform this equation into the body frame, what we must project is the effect of gravity, since the thrust force will always be present on the vertical axis of the drone:

$$F_{BZ} - mg \cos\phi \cos\theta = m\ddot{z} = m\dot{v}_z$$

The top speed in said axis is achieved with the assumption that the vehicle moves completely parallel to the ground, so

$$\phi = \theta = 0$$
$$F_{BZ} - mg = m\dot{v}_z$$

As the speed of a body is modified by the environment in which the body moves, we will include some aerodynamic characteristics in the design (air density, vehicle shape, and drag coefficient).

With such considerations, the previous equation seen from the body frame is modified with the following term known as drag force to be (also shown in Figure A-4):

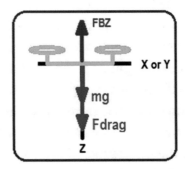

Figure A-4. *A quadcopter with vertical motion and the forces acting on it*

$$F_{BZ} - mg - F_{drag} = m\dot{v}_z$$
$$F_{BZ} - mg - \frac{\rho}{2}C_d A v_z^2 = m\dot{v}_z$$

where rho is the density of the fluid (in this case the air), Cd is the drag coefficient, and A is the effective area of the quadcopter. As the maximization of a quantity is achieved by setting its derivative equal to zero, we make this equality (also the minimization, but in a physical sense, and since the minimum velocity of the drone is zero, here it is considered as a maximization). Note that a quadratic drag model is used because we want to calculate a maximum velocity, that in general is greater than one, and this implies the dominance of the quadratic model.

$$F_{BZ} - mg - \frac{\rho}{2}C_d A v_z^2 = 0$$

From this equation, the velocity must be solved:

$$v_z = \sqrt{2\frac{F_{BZ} - mg}{\rho C_d A}}$$

And the vehicle's vertical top speed is obtained. The rho and A values generally do not represent a problem because rho is usually equal to 1.2 kg/m³ and the area is calculated with the following approximation (also see Figure A-5; https://rechneronline.de/pi/X-shape.php):

$$A \approx 2lb \sin \vartheta - x^2 \sin \vartheta + 4\pi r^2$$

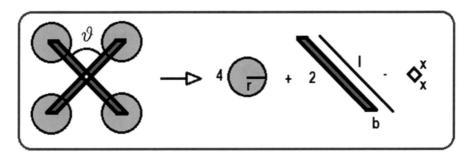

Figure A-5. *The approximate area of a quadcopter*

The problem is the drag coefficient. Some designers from experience establish it as 1.3, while others use auxiliary formulas, as established for example in the Quan Quan book in its section on the drag model. Finally, remember that if the aircraft is a quadcopter in which is assumed that its four motors are the same or that they have similar characteristics, FBz is the sum of the individual thrusts:

$$v_z = \sqrt{2\frac{4F_{mz} - mg}{\rho C_d A}}$$

Regarding the maximum horizontal speed, since the horizontal motion is divided into the X and Y axes, it is convenient to analyze this problem in just one axis (for obtaining a maximum horizontal component). In this way, we avoid a complicated analysis concerning the roll and pitch angles in the body frame, and we only use the scenario in Figure A-6.

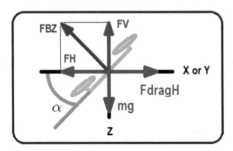

Figure A-6. *A quadcopter with horizontal motion and the forces acting on it*

With the thrust vector, its horizontal and vertical components, and also the gravity vector, we can make a Pythagorean relationship:

$$F_{BZ}^2 = F_V^2 + F_H^2$$

$$F_H = \sqrt{F_{BZ}^2 - F_V^2}$$

Also note that in order to simplify and maximize the drag, this is considered only in the horizontal axis, assuming that in the vertical axis the vehicle only floats. Otherwise, we must consider vertical drag:

$$F_V = mg$$

$$F_H = \sqrt{F_{BZ}^2 - (mg)^2}$$

As per Figure A-6, by analyzing the motion in the horizontal axis we have

$$F_H - F_{dragH} = m\dot{v}_H$$

$$\sqrt{F_{BZ}^2 - (mg)^2} - \frac{\rho}{2}C_dA_Hv_H^2 = m\dot{v}_H$$

where

$$A_H = A\sin\alpha$$

In this case, alpha is the vehicle's inclination, which is related to the roll, pitch, and yaw. For simplicity and in order to calculate a maximum speed value, it can be assumed that the motion occurs around one axis. It is also assumed that the vehicle does not rotate around its vertical axis (yaw angle equal to zero). Therefore, the roll or the pitch angles can be used indistinctly as alpha. Maximizing (making the derivative equal to zero and solving for the velocity), we have

$$\sqrt{F_{BZ}^2 - (mg)^2} - \frac{\rho}{2}C_dA_Hv_H^2 = 0$$

$$v_H = \sqrt{\frac{2}{\rho C_d A_H}\sqrt{F_{BZ}^2 - (mg)^2}}$$

APPENDIX   ADDITIONAL RESOURCES

Again, considering the assumption of the four similar motors,

$$v_H = \sqrt{\frac{2}{\rho C_d A_H}} \sqrt{(4F_{mZ})^2 - (mg)^2}$$

Observe that the horizontal speed will depend on the angle of inclination (it is clear that this angle modifies the horizontal area). In this case, we cannot assume an angle equal to zero because in this condition the vehicle is not able to move horizontally, nor an angle of 90 degrees because the vehicle would fall down (at least with this kind of aircraft configuration, and specifically with this arrangement of motors).

However, since we are looking for a top speed value, in Figure A-6, we can also note that

$$\sin \alpha = \frac{mg}{F_{BZ}}$$

This implies

$$A_H = A \sin \alpha = A \frac{mg}{F_{BZ}}$$

Then, if you replace this value into the horizontal speed equation, the top horizontal speed is

$$v_H = \sqrt{\frac{2}{\rho C_d A \frac{mg}{F_{BZ}}}} \sqrt{(F_{BZ})^2 - (mg)^2}$$

Now we will calculate the maximum torque and angular velocity. This will be done exclusively for the case of the yaw rotation due to the kind of vehicle. You must consider this in your designs if you plan to work with other vehicles with vertical and horizontal force/torque components or acrobatic and aggressive motion.

Observe that the rotational equations previously deduced in this book are used without modifying them, since they are directly developed in the body frame.

The torque in the Z axis of the body frame for this type of vehicle is defined as

$$\tau_z = \sum \tau_c - \sum \tau_{cc}$$

That is, the sum of the clockwise torques minus the sum of the counterclockwise torques. Assuming that we have motors with a similar behavior, and that we are using of a quadcopter, we have

$$\tau_z = 2\tau_c - 2\tau_{cc}$$

The best thing that can happen in this situation is that the absolute value of the maximum torque reaches the following value (either clockwise or counterclockwise):

$$\left|\tau_{z\,max}\right| = 2\tau_m$$

In other words, two motors with the same sense of rotation are turned off so that the maximum torque is achieved in the opposite direction. As mentioned, Tao m has a fixed relationship with the respective thrust in each motor, and this is obtained directly from the motor datasheet. The relationship is fixed because the propeller behaves like a screw transmission, and in this type of mechanism, the force and torque are linked. In general, in the case of a multicopter, the most important design parameter is the thrust force and the secondary is the torque. However, if you need more torque, you can add additional thrusters or motors to provide it.

Once the maximum torque has been calculated, we can determine the maximum angular velocity, which is a not a trivial calculation, but here it is done with a lot of assumptions, simplifications, and omissions (we will indicate them on the way, but you must be careful with these details in your own design).

We start with the following equation that is already expressed in the body frame:

$$\tau_z = J_{zz}\alpha_z = J_{zz}\dot{\omega}_z$$

The aerodynamic drag effects are added. Basically it is the drag force multiplied by the lever arm (the distance between the vehicle's center and each propeller), which is also multiplied by the N arms of the multicopter:

$$\tau_z - N_T r \frac{\rho}{2} C_d A_T v_T^2 = J_{zz}\dot{\omega}_z$$

where Nt is the number of arms that support each propeller, r is their radius measured from the center of the vehicle to the center of gravity of each arm (which is usually located in the motor since the mass of the arm is concentrated there), and vt and At are the linear speed reached by the arms and their effective drag area opposite to the circular motion.

There are several assumptions here. The first is that torque is defined in its simplest form as a force (the drag force, in this case) multiplied by a lever arm (we are also assuming a rotation parallel to the floor). Also observe that the lever arm, instead of being determined by a simple radius, should be determined by a load distribution, but the calculations would be more complicated by the presence of integrals. Finally, if the rotation was not parallel to the floor, there would be a cross product instead of the direct scalar product between the force and its lever arm.

On the other hand, here we consider only the case in which the drone rotates while it is floating. If the aircraft moves along the plane, there will be planar components in the following equality, and they should be presented as a cross product:

$$v_T^2 = r^2 \omega_z^2$$

This way

$$\tau_z - N_T r \frac{\rho}{2} C_d A_T r^2 \omega_z^2 = J_{zz} \dot{\omega}_z$$

The remaining steps are already known. We maximize the angular velocity by making the derivative equal to zero and then we solve for the angular velocity in this equation:

$$\tau_z - N_T r \frac{\rho}{2} C_d A_T r^2 \omega_z^2 = 0$$

Remember that the maximum torque is achieved by two clockwise motors, or by the opposite motors:

$$\left| \tau_{z\,\max} \right| = 2\tau_m$$

Also, remember that Nt = 4 because we are analyzing a quadcopter. Notice that the more arms our multicopter has, the more drag torque they will produce, in the same way that the number of blades affect the performance of a propeller. This is because of the drag contribution of each arm.

Now we will proceed to estimate the previous values using a simulation. Note that instead of carrying out a lot of calculations, the required terms must be added to the simulators described in the previous chapters of this book. These terms must be the drag forces. Observe that a simulation is a numerical approximation that describes the analysis of a system and avoids the direct analytical calculation.

For example, we will modify the first simulation (the one that refers to the robot mode control with yaw angle required to be zero). To simplify, we will only adjust the dynamics of the vertical axis by adding the drag force in the Z axis. The modification of the .m file is done in the way presented in Listing A-1.

Listing A-1. Quadmodel File Modification for Simulating a Quadratic Drag on the Altitude Dynamics, quadmodeldrag.m

```
%x6p=(Fbz/m)-g;
%we just rewrite the previous line, observe the quadratic drag
x6p=(Fbz/m)-g-(0.2*x6*x6/m);
```

The .slx file is changed as indicated in Figure A-7, blockquadmax.slx.

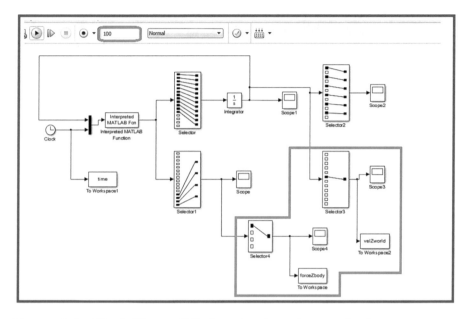

Figure A-7. *Block file modified to simulate the required power*

Once the simulation is finished, type the code from Listing A-2 in the command window. Something similar to Figure A-8 should appear.

Listing A-2. Plotting the Power from the Command Window

```
plot(time,forceZbody.*velZworld,'r')
```

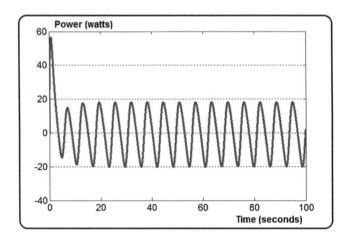

Figure A-8. *The required power plotted from the command window*

As a result, you can notice that according to the control used, the task performed, and the established parameters, only 60W were required (remember that this is only the estimated power on the Z axis; the other powers must be added to calculate a required battery or motors). The negative power only implies changes on the speed direction (by ascending and descending).

Note that this type of flight allows us to make these measurements directly. Otherwise, we would need to obtain the speeds in the body frame or translate the forces into the world frame by adding the lines of code of the kinematics (see the corresponding chapter). In this way, the power should be the vehicle force multiplied by the vehicle speed, or the world frame force multiplied by the world frame speed, but not a mixture as in this particular case in which this is valid for the linearized operation.

The previous simulation displays the estimated power for a given task, but how do we get the maximum values of force and speed?

We start by calculating the required forces to achieve a motion (for example, the drone's takeoff). Without removing the aerodynamic parameters, we are going to modify Fbz as indicated in Listing A-3 in a stepwise manner until we observe that the vehicle is lifted (if we remove these parameters, the vehicle will move with almost no effort as the simulation has zero friction or vacuum conditions).

Listing A-3. A Modification of the Quadmodel File for Obtaining the Takeoff Value by Using Constant Values Instead of a Controller

```
%Fbz=PDz+(m*g);
%we replace the upper line with constant values until drone
takesoff
Fbz=9.8;
```

In this case, since the vehicle weighs 1kg, and in the simulation we defined the gravity equal to 9.8 (see Listing A-4), around 9.8N are required for the simulator not to display errors. With this value we will simply see that the vehicle remains on the ground; with more than 9.8N, the vehicle will take off.

Listing A-4. A Fragment of the Quadmodel File for Observing the Required Force for Overcoming the Vehicle's Weight

```
%constant parameters: mass, inertial values, gravity
m=1;
g=9.8;
```

Applying different thrust values higher than 9.8, we will see a particular speed limit for each case. Given a thrust of 9.82N (Listing A-5), the vertical top speed with the set aerodynamics is 0.3 m/s (Figure A-9); given 15N

(Listing A-6), we will see a speed limit of 5.1 m/s (Figure A-10); and so on. Notice that the greater the force injected into the vehicle, the more abrupt its performance.

Listing A-5. A Modification of the Quadmodel File for Obtaining the Top Speed Value by Using a Constant Force of 9.82N

```
%Fbz=PDz+(m*g);
%we replace the upper line with constant values until drone
takesoff
Fbz=9.82;
```

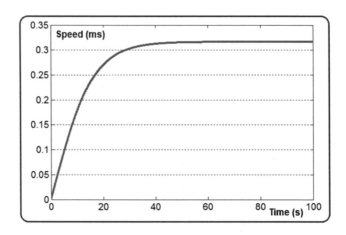

Figure A-9. *Vertical top speed simulated when 9.82N are applied*

Listing A-6. A Modification of the Quadmodel File for Obtaining the Top Speed Value by Using a Constant Force of 15N

```
%Fbz=PDz+(m*g);
%we replace the upper line with constant values until drone
takesoff
Fbz=15;
```

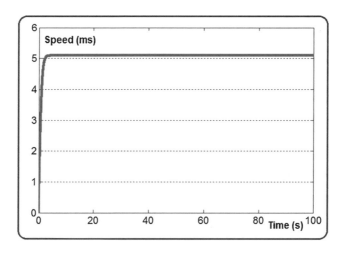

Figure A-10. *Vertical top speed simulated when 15N are applied*

Of course, in this simulation we only modified the behavior of the Z axis, but you should be able to change the three-dimensional behavior to calculate your own parameters. For example, we assigned to the combined factor of the drag force a value of 0.2, but you could make it dependent on the physical parameters of your vehicle (such as the area). Remember that the simulations will be as realistic as the parameters and equations that you add.

For the real measurement of the consumed power, the discussion is simple. The consumed power is the one that will drain your battery or power supply. So this must be measured directly in the battery or power supply by sensing the current and voltage (you should decide if the more suitable measurements for your tasks are direct values, RMS values, or combined values). After that, both values must be multiplied and the result will be the power consumed by the vehicle. This result will indicate the quality of your calculations and simulations, and it will show if more parameters must be included.

Guided References

Chapter 1

An extensive and very detailed book on design, modeling, and basic control of multicopters:

- Quan Quan, *Introduction to Multicopter Design and Control*, Springer, 2017.

My book published with Apress Springer-Nature:

- Mendoza, *Advanced Robotic Vehicles Programming*, Apress, 2020.

Some additional texts for learning state machines (very useful with the remote control and its combination of sticks and buttons, and also to design the flight procedures of a drone). The first two are drone applications, and the next two present an introduction to the most common types of state machines (Mealy and Moore machines or finite state machines). Notice that the state machines applied to a drone can represent its flight modes and the input or change signals between these states can be the remote control sticks or a timer.

- Vojtech Spurny et al, *Cooperative Autonomous Search, Grasping, and Delivering in a Treasure Hunt Scenario by a Team of Unmanned Aerial Vehicles*, Wiley, 2018.

- Jinhyun Kim et al, "Accurate Modeling and Robust Hovering Control for a Quad–rotor VTOL Aircraft," Springer Selected papers from the 2nd International Symposium on UAVs, 2009.

- https://stackabuse.com/theory-of-computation-finite-state-machines/

- www.youtube.com/watch?v=Qa6csfkK7_I

Also remember that, in general, most of the books on digital systems, digital electronics, or algorithm design explain in some section the machines of Mealy and Moore or the finite state machines.

Maker-style books on components and assembly of a multicopter:

- Robert James Davies II, *Arduino Flying Projects: How to Build Multicopters, from 100mm to 550mm*, 2017.

- Terry Kilby and Belinda Kilby, *Getting Started with Drones: Build and Customize Your Own Quadcopter*, Maker Media, Inc., 2015.

- Vasilis Tzivaras, *Building a Quadcopter with Arduino*, Packt Publishing Ltd, 2016.

- Christian Rattat, *Multicopter selber bauen: Grundlagen - Technik - eigene Modelle*, dpunkt.verlag, 2015, in German.

- John Baichtal, *Drohnen und Multicopter bauen*, mitp, 2016, in german.

A MOOC on multicopters with an introductory level:

- `www.edx.org/es/course/autonomous-navigation-for-flying-robots`

Quan Quan online course on multicopters:

- `http://rfly.buaa.edu.cn/course.html`

A book about the development of hardware and software for drones at a computational level (this is useful for the design of autopilots):

- Singh Neeraj Kumar et al, *Industrial System Engineering for Drones*, Apress, 2019.

More on the autopilot design:

- Lorenz Meier et al, *Pixhawk: A Micro Aerial Vehicle Design for Autonomous Flight Using Onboard Computer Vision*, Autonomous Robots, 2012.

- J Rogelio Guadarrama-Olvera et al, "Hard Realtime Implementation of a Nonlinear Controller for the Quadrotor Helicopter," *Journal of Intelligent and Robotic Systems*, 2014.

- https://es.coursera.org/learn/real-time-systems

A series of intermediate level courses on the design and assisted machining of physical components with applications in a drone (framework and propellers). Although non-free software is used, the knowledge can be extended to open software.

- www.coursera.org/specializations/cad-design-digital-manufacturing

For a suitable selection of materials, or at least to know or have an idea about the maximum forces that can act on the frame, legs, or propellers of a drone, because these are the parts most susceptible to be damaged, see the following set of recommendations.

Texts on the use and selection of materials (the handbook is very useful and with a lot of tips for 3D printing).

- Michael Ashby, *Materials Selection in Mechanical Design*, Butterworth-Heinemann.

- Askeland, *Essentials of Materials Science and Engineering*, Cengage Learning.

- www.makerbot.com/stories/design/3d-printing-materials/

- Ben Redwood, *The 3D Printing Handbook: Technologies, Design and Applications*, 3D Hubs, 2017.

- Amit Bandyopadhyay, *Additive Manufacturing*, CRC Press.

Texts and MOOCs on resistance of materials with concepts such as maximum tensile stresses, compression, torsion, shear, deformation limits, and more. These concepts along with the weight of the material are used to determine the resistance of the frame, propellers, landing gear, and such. They are valuable at the time of purchasing the materials or in comparative tables.

- Wayne Whitman's Mechanics of Material Courses at `www.coursera.org/instructor/whiteman`

- Beer et al, *Mechanics of Materials*, McGraw Hill.

An excellent text on propellers for makers and people interested in technical details (in the modeling section of this book, we also provide propeller references, but focused on designers). Also any other manual from the same collection is recommended.

- McCauley, *Professor Von Kliptip's Propeller Performance*.

This book (focused on airplanes) contains a lot of useful concepts regarding history, standards, sensors, flight physics, international regulations, and more:

- *Pilot's Handbook of Aeronautical Knowledge*, FAA.

This text describes in a visual and understandable way many of the motors used by most electric drones:

- Matthew Scarpino, *Motors for Makers: A Guide to Steppers, Servos, and Other Electrical Machines*, Que Publishing.

For the design of drones based on internal combustion engines, you can consult

- Tomislav Haus et al, *Identification Results of an Internal Combustion Engine as a Quadrotor Propulsion System*, IEEE, 2017.

- Fjare, "Feedback Speed Control of a Small Two-Stroke Internal Combustion Engine That Propels an Unmanned Aerial Vehicle," Thesis, University of Nevada.

- Heywood et al, *The Two-Stroke Cycle Engine*, CRC Press.

A book about LIPO batteries for makers (not scientific details, just implementation):

- Micah Toll, *DIY Lithium Batteries: How to Build Your Own Battery Packs.*

The human power quadcopter from the University of Maryland:

- `www.youtube.com/watch?v=emK-qIbuJ-k`

- Joseph Schmaus et al, *Design and Development of Gamera: A Human Powered Helicopter from the University of Maryland*, 2012.

Chapter 2

Three of the most complete references on the modeling of drones and specifically quadcopters. All of them are easy to extend to other aircraft. The first is quite complete and descriptive. The second is practically a classic in the early days of multi-copters. The last is a fairly comprehensive book, and is one of the first texts to handle the concept of the allocation matrix, which is already used in other types of robots (for example, wheeled robots).

- Jinhyun Kim et al, "Accurate Modeling and Robust Hovering Control for a Quad–rotor VTOL Aircraft," Springer Selected papers from the 2nd International Symposium on UAVs, 2009.

- Teppo Luukkonen, "Modelling and Control of Quadcopter," Independent paper, 2011.

- Quan Quan, *Introduction to Multicopter Design and Control*, Springer, 2017.

Two key references for understanding the quasi-speeds or angular speed relationships between the fixed frame and the body frame of a vehicle. In the first one, it is presented graphically and in a geometric way with projections and diagrams. The other references are analytical views based on properties of rotation matrices (be careful, as they use Euler's rotations other than those presented in this book).

- Beedford et al, *Engineering Mechanics Dynamics*, Addison Wesley.

- https://robotacademy.net.au/masterclass/
  velocity-kinematics-in-3d/

Watch the videos about 3D motion and skew-symmetric matrices. A complementary video is this:

- https://robotacademy.net.au/lesson/derivative-
  of-a-rotation-matrix/

Once the previous ones are understood, or if you have the notion, you can use this resource:

- www.coursera.org/learn/motion-and-kinetics

Specifically the sections Eulerian Angles; Eulerian Angles Rotation Matrices; Angular Momentum in 3D; Inertial Properties of 3D Bodies.

An extension of the models described in this book, just in case you want to analyze not only the position of the drone's center of interest, but also an object placed outside that center of interest such as a camera or a robotic arm:

- Pal Johan, *Vehicle Manipulator Systems*, Springer.

- Caccavale, *Adaptive Control for UAVs Equipped with a Robotic Arm*, Elsevier, 2014.

A complementary analysis on the aerodynamic considerations of the propellers (for the vehicle aerodynamics, see the corresponding section on the maximum flight characteristics of a drone):

- Pierre Jean Bristeau et al, *The Roll of Propeller Aerodynamics in the Model of a Quadrotor*, 2009.

- Moses Bangura et al, *Aerodynamics of Rotor Blades for Quadrotors*, 2016.

From the previous one, his doctoral thesis is deeper and more complete:

- Moses Bangura, *Aerodynamics and Control of Quadrotors*, The Australian National University, 2017.

More about the mathematical modeling of propellers (this is useful if you want to make your own propellers):

- `https://web.mit.edu/16.unified/www/FALL/ thermodynamics/notes/node86.html`

Coupled dynamics that are usually neglected and that increase with the size of the aircraft:

- Reza Olfati-Saber, "Global Configuration Stabilization for the VTOL Aircraft with Strong Input Coupling," IEEE, 2002.

Our recommended text on linear algebra and rotation matrices:

- Shin Takahashi, *The Manga Guide to Linear Algebra*, No Starch Press.

- Ron Larson, *Elementary Linear Algebra*, Cengage Learning.

- Grossman, *Elementary Linear Algebra*, Brooks Cole.

Chapter 3

Classic books on the control of multicopters in robot mode:

- Luis Rodolfo Garcia Carrillo, Alejandro Enrique Dzul Lopez, Rogelio Lozano, Claude Pegard, *Quad Rotorcraft Control: Vision-Based Hovering and Navigation*, Springer Science & Business Media, 2012.

- Pedro Castillo, Rogelio Lozano, Alejandro E Dzul, *Modelling and Control of Mini-Flying Machines*, Physica-Verlag, 2006.

MOOC on modeling and control of quadcopters in geometric vehicle mode:

- https://es.coursera.org/learn/robotics-flight

Two articles that are an abbreviated description of multicopters and particularly quadcopters (the second is based on geometric control):

- Hyunsoo Yang et al, *Multi-Rotor Drone Tutorial: Systems, Mechanics, Control, and State Estimation*, Springer, 2017

- Mahony et al, "Multirotor Aerial Vehicles: Modeling, Estimation, and Control of Quadrotor," IEEE, 2012.

Some articles where dynamic compensation is used. This is the first design of the vehicle mode control based on rudders and guide vectors presented in this book (notice that such an approach is common in combination with sliding modes and H-infinity controllers):

- Bambang Sumantri et al, "Robust Tracking Control of a Quad-Rotor Helicopter Utilizing Sliding Mode Control with a Nonlinear Sliding Surface," JSME, 2013.

- Roger Miranda-Colorado et al, *Reduction of Power Consumption on Quadrotor Vehicles via Trajectory Design and a Controller-Gains Tuning Stage*, Elsevier, 2018.

A document (thesis) generated by one of the researchers of the aforementioned MOOC:

- Daniel Mellinger, "Trajectory Generation and Control for Quadrotors," 2012.

Again this book, which is a great reference since it explains various methods of modeling and control:

- Quan Quan, *Introduction to Multicopter Design and Control*, Springer, 2017.

A very complete reference on introductory control of quadcopters (in Spanish):

- Miranda, Garrido, Aguilar, and Herrero, *Drones: modelado y control de cuadrotores*, Alfaomega, 2018.

Basic document on geometric control:

- Bullo et al, *Geometric Control of Mechanical Systems*, Springer, 2005.

The following are complementary, and understanding each one requires reading the others:

- Taeyoung Lee et al, "Geometric Tracking Control of a Quadrotor UAV on SE(3)," IEEE, 2010.

- Taeyoung Lee et al, "Control of Complex Maneuvers for a Quadrotor UAV using Geometric Methods on SE(3)," 2011.

- Taeyoung Lee et al, "Nonlinear Robust Tracking Control of a Quadrotor UAV on SE(3)," 2011.

- Teyoung Lee et al, *Global Formulations of Lagrangian and Hamiltonian Dynamics on Manifolds*, Springer, 2017.

A brief and concise application of the geometric drone control, based on the previous documents:

- Turpin et al, *Trajectory design and control for aggressive formation flight with quadrotors*, Springer, 2012.

An alternative geometric method based on octonions:

- Abaunza et al, "Quadrotor Dual Quaternion Control," IEEE, 2015.

- Castillo et al, *Indoor Navigation Strategies for Aerial Autonomous Systems*, Butterworth-Heinemann, 2016.

See also the rest of the work of Pedro Castillo and Abaunza.

A course on aerial systems with topics regarding Lyapunov's functions:

- `www.coursera.org/learn/nonlinear-spacecraft-attitude-control`

A thesis for understanding all the previous documents (the title is in Spanish, but the contents are in English):

- Claus Rosito, "Sistema de Control de UAVs con aplicaciones a vuelo en formación," Buenos Aires University, 2013.

Books about control methods based on Lyapunov's theory (they are classic references):

- Slotine et al, *Applied Nonlinear control*, Prentice Hall.

- Khalil et al, *Nonlinear Systems*, Prentice Hall.

- Levine, *The Control Handbook*, CRC Press.

- Ortega et al, *Passivity-Based Control of Euler-Lagrange Systems: Mechanical, Electrical, and Electromechanical Applications*, Springer.

Various resources with specific contents applied on polynomial algorithms for trajectory planning:

- Eric Lengyel, *Mathematics for 3D Game Programming and Computer Graphics*, Cengage Learning.

- Hearn et al, *Computer Graphics with Open GL*, Prentice Hall/Pearson.

In the curves and surfaces section or the splines section:

- Peter Corke, *Robotics, Vision and Control: Fundamental Algorithms in MATLAB*, the first and second editions, Springer.

A complement to the previous one:

- https://robotacademy.net.au/masterclass/paths-and-trajectories/?lesson=110

- Lynch and Park, *Modern Robotics*, Cambridge University Press.

- Spong et al, `Robot Modeling and Control`, Wiley.

- `http://ttuadvancedrobotics.wikidot.com/trajectory-planning-for-point-to-point-motion`

- Mellinger and Kumar, *Minimum Snap Trajectory Generation and Control for Quadrotors*, IEEE, 2011.

This is a MOOC on multicopter modeling and control that has a section on snap-level path planning:

- `https://es.coursera.org/learn/robotics-flight`

Other kind of error definitions (some of them are useful for haptics):

- Rafael Kelly et al, "A Brief Tour on Exotic Control Objectives in Robotics," *Journal of Mechanics Engineering and Automation*, 2018.

A way for regulating the time by using error-based controllers (in this case, sliding modes but the method can be useful for other controllers, even PDs):

- Parra-Vega, "Second order sliding mode control for robot arms with time base generators for finite-time tracking," *Dynamics and Control*, 2001.

This article shows a variable yaw controller based on quaternions:

- Anand Sanchez-Orta et al, "Position–Yaw Tracking of Quadrotors," ASME, 2015.

Chapter 4

Books on state space variables and their block representation:

- Sira-Ramirez et al, *Control de sistemas no lineales: linealización aproximada, extendida, exacta,* Pearson (in Spanish).

- Nise, *Control Systems Engineering,* Wiley.

- www.coursera.org/learn/mobile-robot

- Ogata, *Modern Control Engineering,* Prentice Hall.

On numerical methods for solving systems of differential equations (Euler, RK4):

- Zill, *Differential Equations with Boundary-Value Problems,* Cengage Learning.

- Chapra, *Numerical Methods for Engineers,* McGraw Hill.

- Mathews, *Numerical Methods Using MATLAB,* Pearson.

- Sulaymon L. Eshkabilov, *Practical MATLAB Modeling with Simulink,* Apress, 2020.

About Simulink and user-defined functions:

- Sulaymon L. Eshkabilov, *Beginning MATLAB and Simulink,* Apress, 2019.

- www.mathworks.com/help/simulink/user-defined-functions.html

About Scicos/Scilab:

- Campbell et al, *Modeling and Simulation in Scilab/ Scicos with ScicosLab,* Springer, 2010.

- Sandeep Nagar, *Introduction to Scilab*, Apress, 2017.

- www.youtube.com/watch?v=KgBD52cRNJk

If you prefer to code in a less visual way and more like a text interface programming language (Python for example, but easily transferable to other programming language):

- Svein Linge et al, *Programming for Computations – Python*, ODE and second order ODE sections, Springer.

To facilitate code migration between programming languages, you can read

- www.geeksforgeeks.org/runge-kutta-4th-order-method-solve-differential-equation/

Extended code on ODES solvers. In this chapter, we avoided developing these solvers and we used the preprogrammed Simulink code, but the following user, among many others, provides the developed solvers. The algorithms are usable with any other programming language.

- www.mathworks.com/matlabcentral/fileexchange/73027-euler-algorithm

- www.mathworks.com/matlabcentral/fileexchange/73028-runge-kutta-4-method

The following webpage contains a series of fairly complete courses on control and simulation of systems by using tools such as Python, MATLAB, and others:

- https://apmonitor.com/pdc/

A good book for learning S-Functions and the basis for sliding mode control:

- Jinkun Liu, *Advanced Sliding Mode Control for Mechanical Systems*, Springer.

Chapter 5

About Ardupilot libraries:

- Julio Mendoza-Mendoza et al, *Advanced Robotic Vehicles Programming*, Apress, 2020.

- `https://ardupilot.org/dev/docs/apmcopter-programming-libraries.html`

- `https://blog.owenson.me/build-your-own-quadcopter-flight-controller/`

About PX4 libraries:

- `https://dev.px4.io/master/en/index.html`

- Nestor Alonso Santos-Ortiz, "Analyse de la robustesse de la loi de commande d'un quadrirotor embarquant une charge suspendue par cable," 2017, in French.

About Dronekit:

- `https://dronekit-python.readthedocs.io/en/latest/`

An interesting article on data verification algorithms (and also correction):

- Varinder Singh, "A Review on Various Error Detection and Correction Methods Used in Communication," 2015.

The checksum algorithm made from a binary base (in our case it was enough to perform decimal sums or XOR bitwise sums):

- `www.youtube.com/watch?v=AtVWnyDDaDI`

Functional examples of the UART transmission with Ardupilot libraries:

- Mendoza et al, *Advanced Robotic Vehicles Programming*, Springer-Apress, 2020.

Comparison of the UART transmission with other serial data transmission protocols:

- `www.deviceplus.com/arduino/arduino-communication-protocols-tutorial/`

Other types of checksums based on the Hamming distance. Remember that this involves more processing; consequently this can improve the reception and sending of data, but also implies transmission delays. Also read about the CRC algorithm or cyclic redundancy check.

- `www.youtube.com/watch?v=ppU41c15Xho`

About the closed loop motor control:

- *Real-Time Attitude Stabilization of a Mini-UAV Quad-rotor Using Motor Speed Feedback*, Springer, 2013.

- Franchi et al, "Adaptive Closed-loop Speed Control of BLDC Motors with Applications to Multi-rotor Aerial Vehicles," IEEE, 2017.

- `www.youtube.com/watch?v=tjCJ3MlFt7g`

Appendix References
Differential Flatness and Multicopters

- Hebertt Sira-Ramírez et al, *Differentially Flat Systems*, CRC Press.

- Carlos Aguilar-Ibanez et al, "The Trajectory Tracking Problem for an Unmanned Four Rotor System: Flatness-Based Approach," *International Journal of Control*, 2012.

- Nguyen Thinh et al, "Flatness-Based Nonlinear Control Strategies for Trajectory Tracking of Quadcopter Systems," 2016.

- Sira et al, *Control de sistemas no lineales: linealización aproximada, extendida, exacta*, Pearson, 2005 (in Spanish, but very didactic compared to the rest of the documents).

- Fliess et al, "Flatness and Defect of Non-Linear Systems: Introductory Theory and Examples," *International Journal of Control*, 1995.

- Mistler et al, "Exact Linearization and Noninteracting Control of a 4 Rotors Helicopter via Dynamic Feedback," IEEE, 2001.

This book has a lot of examples on differential flatness and control theory in an easy-to-understand presentation (including a bicopter example):

- Gerasimos G. Rigatos, *Nonlinear Control and Filtering Using Differential Flatness Approaches*, Springer.

Sliding Modes and Multicopters

An introductory textbook that is very easy to understand:

- Jinkun Liu, *Advanced Sliding Mode Control for Mechanical Systems*, Springer.

A text with the history and the general state of the art of the sliding modes:

- Fridman et al, *Continuous Nested Algorithms: The Fifth Generation of Sliding Mode Controllers*, Springer, 2015.

Essential sliding mode references (you should first read the aforementioned ones). These references are ordered from least to greatest complexity:

- Edwards et al, *Sliding Mode Control: Theory and Applications*, CRC.

- Sira-Ramirez, *Sliding Mode Control: The Delta-Sigma Modulation Approach*, Birkhauser.

- Utkin et al, *Road Map for Sliding Mode Control Design*, Springer.

- Levant, "Higher-order sliding modes, differentiation and output-feedback control," *International Journal of Control*, 2003.

- Yuri Shtessel et al, *Sliding Mode Control and Observation*, Birkhauser.

- *Sliding Mode Control in Electro-Mechanical Systems*, Utkin CRC.

Sliding modes applied to multicopters:

- Bambang Sumantri et al, "Robust Tracking Control of a Quad-Rotor Helicopter Utilizing Sliding Mode Control with a Nonlinear Sliding Surface," *Journal of System Design and Dynamics*, 2013.

- Filiberto Munoz et al, *Second Order Sliding Mode Controllers for Altitude Control of a Quadrotor UAS: Real-Time Implementation in Outdoor Environments*, Elsevier, 2017.

- Ha Le Hnu Ngoc Thanh, "Quadcopter Robust Adaptive Second Order Sliding Mode Control Based on PID Sliding Surface," IEEE, 2018.

Applications with sigmoid functions (an alternative to the saturation functions):

- Garcia-Carrillo et al, "Hovering Quad-Rotor Control: A Comparison of Nonlinear Controllers Using Visual Feedback," IEEE, 2011.

- Escareno et al, "Embedded Control of a Four-Rotor UAV," IEEE, 2006.

Helicopters, Omnicopters, Airplanes, and More

For standard helicopters (one main rotor and one tail rotor):

- Mahony et al, "Robust Trajectory Tracking for a Scale Model Autonomous Helicopter," *International Journal of Robust and Nonlinear Control*, 2004.

- Beibei Ren, *Modeling, Control, and Coordination of Helicopter Systems*, Springer, 2012.

- John Koo et al, "Output Tracking Control Design of a Helicopter Model Based on Approximate Linearization," IEEE, 1998.

For airplanes:

- Roskam, *Airplane Flight Dynamics and Automatic Flight Controls*, DARcorporation, 1998.

- Robinson, *A Generic Model of Aircraft Dynamics*, Swedish Armed Forces, 2012.

- Espinoza et al, *Backstepping - Sliding Mode Controllers Applied to a Fixed-Wing UAV*, Springer, 2013.

- Stevens, *Aircraft Control and Simulation*, Wiley.

For unusual multicopters (omnidirectional aircraft):

- Dario Brescianini et al, "Design, Modeling and Control of an Omni-Directional Aerial Vehicle," IEEE, 2016.

- Yangbo Long et al, *Omnicopter: A Novel Overactuated Micro Aerial Vehicle*, Springer, 2013.

Coaxial drones:

- Wang et al, "Flight Dynamics Modeling of Coaxial Rotorcraft UAVs," *Springer Handbook of Unmanned Aerial Vehicles*, 2014.

- Abdelkader Abdessameud et al, *Motion Coordination for VTOL Unmanned Aerial Vehicles*, Springer, 2013.

- Johnson et al, "Modeling, Control, and Flight Testing of a Small-Ducted Fan Aircraft," *Journal of Guidance, Control, and Dynamics*, 2004.

Snake-like aerial manipulators (they are the result of the chained effect of their individual aerial linkages, but they also have the same generic form in their modeling):

- Hyunsoo Yang et al, "LASDRA: Large-Size Aerial Skeleton System with Distributed Rotor Actuation," IEEE, 2018.

- Moju Zhao et al, "Design, Modeling, and Control of an Aerial Robot DRAGON: A Dual-Rotor-Embedded Multilink Robot with the Ability of Multi-Degree-of-Freedom Aerial Transformation," IEEE, 2018.

More applications and information on the concepts of thrust vectoring and omnidirectionality:

- Mendoza et al, "Snake Aerial Manipulators: A Review," IEEE, 2020.

- Mendoza et al, *Advanced Robotic Vehicles Programming*, Springer-Apress, 2020.

- Jeongae Bak, *Positioning Control of an Underwater Robot with Tilting Thrusters via Decomposition of Thrust Vector*, Springer, 2017.

Examples of a quadcopter modeled with the Euler-Lagrange approach, or the generic equation of a robot:

- Danial Hashemi et al, "Trajectory Planning of Quadrotor UAV with Maximum Payload and Minimum Oscillation of Suspended Load Using Optimal Control," 2020.

- Guerrero et al, "IDA-PBC Methodology for a Quadrotor UAV Transporting a Cable-Suspended Payload," 2015.

- Caccavale et al, "Adaptive Control for UAVs Equipped with a Robotic Arm," 2014.

- Jinhyun Kim et al, "Accurate Modeling and Robust Hovering Control for a Quad–rotor VTOL Aircraft," Springer Selected papers from the 2nd International Symposium on UAVs, 2009.

Rotational Representations for Drones

A very complete document but somewhat difficult to read (practice your linear algebra and complex numbers concepts first):

- `https://web.mit.edu/2.998/www/`
  `QuaternionReport1.pdf`

There are sections in this MOOC with useful problems to visualize the advantages and disadvantages of these three types of rotational representations. Note that drones are handled from an extremely linearized point of view.

- `www.edx.org/es/course/autonomous-navigation-`
  `for-flying-robots`

A couple of books with extensive information on the use of these and other rotational representations:

- Quan Quan, *Introduction to multicopter design and control*, Springer, 2017.

- Peter Corke, *Robotics, Vision, and Control: Fundamental Algorithms in MATLAB*, Editions 1 and 2, Springer.

These videos complement the previous book, in particular the one called "Interpolating rotation in 3D:"

- `https://robotacademy.net.au/masterclass/paths-`
  `and-trajectories/`

This book addresses an alternative to the geometric control based on rotation matrices, through the use of octonions (this avoids the redundancy of quaternions):

- Castillo et al, *Indoor Navigation Strategies for Aerial Autonomous Systems*, Butterworth-Heinemann, 2016.

More about the definition of distances between quaternions and rotation matrices (read again the geometric control section in this book and compare with the information presented below; the link is based on the Rodrigues rotation formula):

- www.boris-belousov.net/2016/12/01/quat-dist/

This book also shows interesting and useful results on the aircraft orientation measurement problem:

- Ranjan Vepa, *Dynamics and Control of Autonomous Space Vehicles and Robotics*, Cambridge University Press.

This article shows a variable yaw controller based on quaternion:

- Anand Sanchez-Orta et al, "Position–Yaw Tracking of Quadrotors," ASME, 2015.

Linear Control

Classic and useful references on methods 1 to 5:

- Nise, *Control systems Engineering*, Wiley.

- Brian Douglas' YouTube channel: www.youtube.com/user/ControlLectures/videos

- www.edx.org/course/introduction-to-control-system-design-a-first-look

- www.edx.org/course/introduction-to-state-space-control

All the sections on the next webpage:

- http://ctms.engin.umich.edu/CTMS/index.php?example=Introduction&section=ControlPID

The next set of courses and books:

- `https://es.coursera.org/learn/controle` (in Portuguese)

- `https://es.coursera.org/learn/controle-moderno` (in Portuguese)

- `https://es.coursera.org/learn/resposta-frequencia` (in Portuguese)

- `https://es.coursera.org/learn/controle-s` (in Portuguese)

- Ogata, *Modern Control Engineering*, Prentice Hall.

- Kailath, *Linear Systems*, Prentice Hall.

- Victor Manuel Hernandez Guzman et al, *Automatic Control with Experiments*, Springer.

Useful references on method 6, also related to the indirect method of Lyapunov (this is relatively simple to design, compared to the previous methods, at least it is directly programmable):

- `www.coursera.org/learn/mobile-robot`

- Rugh, *Linear System Theory*, Prentice Hall.

My doctoral thesis, in particular page 42 (in Spanish):

- Mendoza, "Diseño de controladores robustos para sistemas electromecánicos," 2016.

This page, in addition to describing useful commands for the linear calculation of Lyapunov functions, offers excellent references on this method:

- `www.mathworks.com/help/control/ref/lyap.html`

Basic but useful references on method 7:

- Hagan, *Neural Network Design.*

- Lilly, *Fuzzy Control and Identification*, Wiley.

Drone Power Consumption and Maximum Flight Features

A detailed explanation of the drag equations used in vehicles and aircraft can be found in the following book, which uses a theorem called Buckingham Pi:

- Frank White, *Fluid Mechanics*, Mc Graw-Hill.

A very complete and introductory course on aerodynamics is the following (in French) Comment vole un avion?, Eric Poquillon et al:

- www.fun-mooc.fr/courses/course-v1:isaesupaero+25001+session06/about

Again the Quan Quan book but now the "Drag Model" section:

- Quan Quan, *Introduction to Multicopter Design and Control*, Springer, 2017.

The basis of this section:

- https://klsin.bpmsg.com/how-fast-can-a-quadcopter-fly/

The aerodynamic analysis of a drone applied to improve its flight performance:

- www.flitetest.com/articles/aerodynamics-in-racing-multirotors

A couple of articles that indirectly or directly deal with topics about the power consumption of a multicopter from an experimental point of view:

- Nadia Kreciglowa et al, "Energy Efficiency of Trajectory Generation Methods for Stop-and-Go Aerial Robot Navigation," IEEE, 2017.

- Dario Brescianini et al, "An Omni-Directional Multirotor Vehicle," Elsevier, 2018.

More information about the propeller aerodynamics:

- Pierre Jean Bristeau et al, "The Role of Propeller Aerodynamics in the Model of a Quadrotor," 2009.

- Moses Bangura et al, "Aerodynamics of Rotor Blades for Quadrotors," 2016.

From the previous one, his doctoral thesis is much more profound and complete:

- Moses Bangura, "Aerodynamics and Control of Quadrotors," The Australian National University, 2017.

Classic articles on aerodynamic of multicopters:

- Haomiao Huang et al, "Aerodynamics and Control of Autonomous Quadrotor Helicopters in Aggressive Maneuvering," 2009.

- C. Powers et al, "Influence of Aerodynamics and Proximity Effects in Quadrotor Flight," 2013.

- W. Dong et al, "Modeling and Control of a Quadrotor UAV with Aerodynamic Concepts," 2013.

Index

© Julio Alberto Mendoza-Mendoza, Victor Javier Gonzalez-Villela,
Carlos Fernando Aguilar-Ibañez, Leonardo Fonseca-Ruiz 2021
J. A. Mendoza-Mendoza et al., *Drones to Go*, https://doi.org/10.1007/978-1-4842-6788-2

Printed in the United States
By Bookmasters